French Rugby Football

Berg French Studies

General Editor: John E. Flower

ISSN: 1354-3636

French Rugby Football

A Cultural History

Philip Dine

BERG

Oxford · New York

First published in 2001 by
Berg
Editorial offices:
150 Cowley Road, Oxford, OX4 1JJ, UK
838 Broadway, Third Floor, New York, NY 10003-4812, USA

Berg is the imprint of Oxford International Publishers Ltd.

Library of Congress Cataloging-in-Publication Data

A catalogue record for this book is available from the Library of Congress.

British Library Cataloguing-in-Publication Data

A catalogue record for this book is available from the British Library.

ISBN 1 85973 322 0 (Cloth)
        1 85973 327 1 (Paper)

Typeset by JS Typesetting, Wellingborough, Northants.
Printed in the United Kingdom by Biddles Ltd, Guildford and King's Lynn.

Contents

Acknowledgements

The combination of a lifelong personal involvement in rugby football and a more recent professional interest in the sport means that my acknowledgements here must reach further back and be spread more widely than is usually the case in an academic work. It was my late grandfather, Arthur Newsham (my first French teacher and my first rugby coach), who introduced me to the union game at Barnstaple in Devon, together with the subtleties of rugby league at Barrow, in his native Cumbria. Although Barnstaple RFC remains my sporting home, I also need to thank all those who contributed to my development both on and off the pitch at Barnstaple Grammar School, North Devon College, Dundee University, Stirling University, and with the Combined Scottish Universities.

My initiation into French rugby came as a player in the third division of the national championship with the Tours Etudiants Club, and my enthusiasm for the French way of playing is paralleled by my gratitude for the hospitality extended to me by lovers of 'the adopted game', both at that time and since. Friends and colleagues in France whose help and encouragement have proved especially valuable include Pierre Arnaud, Jean Camy, and Thierry Terret at the Centre de Recherche et d'Innovation sur le Sport in Lyons, Patrick Mignon at the Institut National du Sport et de l'Education Physique in Paris, and Jean-Pierre Augustin at the Maison des Sciences de l'Homme d'Aquitaine in Bordeaux. More recently, the encyclopaedic knowledge of Jean-Pierre Bodis and the *passion treiziste* of Robert Fassolette have also been much appreciated. The hospitality and wealth of anecdotes provided by Michel Fodimbi and Guy Etcheberry and their families in Lyons and Vienne were as enjoyable as they were valuable. Olivier Nier, formerly of Grenoble and now at Brive, has also been a precious guide to the modern French game, not least for those Loughborough students who have been able to benefit from the links established between the University and the CA Brive club.

Nearer home, Jean-Pierre Boulé of Tarbes and the Nottingham Trent University was a regular source of advice and local knowledge. In Leicester, Richard Holt, a pioneer of French sports history, offered both inspiration and encouragement, as, from a sociological perspective, did Ken Sheard. For its part, the work of British chroniclers of rugby league – including particularly Geoffrey Moorhouse, Mike Rylance, Phil Fearnley, and Phil Melling – showed me just how much remains to be said by the scholarly literature of rugby union. To Ian Henry, of the Department of Physical Education, Sports Science and Recreation Management at Loughborough University, I owe special thanks, both for helping me to establish contacts with researchers in France, and for coaxing me out of retirement to play for Loughborough RFC's 'Vets' XV. My colleague Jeremy Leaman of the Department of European Studies and Melton Mowbray RFC is similarly to be thanked. Nick Bromell's regularly voiced enthusiasm for the glory days of the Boniface brothers and Gachassin was particularly appreciated, coming as it did from a fellow Devonian, and thus almost in spite of himself.

Invaluable financial support for the early stages of this project was provided by the Nuffield Foundation, and later supplemented by funding from the Faculty of Social Sciences and Humanities at Loughborough University. Without such support this project could never have been brought to fruition. Mark Szegner, Information Technician in the Department of Geography at Loughborough University, very generously gave of his time and expertise to produce the distribution map included in the appendices. Mick Cleary of the *Daily Telegraph*, Philip Burnham-Richards of the Hulton Getty Picture Collection, and Justin Davies at Allsport were all extremely helpful in the hunt for a suitable jacket illustration. At Berg Publishers, the guidance (and patience) of Kathryn Earle, Sara Everett, and their colleagues must also be gratefully acknowledged.

However, those who have done the most to allow this book to be completed are, as always, my wife Carol, my son John, and my daughter Morag. On this occasion, the combined exertions, in a sporting context far removed from the rugby pitch, of Brian Askew, Mark Webber, and the Peloton de Gendarmerie de Haute Montagne de Chamonix also proved decisive. I am fortunate indeed to be in a position to record my thanks to them all here.

Introduction: 'Only fabulous French can do this'

If there is one thing upon which observers of the French people past and present are generally agreed, it is that France is different. This truism, if nothing else, unites historians, economists, political scientists, and a wide variety of cultural commentators, both in France itself and abroad. The concept of the 'French exception' has consequently been widely used to describe the paradoxical development of the modern French nation-state, the territorial and social entity born of the Revolution of 1789. Indeed, this notion has become a central tenet both of the contemporary French world-view and of the academic discipline of French studies.[1] At the core of the French paradox – be it in the geo-strategic, economic, political, or conventionally regarded 'cultural' domains – is a tradition of success of a distinctly idiosyncratic kind, often achieved in spite of obvious structural handicaps. Nowhere has this long-term phenomenon been more readily apparent in recent years than in a public sphere that might legitimately be regarded as the modern world's most visible, because most intensely mediatized, field of international relations: namely, competitive sport. So, to take only the most recent and obvious example, the conspicuous success of the French association football team, world champions in 1998 and European champions in 2000 – an unprecedented double – has been achieved against the background of a historically weak domestic league, with virtually all members of the current squad based not in France, but rather in Italy, Spain, Germany, or Great Britain. The mediatic representation and political recuperation of this 'multicultural' national side's achievements are themselves part of a narrative of state-sponsored investment, both moral and material, in competitive sport that, for all its modern glamour and glitz, has its roots in the dark years of the Second World War, and even the Franco-Prussian war of 1870.[2] In Olympic sports, which have been systematically encouraged by French governments since General Charles de Gaulle's outraged reaction to the poor national performance at Rome in 1960, France has had an outstanding record in recent years, finishing fifth overall at Atlanta in 1996 and sixth overall at Sydney in 2000. Even the relative weakness of French competitors in the country's premier sporting spectacle, the annual Tour de France cycle race, has not prevented the successful transformation of an event based essentially on pre-First World War technology into a thoroughly modern global media commodity, while at the same time maintaining its role as a mobile celebration of French unity in diversity.[3] In sport as in so much else, in short, there is an identifiably French way of doing things, and it is one that has regularly triumphed in spite of the odds.

The truth of this observation is all the more marked as regards the French approach to rugby football, a game that should not, in all logic, have taken root in the country at all. Yet rugby is properly regarded as a monoculture in the south-west of the country, such is the game's hegemony in what has become established as its French heartland. For in much the same way as France may be divided in terms of the historical development of its productive infrastructure into an industrialized north and east and a still predominantly rural south and west,[4] so the national territory can be split into a rugby-playing zone to the south and west of the river Loire, and the rest. As Jean Lacouture, biographer of de Gaulle, and rugby correspondent of the national journal of record, *Le Monde*, has put it: '[rugby] has become in a century the "national" sport of a France whose northern boundary is marked by a line drawn from the Charente to the Jura'.[5] Although a number of important rugby-playing enclaves exist, as Lacouture's description suggests, in the south-east of the country (as well as in Paris), it is in the south-west that the game is most deeply rooted. The clear overlap between the two zones is not coincidental, and we shall see that the cultural specificity of French rugby resides more than anything else in its close association with both the reality and the mythology of rurality. For in what follows, this longest established French team game will be regarded not just as a physical *practice*, but also as a system of signification or *discourse*. Viewed in this light, rugby football may legitimately be considered as a means of representing and making sense of the world, and thus may even be regarded as *un mode de vie* or a way of life.[6]

Like the industrial and agrarian revolutions, modern sports came late to France, and it is only with the Franco-Prussian war of 1870 that the era of the new games can be said to have begun. Yet it will be argued that French rugby football draws for its vitality on much deeper roots, and particularly on the traditional social structures of the south and west. This study will consequently concern itself with both poles of what has become a standard dichotomy in French historiography: *l'histoire événementielle*, the conventional narrative of names, dates, and deeds; and the thematically organized study of *la longue durée* [the long term]. This longer time-scale is the basis of Fernand Braudel's celebrated study of *The Identity of France*, a monumental work that privileges the analysis of the 'deep structures' of French society, often referred to more commonly as *la France profonde* [deep France].[7] Recent cultural commentators have drawn attention to the 'acceleration' and even the 'end' of history in the putatively 'post-modern' world, with the implication that both of these schools of historiography have been overtaken by the collapse of the apparent certainties that shaped the mental landscape not only of French society but also of the Western world as a whole in the half-century after the Second World War.[8] While not itself endorsing this apocalyptic analysis, the present study will seek to show that rugby union has, in its modest way, undergone its own crisis of (post-)modernization since the decision by the game's international governing body in August 1995 to allow full professionalism in a sport that was until that time – at least officially – wholly amateur. The game in France, as elsewhere, has thus been in the throes of a television-led revolution since 1995, with *la longue durée* effectively meeting head-on with the forces of globalization.

Yet, as was made wonderfully clear at the most recent manifestation of rugby's new world order, the 1999 World Cup, French sporting exceptionalism is alive and well. Having struggled unconvincingly through the early rounds of the competition, France just managed to scrape past lowly Fiji to progress into the semi-finals, where they came up against the tournament's outstanding side and clear favourites, New Zealand. It was then that a characteristically French variety of magic, familiar to rugby lovers around the world, was conjured up. Just over a year after France's triumph in the 1998 football World Cup, a French side was again to inflict a dramatic defeat on a team hitherto perceived to be the best in the world. In this case, the footballers of Brazil were replaced by the mighty All Blacks. As if merely beating the odds-on favourites – hitherto regarded as wellnigh invincible – was not enough, the unfancied French XV gave a dazzling display of running rugby and brilliant counter-attacking play that had the English crowd on its feet and roaring for the traditional enemy: 'everyone [in the Twickenham stadium] was French for one day'.[9] For *The Daily Telegraph*, the most right-wing and anti-European of the British broadsheets, but also generally regarded as the most authoritative in terms of its sports coverage, the event was front-page news, as 'France created the biggest upset in the history of the Rugby World Cup'.[10] The paper's senior rugby correspondent, Mick Cleary, went on to explain how the French had comprehensively out-thought and out-played the New Zealanders, defeating them by a record score (43–31), under a banner headline proclaiming 'Only fabulous French can do this':

This was an upset on a colossal scale. [. . .] But the deed of victory is only part of the story. The manner of it will warm many a night by the fireside to come.
[. . .]
Where did they find this from? From within their soul, that remote corner where only truth resides. They knew deep down that it was death or glory, oblivion or immortality.

Logic was given leave of absence. They played with the heart and with instinct. They cared not a jot about All Black reputation. [. . .]

The French were fired by self-belief. They were audacious as well as outrageous. [. . .] God was wearing blue.[11]

At one level, this is a standard example of journalistic hyperbole, complete with the military metaphors that so often dominate sporting rhetoric. However, we are also presented here with a conception of an essential sporting 'Frenchness' – a myth of the French as rugby's chosen people – that is quite as important historically as the 'rainbow nation' discourse associated with France's all-conquering football team.[12] For while French rugby may never have produced a single moment with the social and political impact of the victory of the ethnically diverse home team in the France 98 tournament, this particular sport may reasonably be represented not only as the oldest but also as the most culturally specific team game in France. Only cycling, in fact, could be said to be more significant in terms of its national cultural resonance, principally through the special place accorded to the annual Tour de France. Indeed, the national victory in the global sport of football may point the way forward to a brighter, more socially inclusive, future; but the exploits of the *XV de France* come steeped in the complex mythology of the past. Moreover, not only has the 'manner' of French rugby 'warmed many a night by the fireside', it has actually played a significant role in the imaginative construction of the contemporary French nation. This is the principal argument of the cultural history proposed here.

Of course, French rugby's continuities extend well beyond the positively depicted achievements of its representatives in international competitions, and a critical examination of the game's 'deep structures' may well encourage negative readings of its most cherished images and institutions. For if French rugby is undoubtedly an important site for the construction of local, regional, and national identities, it is first and foremost a means of establishing or reinforcing conventionally gendered personal identities for its overwhelmingly male practitioners, administrators, and spectators. As John Nauright and Timothy Chandler put it in the introduction to their *Making Men: Rugby and Masculine Identity*: 'we feel it is important to begin with an examination of sport, in this case the sport of Rugby Union, from the position that it has been, and largely remains, an activity controlled by males, played by males, written about by males and utilized by male politicians'.[13] This 'game' may therefore legitimately be regarded as one of the most obviously gendered of activities, fully inscribed within the entrenched power structures of patriarchy, and often sharing its most socially conservative – and even unpleasantly reactionary – assumptions. Indeed, as a general principle, sport may prudently be regarded as 'a repository for dominant ideology in its celebration of ruthless nationalism, racism, militarism, imperialism and sexism'.[14] Yet if rugby, like sport as a whole, is part of a patriarchal system of domination and control, then it would seem to make sense to attempt to understand the historical origins and modern manifestations of that system, with a view to demonstrating its failings and thus effecting change. By the same token, given that rugby has played and continues to play such an important role in the construction of masculine identities, it is surely worthwhile to establish the specific processes by which men have been and continue to be 'made' in France, and particularly in the traditionally rugby-playing south-west of the country. Moreover, the fact that rugby union, like all sports, is ideologically loaded does not mean that its values are immutably fixed.[15] More specifically, rugby may be a highly gendered practice – in spite of a small but significant history of female participation in the game in France, as elsewhere[16] – but it is by no means straightforwardly predetermined in its other social and symbolic values.

However, in order to make sense of the story of French rugby, from the game's early days in the 1880s to the present, it is first necessary to say something about the social context of this particular sport. An informed awareness of historical transformations in patterns of work and leisure, as of the evolution in mentalities that such changes imply, will therefore be adopted as a necessary precondition for an understanding of elements of continuity and change in the evolution of sporting organizations, policies, and practices in France. Much important work has already been done in this area, as social historians such as Eugen Weber, Pierre Arnaud and Richard Holt have illuminated French sport's existence as a socio-economic, political, and cultural nexus.[17] The present survey will seek to build on this solid foundation with a detailed case-study of French rugby, invoking such tried and tested explanatory paradigms as the role of modern games in the communication of ideology and their function as sites of sociability. Additionally, the discussion will develop as a key concept the thematic of festivity, drawing on insights from both leading practitioners such as Jean Gachassin and professional sociologists like Pierre Sansot, who are united in their belief that, at the most basic level, 'le rugby est une fête' [rugby is a feast or festival].[18] The game's festive dimension will be considered in more depth a little later in this introduction.

To the outsider, France is primarily remarkable as the great exception to the pattern of rugby union's dissemination in the later nineteenth and early twentieth centuries; a fact still reflected in its current status as the only major rugby-playing nation outside what we might call the British imperial *bloc* of the 'home' countries – England, Scotland, Wales, and Ireland (north and south famously playing together as a single national side) – and the former dominions of Australia, New Zealand, and South Africa. This historical difference has, over the years, been reflected in the emergence of a distinctively French rugby culture, which has not infrequently brought the Fédération Française de Rugby (FFR), the national organizing body for the union game, into sharp conflict with the other rugby-playing nations, and in particular the British; a situation not helped by France's obvious linguistic and cultural isolation in this particular context. Rugby thus represents a very specific example of the exceptionalism appealed to by commentators on French society of all kinds. As a result, this particular sport, France's first modern team game, complete with its regularly vaunted glories and its less often examined darker side, provides a privileged site for examining profound changes in French society over the past century and a quarter.

Both the general historical development and the specific geographical implantation of rugby union in France present difficulties to the foreign observer. Why, after all, should rugby have ever been adopted at all as a national game in France, Britain's foremost imperial rival, when its expansion elsewhere has largely been limited to the British Isles and the major centres for British colonial emigration (the basis for the game's contemporary power-base in the southern hemisphere)? Why should French rugby have rapidly, and unusually, have become established as a popular rather than a socially elitist sport? Why should French rugby have become both so attractive to spectators in France and abroad (the much lauded *beau jeu*, or 'beautiful game') and so regularly brutal (the less easily avowed *jeu dur*, or 'hard game')? Why should this sport have flourished not, as did so many other sporting imports, in the industrial population centres of the north and east, but rather in the cities, towns, and, especially, villages of the still predominantly rural south-west? Why, above all, should rugby have been elevated to a position of central significance in the construction of local and regional identities throughout its heartland in the *Midi*, before becoming adopted as an authentically national sporting spectacle?

A variety of more or less plausible solutions have been suggested to the enigma of French rugby's distinctive pattern of geographical implantation and cultural assimilation. These will be examined in the following chapters, together with a number of my own observations. What is certain, however, is that just as French rugby has become synonymous internationally with a cavalier attitude to both regulation ('French indiscipline') and playing styles ('French flair'), so it is beyond doubt that the game is firmly associated in French minds with the south-west, often mythified as *l'Ovalie*, the land of the oval ball. Although this generally unquestioned self-image of the French game does have its roots in a certain historical and sociological reality, it nevertheless remains essentially mythic. It may thus be subjected to critical scrutiny, so as to reveal the broader social significance of the ideological messages communicated by such apparently innocent and reassuring sentiments.

French rugby may now be threatened by the forces of globalization; but its development was undoubtedly assisted by the broadly simultaneous rise of industrial capitalism and political nationalism. This link will be examined throughout the discussion, with key analytical tools being provided by, on the one hand, an understanding of the new modes of sociability that accompanied industrialization and urbanization, and, on the other, an appreciation of the ideological and structural linkage between modern sports and the rise of the nation-state. More specifically, the material existence and cultural resonance of this particular sport in modern France will be considered in terms of its uniquely privileged relationship with the state (most clearly revealed during the Vichy period and under de Gaulle). French rugby will thus be examined as evidence in favour of the argument that 'Sporting competition . . . provides the primary expression of imagined communities; the nation becoming more "real" in the domain of sport.'[19]

What precisely is meant by the term 'cultural history' as applied in this book? The approach adopted is, in fact, a double one, in that the case-study is intended both to reveal the sport's specificity as a micro-culture, and to illuminate its particular contribution to broader local, national, and even global cultures. The analysis will, of necessity, focus primarily on the construction and reconstruction of a variety of masculine identities, typically informed by dominant patriarchal and ethnic models: the story of French rugby football is overwhelmingly a story of white males, after all. The insights provided by recent feminist and post-colonialist critiques of modern sport will not, for all that, be ignored, any more than will the earlier critiques offered by both Marxist and non-Marxist historians and sociologists. The architecture of this study is intended to combine a clearly delineated and chronologically ordered narrative of the game's introduction and development with a theme-driven analysis of rugby's interest to the cultural historian. In addition, each chapter will seek to illuminate rugby's role as a privileged site for the construction of local and national identities by focusing on the contribution made to the on-field development and off-field perception of the sport by a number of emblematic clubs and players. In this way, the sport's evolution will be traced from the early years in Paris, through its subsequent development in the Bordeaux region, to the abiding playing and cultural hegemony of the south-west. Underpinning the discussion will be the hypothesis that rugby has operated throughout as a means of linking tradition and modernity, providing a reassuring (if frequently spurious) continuity in a period of rapid and radical socio-economic and political change. At the most basic level, this book is thus conceived as a contribution to the broader process of understanding the often troubled recent history of Britain's nearest neighbour.

Central to this examination will be such broad historical movements as industrialization and urbanization, the commodification and professionalization of leisure, and the mediatization and globalization of economic and cultural exchanges. A particular focus for discussion will be the relative failure of rugby union, in spite of conspicuous early successes, to establish itself durably in the south-east of France, where it has had to compete with both association football and rugby league. This will in turn be considered as part of the broader history of relations between the rival codes of rugby union (fifteen-a-side, and officially amateur until 1995) and rugby league (thirteen-a-side, and openly professional since its introduction to France in the early 1930s), including particularly the immediate circumstances and abiding legacy of the suppression of the latter code by the collaborationist Vichy administration. This book thus draws upon the extensive literature, in the broadest sense, devoted to rugby in France from the early 1900s to the present, to cast light on some of the shadier aspects of the sport's history in that country, as well as its much-lauded public face. In the light of the current reconfiguration of rugby football – most obviously the reorganization, remarketing and remediatization, in France as elsewhere, of the formerly amateur union game – it is hoped that this survey will have a particular relevance at present and may contribute in a modest way to the understanding of a sport with deep local roots that stands on the threshold of a new, thoroughly professionalized and globalized, era.

Before embarking on the discussion proper, it is worth underlining that where some historians might be inclined to dismiss the legends, anecdotes, and fantasies to which French rugby has so often given rise, this study will seek to make such representations an integral part of what is intended at least as much as a study of a sporting discourse as of a sporting practice (in so far, that is, as the two can be separated at all). Indeed, it is in its consistent ability to generate epic narratives that French rugby most readily reveals both its micro-cultural specificity and its broader cultural significance. 'Sports', as Fred Inglis has argued, first and foremost 'tell us stories; they make sense of the world.'[20] It is this, in fact, that leads Inglis to assert that 'sport is one of the main cultural experiences', and, moreover, 'that, at least since about 1880, the meanings and functions of art and sport in industrial society have lain very close together, and that at the very least something of what sport means to us will be revealed by a consideration of how we see our artists'.[21] Indeed, for Inglis, it is precisely the overlap between sport and art in the popular cultural sphere that helps to explain the deeper significance of the seemingly trivial: 'The "purposefulness without purpose" by which Kant defined the aesthetic is as readily found in games as in art. It is what brings them together in the single realm of . . . popular aesthetics.'[22] The link between sport and art is regularly to the fore in French rugby, where it has, among other things, led to the production of a body of creative writing that has no equivalent in the English-speaking rugby world.[23] A single incident from the imaginative literature of the French game will be enough to give a foretaste of its very particular flavour. This will also help to explain the third major theme of this analysis – which is intended to complement the more familiar issues of ideology and sociability – namely, festivity, and its particular links with French rugby's micro-culture.

'The Strange Sancey–Soro Duel' is drawn from *Les Contes du rugby* (1961), a collection of historically accurate, if undoubtedly picaresque, tales assembled by Henri Garcia, one of the French game's most prolific and respected chroniclers.[24] The duel in question involves a match between Lourdes, the dominant force in French rugby from the later 1940s to the early 1960s, and a side closely associated with the theory and practice of *le beau jeu*, and Toulon, a club with a reputation for rugged forward play from the south-east of the country, and thus from the periphery, in French rugby terms. More specifically, the encounter centres on the clash between two of the most formidable players on the pitch, the celebrated Lourdes lock forward, Robert Soro, and his almost equally ferocious opponent, Raymond Sancey, in Toulon's second row. The two teams' battle for physical and territorial supremacy is reduced in Garcia's *conte* to a personal challenge issued to Sancey 'by the good town of Toulon', and it is with its ringing ribaldry that the tale opens: 'No! Playing away at Lourdes, you'll never stick your finger up Big Soro's arse!'[25] The narrative that follows first establishes the general character of the two towns and their respective clubs, and explores their long-standing rivalry, before switching attention to the build-up to the great game, and then describing the match itself. Predictably, the *dénouement* centres on Sancey's final achievement of the grotesque goal set for him by the assembled *Toulonnais*. Profiting from a generalized outbreak of fighting between the two packs of forwards, Sancey assaults the distracted Soro in a fashion that the Lourdes player and his team-mates could never have suspected. Initially stunned, the Lourdes supporters quickly launch their own verbal and then physical attack on 'those queer bastards' from Toulon.[26] The resulting pitch invasion leads to the abandonment of the match and forces the Toulon side to take refuge in their changing-room. Their escape route to the local railway station is subsequently blocked by a furious, stone-throwing mob, some thousand strong, which overwhelms the attempts by the local *gendarmes* to restore order. It is only with the intervention of the Toulon hooker, Henri Laugier, a serving police inspector, who brandishes his service revolver to cover the team, that the Toulon 'homos' are able to make good their escape in an armoured *gendarmerie* lorry: 'And all that happened because Sancey had had the crazy idea of sticking his finger up Big Soro's arse, on his home patch, in Lourdes . . . '.[27]

We are far removed here from rugby's origins in the English public school system,[28] and also a good distance from the sporting ethos of those Parisian aristocrats, such as Baron Pierre de Coubertin, the founder of the modern Olympic games, who first imported the game into France. For, as we shall see, in the process of its diffusion and popularization, French rugby took on its own distinctive characteristics – many of them attractive, some considerably less so – to which we may conveniently refer, following Sébastien Darbon, as 'the traditional culture of [French] rugby'.[29] We shall examine this nationally specific rugby culture, or more accurately micro-culture, in more detail when we come to consider the French game's peculiar rootedness in the south-west. However, for the time being we might simply link the above tale to Darbon's ethnographic observations regarding French rugby and 'a certain conception of the group', in which solidarity both on and off the pitch is central to the communitarian way of life still prevailing in the game's south-western strongholds. The two most basic laws of rugby football – the bans on passing the ball forward, and (at its most simply stated) being in front of the ball when it is played (and thus 'off-side') – mean inevitably that rugby is a game characterized first and foremost by 'a permanent front-line', with a direct impact on the states of mind of its players and (community-based) supporters:

> Much more than in football or basketball, we find in rugby this idea of a territory to be defended, which is exacerbated by the violence of the physical contact involved. It is clear that this constitutes an important factor in the reinforcement of identity-based behaviour, which is expressed through the valorization of the club jersey or of the village . . . Who do they think they are these 'foreigners' (sometimes the inhabitants of a village just a few kilometres away) who dare to tread upon the soil of our village, and to penetrate the sacred space of our stadium? . . . That surely deserves punishment![30]

Darbon links this parochial siege mentality to the objectively disproportionate difficulty of winning away from home in rugby in general and French rugby in particular,[31] and thus helps to explain the real and abiding local rivalries evoked by Garcia's comic tale.

So much, then, for the communitarian and territorial aspects of Sancey's very specific penetration of Soro's 'sacred space'; but what of its grotesque physicality? For this we need to note Darbon's comments regarding a number of other constitutive features of French rugby culture, including particularly 'the taste for violence, a relationship with food and drink that some would consider excessive, [and] a marked valorization of the epic narrative'.[32] These characteristics may be understood in terms of the third major pole of the analysis of the French game proposed here: for no examination of rugby in France would be complete without a consideration of its festive dimension, with all that this term implies in the way of a 'carnivalesque' celebration of excess. For there are distinctly Rabelaisian overtones to Garcia's mock epic of sexualized violence, the pricking of immoderate local pride, and the spontaneous popular overthrow of the established order (both in sporting terms and as regards the officers of the state). Moreover, there is a good deal to be learnt about these and related aspects of French rugby culture from the principal commentator on this aspect of François Rabelais's work and world, Mikhail Bakhtin, particularly in so far as his concept of 'carnival' has subsequently been applied to various fields of social scientific enquiry.

In his hugely influential re-reading of the sixteenth-century French writer,[33] Bakhtin stressed that the feasts and fairs of the late-medieval world depicted by the author were not merely confined to the enjoyment of copious amounts of food and drink, and of a variety of associated popular entertainments, but also involved the symbolic overthrow of established power structures and their ways of making sense of the world. Indeed, for the Russian cultural critic, the carnival's ritual transgression of social order, its periodic inversion of prevailing hierarchies and orthodoxies, was its real driving force, and the reason for the remarkable longevity and intensity of popular cultural manifestations. Thus regarded, the Bakhtinian concept of the 'carnivalesque' becomes a powerful tool for understanding the generally unsuspected grip on supposedly modern mentalities of much older ways of imagining the world. This is particularly true as regards deep-rooted attitudes to the body, sexuality, violence, food and drink, and social authority. Although these apparently atavistic responses generally remain hidden, they may reappear in times of social stress, or, conversely, in moments of communal relaxation.[34] It is this, above all, that explains the relevance of

Bakhtin's work to our study of French rugby football in general, and to Henri Garcia's literary representation of the game in particular. For in Garcia's tale of the Soro–Sancey duel we can find elements of 'carnivalesque' laughter and 'grotesque' realism, as identified by Bakhtin, together with the hostility to order that could, in the right circumstances, transform carnival into a potent political force. As we shall see, the French rugby supporters who turned a premature celebration of victory into a riot through the streets of Paris following the national side's unexpected defeat by Scotland at Colombes in 1913 – the so-called 'Baxter Affair' – provide only one example of this periodic tendency of French rugby to destabilize, if only temporarily, the broader society in which it exists. In what follows, in fact, it will be argued that French rugby is capable of incarnating both order and its transgression, both the exalted and the base, both the modern and the pre-modern. The French version of the game – and this is the key to its unique character – is equally at home in the classically athletic body celebrated by Coubertin and his fellow advocates of a reinvented Olympic ideal, and in the grotesquely disported body prioritized by Rabelais and Bakhtin,[35] and given a comic sporting incarnation here in the person of the unfortunate Robert Soro.

While French rugby players (and especially forwards) may, as here, be affectionately depicted as grotesque, the French *rugbyman* may just as easily be represented by the game's prevailing discourse as wholly classical: the regular celebration (typically in the formal purity of photographic isolation) of the dashing centre-three-quarter or the diving winger makes this only too clear. Indeed, it is precisely in the creative tension between these 'high' and 'low' symbolic poles that the real interest of French rugby's micro-culture is to be found. For it is this that enables an apparently trivial game to participate so powerfully in 'the logic of identity-formation' in 'domains of transgression where place, body, group identity and subjectivity inter-connect'.[36] Rugby is thus every bit as appropriate to the expression of the communal solidarity characteristic of the still essentially organic communities that constitute its south-western heartland – where *le rugby des villages* may even be perceived as a bastion against the excesses of globalization[37] – as to the 'communicative contact of an obviously modern kind, embodied in the "mass" media' that is so typical of the 'imagined community' of the modern nation-state.[38] The particular combination of ideology, sociability, and festivity promoted by French rugby football may thus be seen to be both historically rooted and capable of adaptation to dramatically changed social circumstances. It is this particular sporting paradox that we shall now begin to explore by examining the early years of rugby football in France.

Notes

1. A useful overview of 'The background to French cultural exceptionalism' is provided in William Kidd and Siân Reynolds, *Contemporary French Cultural Studies* (London, Arnold, 2000), pp. 21–65.
2. See Hugh O'Donnell and Neil Blain, 'Performing the Carmagnole: negotiating French national identity during France 98', *Journal of European Area Studies*, vol. 7, no. 2, November 1999, pp. 211–25; also Philip Dine, 'Sport and the State in contemporary France: from *la Charte des Sports* to decentralisation', *Modern & Contemporary France*, vol. 6, no. 3, 1998, pp. 301–11.
3. The succession of drugs scandals that have recently afflicted the Tour would not, in spite of appearances, seem to constitute a major threat to the event's durability. On the Tour's unique contribution to French culture see especially Georges Vigarello, 'Le Tour de France' in Pierre Nora (ed.), *Les Lieux de mémoire: III. Les France: traditions* (Paris, Gallimard, 1992), pp. 884–925.
4. Patrick Le Galès, 'The regions' in Malcolm Cook and Grace Davie (eds), *Modern France: Society in Transition* (London, Routledge, 1998), pp. 91–112, at p. 96.
5. Jean Lacouture, *Le Rugby, c'est un monde* (Paris, Seuil, 1979), p. 22.
6. Sébastien Darbon, *Rugby, mode de vie: Ethnographie d'un club, Saint-Vincent-de-Tyrosse* (Paris, Editions Jean-Michel Place, 1995).
7. Fernand Braudel, *The Identity of France: II. People and Production* (trans. Siân Reynolds; London, Collins, 1990), p. 678.
8. Francis Fukuyama, *The End of History and The Last Man* (London, Hamish Hamilton, 1992). See also Jean-François Lyotard's classic definition of post-modernism as 'incredulity towards meta-narratives', as discussed by Grant Jarvie and Joseph Maguire, *Sport and Leisure in Social Thought* (London, Routledge, 1994), p. 213.
9. The words of French centre Emile Ntamack, as reported in *The Daily Telegraph*, 1 November 1999, p. 1.
10. Ibid.
11. Mick Cleary, 'Only fabulous French can do this', ibid., p. S1. See also Paul Hayward, 'Was this the greatest game ever played?', ibid., p. S11.
12. The term 'rainbow nation' is suggested by Nelson Mandela's association of the whole of the newly democratic South Africa with the fortunes of the Springboks in the 1995 rugby World Cup. See Grant Jarvie and Irene Reid, 'Sport in South Africa' in James Riordan and Arnd Krüger (eds), *The International Politics of Sport in the Twentieth Century* (London, E. & F. N. Spon, 1999), pp. 234–45; also Douglas Booth, 'Recapturing

the moment? Global rugby, economics and the politics of nation in post-apartheid South Africa' in Timothy J. L. Chandler and John Nauright, *Making the Rugby World: Race, Gender, Commerce* (London, Frank Cass, 1999), pp. 181–207.

13. John Nauright and Timothy J. L. Chandler (eds.), *Making Men: Rugby and Masculine Identity* (London, Frank Cass, 1996), p. 2.

14. Jennifer Hargreaves, cited in Roger Horrocks, *Male Myths and Icons* (London, Macmillan, 1995), p. 147.

15. On this subject see Jarvie and Maguire, *Sport and Leisure*, p. 189. Their approach draws in this respect on Pierre Bourdieu, *La Distinction: critique sociale du jugement* (Paris, Minuit, 1979) and 'Comment peut-on être sportif?' in the same author's *Questions de Sociologie* (Paris, Minuit, 1981). For Bourdieu's characterization of the *habitus* of French rugby football, see *Distinction: A Social Critique of the Judgement of Taste* (trans. Richard Nice; London, Routledge & Kegan Paul, 1984), p. 213. For a discussion of Bourdieu's analysis see Philip Dine, 'The historical development of rugby in south-east France: *En marge de l'Ovalie?*' in Maurice Roche (ed.), *Sport, Popular Culture and Identity* (Aachen, Meyer & Meyer Verlag, 1998), pp. 211–24.

16. See Alison Carle and John Nauright, 'Crossing the line: women playing rugby union', in Chandler and Nauright, *Making the Rugby World*, pp. 128–48. On rugby and gender more generally see especially Anne Saouter, *"Etre rugby": Jeux du masculin et du féminin* (Paris, Editions de la Maison des Sciences de l'Homme, 2000).

17. Eugen Weber, 'Gymnastics and sports in *Fin-de-Siècle* France: opium of the classes?', *The American Historical Review*, 76/1, February 1971, pp. 70–98; Pierre Arnaud (ed.), *Les Athlètes de la République: gymnastique, sport et idéologie républicaine 1870–1914* (Toulouse, Privat, 1987); Pierre Arnaud (ed.), *Le Militaire, l'écolier, le gymnaste: Naissance de l'éducation physique en France (1869–1889)* (Lyons, P. U. de Lyon, 1991); Richard Holt, *Sport and Society in Modern France* (London, Macmillan, 1981).

18. Jean Gachassin (with Emmanuel Cazes), *Le Rugby est une fête* (Paris, Solar, 1969); Pierre Sansot, *Le Rugby est une fête* (Paris, Plon, 1990).

19. Joseph Maguire and Jason Tuck, 'Global sports and patriot games: rugby union and national identity in a United Sporting Kingdom since 1945' in Mike Cronin and David Mayall (eds), *Sporting Nationalisms: Identity, Ethnicity, Immigration and Assimilation* (London, Frank Cass, 1998), p. 106.

20. Fred Inglis, *The Name of the Game: Sport and Society* (London, Heinemann, 1977), p. 71.

21. Ibid., pp. 72 and 77.

22. Fred Inglis, *Popular Culture and Political Power* (London, Harvester Wheatsheaf, 1988), p. 132.
23. In this, French rugby is more akin to cricket and baseball, with their particularly rich literatures in English, as well as cycling, especially in French. It is no coincidence that the celebrated novelist Antoine Blondin concentrated on these two sports in his journalism for *L'Equipe*. See Chapter 8.
24. Henri Garcia, *Les Contes du rugby* (Paris, La Table Ronde, 1961), pp. 25–38. All translations from French sources are my own unless otherwise stated.
25. Ibid., p. 27.
26. Ibid., p. 35.
27. Ibid., p. 38.
28. In fact, a counter-argument can be made, linking the rise of modern games precisely to the sexual mores of these boarding schools, to the effect that 'sport arose out of a desire to channel homosexuality in a socially acceptable manner': see Arnd Krüger, 'The homosexual and homoerotic in sport' in Riordan and Krüger (eds), *The International Politics of Sport*, pp. 191–216; p. 204 for the quotation. See also P. G. White and A. B. Vagi, 'Rugby in the 19th-century boarding school system: a feminist psychoanalytic perspective' in M. Messner and D. Sabo (eds), *Sport, Men and the Gender Order: Critical Feminist Perspectives* (Champaign, IL, Human Kinetics, 1990). The theme of homosexuality in French rugby is also discussed in Chapter 10.
29. Sébastien Darbon, *Rugby d'ici: Une manière d'être au monde* (Paris, Editions Autrement, 1999), p. 13.
30. Ibid., p. 42.
31. Ibid. The relatively predictable nature of rugby games, compared with football matches, for instance, explains why the French national lottery's short-lived experiment with the game as the basis for its *Loto Sportif* in the mid-1980s was such a failure.
32. Darbon, *Rugby d'ici*, pp. 43–4.
33. Mikhail Bakhtin, *Rabelais and His World* (trans. Hélène Iswolsky; Cambridge, MA and London, MIT Press, 1968).
34. In the French context, the theory of carnival has notably been invoked to try to explain such uncomfortable occurrences as the *épuration* or 'cleansing' that followed the Liberation of France in 1944 and the quasi-revolutionary Paris 'events' of May–June 1968.
35. See Peter Stallybrass and Allon White, *The Politics and Poetics of Transgression* (London, Methuen, 1986), pp. 21–2; cf. Ann Jefferson, 'Bodymatters: self and other in Bakhtin, Sartre and Barthes' in Ken

Hirschkop and David Shepherd (eds), *Bakhtin and Cultural Theory* (Manchester, Manchester University Press, 1989), pp. 152–77.
36. Stallybrass and White, *The Politics and Poetics of Transgression*, p. 25.
37. S. Fleuriel, 'Forms of resistance to the economic hold on sport: a national spirit versus the world market – the case of French rugby', *Culture, Sport, Society* 1(3), 2000.
38. Jefferson, 'Bodymatters', p. 17.

PART I

The Rise of *le rugby-panache*, 1880–1914

– 1 –

Pioneers and Patriots in Paris

In the winter of 1892, against a backdrop of anarchist bomb outrages, social strife, insurrection in the colonies, and increasingly strained relations between the French state and the Roman Catholic Church, Edmond Renoir, a correspondent for the popular journal *L'Illustration*, chose to focus his readers' attention on 'Un match de foot-ball'. The football in question was of the rugby union variety, and was still very much a novelty to a mass-market readership that generally remained unfamiliar with the athletic sports that had made their first appearance in the capital a decade or so earlier. However, the account provided of the encounter between the leading local club Stade Français and the touring Rosslyn Park side is primarily of interest for the light it casts on the linkage between the new games, the nascent popular press, the class system, and Franco-British relations at this time:

> On Monday, for the initiated, Paris received a great honour. An English team deigned to cross the Channel, under the auspices of Lord Dufferin in person, to give a master-class to one of the best teams that we are able to muster. The result was a foregone conclusion. The English scored all the points; our players scored none – and they were no less satisfied for that. The way in which they were defeated honoured them.[1]

At this time, as Eugen Weber was the first to point out, 'football was rugby', and would continue to be so for at least another two decades. So, 'when, in 1909, the Douanier Rousseau painted his *Joueurs de football*, the players were obviously rugby players, and so were those of later painters who depicted ball games, like André Lhôte, Albert Gleizes, and Robert Delaunay'.[2] Yet for all the enthusiasm of cultured Parisian society for the new game, the British upper classes remained its undisputed masters, both on and off the pitch.

Rugby union, the fifteen-a-side version of the various handling forms of 'football' currently in existence,[3] may well be unique among modern athletic sports in possessing a detailed creation myth. For while devotees of other sporting disciplines may look back fondly to pioneering individuals and associations, only rugby – if we exclude the consciously invented tradition of the modern Olympic marathon[4] – claims to be able to trace its origin to a single heroic exploit. As commemorated since 1900 by the plaque set into the Headmaster's Wall at Rugby School in Warwickshire, it was in 1823 that a senior pupil, William Webb Ellis, 'with a fine disregard for the rules of football as played in his time, first took the ball in his arms and ran with it, thus originating the distinctive character of the Rugby game'.[5] This, at least, is the received wisdom, and the reason why today's rugby World Cup competition is contested every four years for the William Webb Ellis trophy.[6] Webb Ellis himself would never know of his rise to fame, which was posthumously decided by the school's authorities. After Rugby, he read divinity at Oxford, and became rector of a parish in Essex, as well as seeing service in the Crimean War. However, for reasons that remain obscure, he elected to spend his later years on the Mediterranean coast of France, and, on his death in 1872, was buried in Menton, in the *département* of the Alpes-Maritimes.[7] This is a French connection that would appear to have little, if anything, to do directly with the spread of the game that Webb Ellis is popularly supposed to have created.[8] Nevertheless, the coincidence has a definite symbolic value, as the Fédération Française de Rugby (FFR) is evidently well aware: a delegation annually visits the grave to commemorate the passing of this very first rugby-playing British expatriate.

For Thomas Arnold, the reforming headmaster of Rugby School, and for other leading educators such as H. H. Almond, at Loretto College in Scotland, the new handling game was rapidly to take on a significance that went far beyond its value as a physical exercise. Arnold, subsequently immortalized in Thomas Hughes's *Tom Brown's Schooldays* (1858), encouraged participation in the sport, believing it to be capable of reinforcing his young charges' combative instincts, whilst simultaneously inculcating a sense of discipline: it thus prepared them for the leading role that they would in due course be asked to play in the life of the nation. Whether or not Waterloo – the battle that had, a mere thirteen years earlier, ended Napoleon's territorial ambitions in Europe – had really been won on the playing-fields of Eton, Arnold and those of like mind were confident that the military, diplomatic, and commercial future of the burgeoning British Empire would be assured on the rugby pitches of the public schools, the universities, and, increasingly, the suburban clubs that 'old boys' and 'former pupils' were establishing in London, Edinburgh, and elsewhere. The founding of the (English) Rugby Football Union in January 1871 thus marked a key moment in the game's early development, as did the playing of the first international match, between England and Scotland, at Raeburn Place in Edinburgh, in March of the same year. Britain now looked to export rugby and its other school-based athletic sports – including particularly association football (or 'soccer'), which had officially parted company with rugby in 1863 – to the Empire and beyond.

It is difficult to overstate the contrast between the all-encompassing confidence of Victorian Britain and the cultural climate prevailing in the France that emerged from the Franco-Prussian War. The circumstances in which the discredited regime of the Second Empire had collapsed, to be replaced by a new Republic, were grave indeed, and the outlook seemed correspondingly bleak. Yet, paradoxically, the concrete necessities of this critical moment in French history were to give rise to remarkable developments in both the political and the cultural life of the nation. Jill Forbes and Michael Kelly have persuasively summarized this complex phase in French social development as follows:

> The Third Republic was born in blood with the Prussian invasion and occupation of 1870, the capitulation of the French army, the loss of Alsace and parts of Lorraine, and the short-lived and bloody experiment in socialism of the Paris Commune in the spring of 1871. Thereafter the regime moved from political crisis to political crisis as the republican party, itself by no means homogeneous, put in place the framework which eventually ensured that a secular Republic would endure, and its assorted opponents – monarchists, Orléanists, and Bonapartists on the Right, syndicalists and anarchists on the Left – would all, finally, come together in a 'union sacrée' to fight Germany again in 1914. Yet during this truly remarkable half-century important and lasting developments took place in the fields of painting, sculpture, literature, music, and architecture as a whole host of conventions, beliefs, and traditions were questioned, found wanting, swept away, and replaced by a completely new set of values, techniques, and approaches which can now be recognized as the first tentative manifestations of modern art.[9]

It is, perhaps, only to be expected that academic studies of 'this extraordinary coexistence of political and cultural experiment'[10] should have tended to focus on the rise of artistic modernism as the primary indicator of the profound changes that French society underwent in the period 1870–1914, not the least of which was the continuation of a technologically-driven transformation of the economy that had begun under the Second Empire. While it is undoubtedly the case that French economic growth was to lag behind that of the other European powers during the nineteenth century – precisely because, as Hervé Le Bras has put it, 'the industrial imperative was eclipsed by the political imperative of unity'[11] – the emergence of qualitatively new modes of production and consumption would result in radical social restructuring, at least in the industrialized north and east of the country. The renegotiation of individual and collective identities that such processes jointly necessitated extended well beyond such conventionally legitimate areas of national achievement (and scholarly enquiry) as the 'high-cultural' fields identified by Forbes and Kelly. Among the many social developments that merit examination in this regard, the growth of mass leisure is of particular importance. It is therefore no coincidence that the foremost historian of the social and cultural transformation of France in the period 1870 to 1914, Eugen Weber, should also have been a pioneer of that country's sports history.

As Weber was the first to demonstrate, the rise of modern sports in France began essentially in the wake of the Franco-Prussian War of 1870, with military-style gymnastics providing the first real alternative to traditional, village-based forms of amusement.[12] However, the appeal of gymnastics, although strongly encouraged by political nationalists as the basis of both a physical and a moral regeneration, and thus of a future *revanche* [revenge] against the Germans, would wane as other sports were introduced into France in the 1880s. Where gymnastics had, ironically, been imported from Germany itself, these new sports – athletics, football, and rugby, as well as others such as rowing – came from Great Britain, and specifically from the English, and Scottish, public schools. They offered new opportunities and new roles to both individuals and the group, and were well adapted to the rapidly changing lifestyles of the inhabitants of the major French population centres of the later nineteenth century, as France's belated industrial revolution saw centuries-old patterns of rural and agriculturally-based work and leisure begin to give way to new, urban, and technologically-dependent modes of sociability, including notably participating in and spectating at sports events. No less a commentator on the identity of France than Fernand Braudel has drawn attention to the key role played in the long-term evolution of what he terms the 'oneness' of France by 'the need for social intercourse, *la sociabilité*, the need to meet other people', alongside economic and political constraints. 'The trouble' as he goes on to note 'is that sociability does not leave behind as much historical evidence as economic [and political] constraints do.'[13] Fortunately, this is less true in the modern period than in the pre-industrial times that are the real focus of Braudel's analysis, and students of French sporting sociability are particularly fortunate in having had solid foundations laid by the work of commentators like Eugen Weber, and, perhaps even more obviously, Richard Holt.[14] Jean-Paul Callède, following Maurice Agulhon, has persuasively argued that the rise of sports clubs, and thus what he calls 'associative sociability', was a key moment in 'the emergence and affirmation of cultural modernity', through its creation of a distinct, and previously unknown, public sphere 'in which new identities and new forms of independence could be constituted'.[15] The importance of the new games 'simply' as a way of socializing should not, therefore, be forgotten as we look now in greater detail at the more overtly ideological component of French sporting discourse in the later nineteenth century.

From the outset, the dissemination and development of the major modern sports was characterized in France by a combination of class divisions and regional antagonisms, both of which were fuelled by the competing ideologies of the day, the foremost of which was a variously inflected but uniformly belligerent nationalism. It is with the role of the new games as what Weber termed 'the opium of the classes'[16] that we shall primarily concern ourselves in the rest of this chapter. Where gymnastics on the military model had served as a conduit for popular germanophobia, the 'English' sports were underpinned by an aristocratic anglophilia predicated upon a desire to emulate the empire-building achievements of France's nearest neighbour and principal colonial rival. The most prominent advocate of sport as a means of simultaneously defending the class interests of the upper echelons of French society and furthering the country's imperial ambitions was undoubtedly Baron Pierre de Coubertin, the founder of the modern Olympic Games. Through the umbrella organization that he established in 1887 to oversee the newly imported athletic sports – the Union des Sociétés Françaises des Sports Athlétiques (USFSA) – Coubertin was able to exert a powerful influence on their early development.[17] On the basis of his personal observation of the workings of the English public school system, Coubertin would attach the greatest importance to large-scale participation in the new games (albeit by a carefully delineated social elite), and thereby to the principle of strict amateurism. This 'Corinthian' sporting ethos[18] had its roots in the desire of Coubertin and his supporters to draw upon what they saw as a successful British model of aristocratic adaptation to the challenges of a newly democratic society. For the *débâcle* of 1870 represented not only a humiliating military defeat (resulting in the loss of the two eastern provinces of Alsace and Lorraine), but also a definitive reverse for the monarchy. Instituted in the wake of the siege of Paris and an armistice that had led to the bloody class conflict of the Commune, the Third Republic would, by the manner of its consolidation, render unthinkable a return to anything like the pre-Revolutionary *ancien régime*. In the face of the secular religion that militant Republicanism soon became, the aristocracy sought new ways of defending its class interests. For Coubertin and those of like mind, the solution was to be found in the new athletic sports. Richard Holt explains this 'serious social purpose behind the introduction of the English sports':

The answer lay in the formation of a more open élite composed of the sons of the nobility and of the bourgeoisie, an aristocracy of birth and wealth of the kind which those flexible upper-class reformers, the Whigs, had created in Britain. Barriers between the upper and middle classes were broken down at the public schools and particularly on the playing fields. Games like rugby taught the virtues of group cohesion whilst still imbuing the schoolboy with a strong sense of individualism. Sport not only helped to produce practical, resourceful people as opposed to ivory tower intellectuals and time-serving officials, it was also thought to generate group solidarity.[19]

Thus the new games became 'one of the tributaries through which the wider debate on the alleged decadence of French society flowed'.[20]

The received view of the *belle époque* (1890–1914) as an era of unbridled gaiety and amusement is strikingly at odds with the evidence now available of the national soul-searching prompted by defeat, occupation, and the loss of territory, together with the scarcely less challenging experiences of industrialization and urbanization. The post-1870 obsession with the physical and moral regeneration of the nation – exacerbated by renewed fears about the country's historically low birth-rates – must therefore be borne in mind as the immediate context for the introduction of the modern athletic sports. This background also hints at the key role that would be played in their dissemination and development by an educational system itself destined to become an ideological battleground, as the 'République des instituteurs' [the Republic of the schoolmasters] embarked on its mission of establishing a unitary national culture in France. By the same token, we need to be conscious of the broader pattern of social restructuring that had begun under the Second Empire (1852–70) and that became ever more intense as the century wore on. Indeed, such were the wide-ranging technological and cultural changes affecting Paris at this time that 'modernity' itself could actually be said to have come into being in the city. For it was in this specific context that 'modern life' was born, or at least this was the view of that most acute of contemporary social observers, the poet Charles Baudelaire. Here, in fact, the familiar 'talismanic innovations [or] emblems of modernity': 'the telegraph and telephone, railroad and automobile, photograph and cinema'[21] would be given full rein and enshrined as the markers of a qualitatively distinct and historically specific metropolitan culture, peopled by newly mobile and self-aware individuals, who together would constitute the mass audience for the many, varied, and, overwhelmingly, commercially motivated and technologically mediated forms of distraction now on offer to them, on the basis of their newly acquired leisure hours and leisure budgets.

It was thus into the new urban reality of the city – and specifically the 'Haussmanized' cityscape (both architecturally reordered and socially controlled) of post-1850 Paris – the undisputed 'capital of the nineteenth century' – that the first athletic sports would be introduced and would have to compete for attention. For the truly modern phenomenon of sport was only one among the very many diversions on offer to the population of the city in the later nineteenth century.[22] As personified by an entrepreneur such as Joseph Oller – who invested as much in swimming pools, skating rinks, and cycle-tracks as he did in circuses, music halls, and cinemas[23] – the commercially motivated breaking down of barriers and boundaries that began to occur at this time was characteristic of the Parisian cultural scene, in both its 'high' and 'low' manifestations. However, a determinedly rearguard action against such unprecedented social mixing was waged by the aristocratic advocates of the new athletic sports. More specifically, the social prejudices of the USFSA's natural constituency were to give rugby football a significant early advantage over its most obvious rival, the non-handling game of association football or 'soccer'. As Weber puts it: 'The USFSA [was] addicted to rugby, which was "more highly regarded in the upper classes of [English] society".'[24] Such was the USFSA's hostility to football that the game's development was effectively blocked for the better part of forty years, that is to say until after the Great War:

> . . . the slow progress of soccer with its narrow, foreign base contrasts with the swifter adoption of rugby, introduced less by foreign residents than by French schoolboys. It was only after 1919, with athletic sports no longer a preserve of upper-class teenagers, that the spread of ball games at the popular level meant the spread of soccer . . .[25]

This said, British expatriates had undoubtedly been responsible for the establishment in 1872 of the very first French sports club – the Le Havre Athletic Club, which included a form of rugby football among its various activities[26] – and in the 1870s and 1880s they would continue to be active, forming associations such as the English Taylors Club in 1877 and the Paris Football Club in 1879.[27] Although short-lived, the latter club even managed to tour London, where it was comprehensively outplayed by Old Millhillians, the Civil Service, Hornsey Rise, and Graversant.[28] Yet the membership of these expatriate associations displayed no determination to proselytize, and we thus need to look elsewhere to trace the real rise of French rugby, and specifically to those clubs formed by schoolboys from the fashionable Parisian schools.

Jean-Pierre Bodis has suggested that initial French interest in the sporting activities of these displaced Anglo-Saxons was sparked by a combination of natural curiosity and a wide-ranging 'anglomania' inspired by the obvious might of Victorian Britain, and reflected in the writing of Jules Verne, among others.[29] The mimetic character of much early French sporting activity is accurately reflected in the name chosen for the first indigenous sports association: the Racing Club de France, founded in 1882 by students from the *lycées* Condorcet, Janson-de-Sailly, and Rollin, together with the private Ecole Monge (which was to become the modern *lycée* Carnot). The following year would see the establishment of this senior French club's great rival, Stade Français, which was formed by pupils from the *lycée* Saint-Louis, together with students from other institutions. Other prestigious schools that took up the game included the *lycée* Michelet, which became the principal recruiting ground for the Olympique club, and the *lycée* Henri IV, as well as the private Ecole Alsacienne, Ecole Albert-le-Grand, and Académie Jullian.[30] These and other educational establishments fed into the existing associations or were involved in the founding of new ones, such as the Inter Nos club. Of particular interest is the *lycée* Lakanal at Sceaux, near Paris, which still has on display a 43-foot-long mural painting of a match played in 1897, in which such important figures in the game's early development as Frantz Reichel, the future secretary-general of the USFSA, and sporting correspondent of *Le Figaro*, are clearly visible. According to Potter and Duthen, the work 'was commissioned by the French Director of Fine Arts from O. D. V. Guillonet in 1897, and shown at the Salon des Artistes Français two years later'.[31]

It is worth pointing out here that while free, secular, and compulsory education had been established for children of primary school age by the Ferry laws of 1881–1882, secondary education continued to be restricted to the more privileged strata of French society. Indeed, the secondary education provided in the state-run *lycées* remained optional and fee-paying until the Tardieu ministry of the early 1930s, and was scarcely less expensive than the Catholic upbringing provided by private institutions. This inevitably meant that the lower orders were excluded from the new sports being played by the most fashionable *lycéens*, which encouraged rugby's development as the preserve of the Parisian *gratin* [upper crust]. However, this is not to suggest that the apprentice rugby players were exclusively, or even predominantly, drawn from the aristocracy. After all, this class had its own deep-rooted sporting traditions – especially those associated with equestrianism – whereas the middle and upper-middle classes were to provide a particularly rich recruiting ground for the new athletic sports, led by rugby.[32] A number of British expatriates would also be involved in these first indigenous clubs, both as leading players and as strategically placed administrators. One such figure was C. F. Rutherford, a Scot who came to Paris from Epsom College in 1895 and went on both to captain the Racing Club and to become the French rugby federation's first secretary.[33] A glance at the team-sheets for the earliest encounters of the Paris clubs, sprinkled as they are with family names that are hyphenated or contain the aristocratic particle 'de', together with a number of Anglo-Saxon ones, is suggestive of the social recruitment that characterized the French game in these early days. The sides that disputed the first 'national' championship final provide a suitable sample. Played on the Bagatelle pitch in the Bois de Boulogne on 20 March 1892, the match involved both of the capital's senior clubs – indeed, they were the only two teams in the championship – with the Racing Club beating Stade Français 4–3 in a match refereed by Baron Pierre de Coubertin himself and watched by a crowd estimated at 2,000. The teams were as follows:

Racing Club: J. S. Thorndike; G. Duchamps, Wiet, C. de Candamo (captain), G. de Candamo; Frantz Reichel, Feyerick; H. Moitessier, A. de Palissaux, d'Este; Sienkiewicz, Blanchet; R. Cavally, C. Thorndike, L. Pujol.

Stade Français: Venot; Munier, Pauly, de Pourtalès, Dobree; Amand, de Joannis; Heywood (captain), Herbet, F. Puaux; Braddon, L. Dedet; P. Dedet, Saint-Chaffray, Garcet de Vauresmont.[34]

While these names are by themselves enough to give a flavour of the occasion, a little additional detail may usefully be included here. For the first meeting of these two clubs had taken place only the previous year, on 19 May 1891, club activities until this date having been purely internal, involving matches between fellow-members of each club. Watched by a mere three hundred spectators, this historic encounter took place near the Saint-Cloud race-course, again in the fashionable western suburbs of the city, and involved several names who would feature in subsequent meetings of the two clubs, and who represented a distinctly varied group:

. . . for Stade Français, Heywood, an English teacher; Oudot, a journalist; Saint-Chaffray, a colonial administrator; Frank-Puaux, a journalist; Dobree, a *notable* and justice of the peace in Guernsey; Dedet, *chef de bureau* in the Ministry of Commerce; Herbet, a merchant. For the Racing Club, Reichel, a journalist; Wiet, a diplomat specializing in the Middle East, and with qualifications in Arabic, Persian, and Turkish; the de Candamo brothers, from Peru, were members of high society and spent their time playing golf and tennis; de Zevallos went back to his native Chili; while Potter and Thorndike probably returned to the United Kingdom.[35]

The importance of Frantz Reichel, who would go on to become a leading player at both club and national level, as well as an influential commentator on and administrator of the French game, has already been noted. Jean-Pierre Bodis underlines the fact that while a few aristocrats were among the players in these early encounters, they were significantly outnumbered by members of the upper-middle-classes. However, such members of the nobility as the de Pourtalès family and the Martel de Janville brothers are worthy of note in spite of their relative rarity. Roland de Pourtalès would join Coubertin, Reichel, and the Racing Club's moving spirit, Georges de Saint-Clair, together with other leading figures such as Jules Marcadet and Michel Goudinet, in an influential band of *animateurs*, who acted as promoters or sponsors of the new game.[36] The Martel de Janville brothers, for their part, are primarily remarkable as the sons of the celebrated literary figure 'Gyp', the pseudonym of Sibylle-Gabrielle-Marie-Antoinette de Riquetti de Mirabeau, the wife of Count Martin de Janville. One of the brothers, Thierry, would go on to become a pioneer of neurosurgery before committing suicide following the fall of France in June 1940. More typical of the social complexion of these first French championship matches were the future professor of surgery, Antonin Gosset (a member of Stade Français's championship-winning side of 1895), and Jean-Baptiste Charcot, the son of a leading medical figure and himself a future polar explorer, as well as a French champion with the Olympique club in 1896.[37]

Given the highly restrictive recruitment practices of both the Racing Club and Stade Français – in both of which an approval system based on personal recommendation was reinforced by the charging of substantial membership fees – the early development of French rugby was inevitably characterized by its social exclusivity.[38] With private facilities in the Bois de Boulogne, and with the generous and influential support of former pupils now well established in the professions and public life, these clubs were less concerned with extending the game's base (either socially or geographically) than with using it to reinforce an established system of class-based privilege. The cultural historian Pascal Ory has linked this preoccupation with the cohesion of an elite group to the tendency of French sports clubs, including Racing Club and Stade Français, to be multisport rather than single-sport associations, thus favouring sociable participation rather than specialization in the pursuit of performance.[39] Regarded in this light, the Parisian domination of the national championship in the 1890s may be seen to be simply the logical outcome of the elitist ethos of French rugby's first practitioners. It is only with the victories of Stade Bordelais in 1899 and Stade Toulousain in 1912, in fact, that we see the emergence of French rugby's long-term power-bases, firstly in the Gironde, and then in the far south-west. (These two stages in the shift of the spotlight away from Paris will be examined in Chapters 2 and 3 respectively.)

Present among the distinguished guests at the opening of the Racing Club's new premises in the Bois de Boulogne in 1886 was the controversial Minister of War, General Georges Boulanger, then at the height of his public prominence.[40] A Catholic populist whose *revanchard* belligerence attracted elements of the new urban working class, Boulanger was primarily supported by the reactionary nationalist Right, such as the writer Maurice Barrès and Paul Déroulède's militantly anti-republican League of Patriots. For all its anglophilia, Coubertin's USFSA was not much less vocal in its regular proclamation of its patriotic credentials. To celebrate its fifth anniversary, the organization hosted an enormous banquet, with the President of the Republic, Sadi Carnot, and Grand-Duke Vladimir of Russia as its principal guests. Held in the main amphitheatre of the Sorbonne, the event was dominated by nationalist themes and patriotic speeches, including one by the former head of the government, Jules Simon. Such sentiments were permanently enshrined in the USFSA's motto – 'Ludus pro patria' [the game for the fatherland] – which figures to this day on the celebrated 'Bouclier de Brennus', a shield presented to the USFSA by the Parisian sporting enthusiast and administrator Charles Brennus, and now the trophy awarded annually to the French national rugby champions.[41]

Although the focus for the development of French rugby would shift decisively away from Paris after the turn of the century, the years leading up to the Great War would see the game firmly established as part of the capital's social, political, and cultural scene. Its impact on the visual arts has already been noted; it would also be celebrated in a string of literary works that began with Pierre Mac Orlan's *La Clique du Café Brebis* in 1918, and was continued in the inter-war years by such established figures as Alexandre Arnoux, Jean Giraudoux, and Jean Prévost.[42] Even more remarkable was the establishment in 1913 of the Club Sportif de la Jeunesse Littéraire, on the initiative of someone whose imaginative universe might reasonably be expected to be the antithesis of contact sports, namely Henri-Alban Fournier, better known as 'Alain-Fournier'. That the author of *Le Grand Meaulnes* (1913) should have brought together a group of rugby enthusiasts that also included Giraudoux, Mac Orlan, and Gaston Gallimard – the publisher and founder of the highly influential *Nouvelle revue française* – along with Alain-Fournier's brother-in-law, the writer Jacques Rivière, is remarkable enough; but the irony of the situation was underscored by his playful habit of signing club notices as 'Augustin Meaulnes' or 'Frantz de Galais'.[43] What is more, the very existence of such a group of literary *rugbymen* points very clearly to significant differences between British and French constructions of sporting masculinity at this pioneering stage in rugby's development. Thierry Terret, following Jacques Defrance, has usefully drawn attention to the social definition of physical excellence prevailing in France in the later nineteenth century, establishing four distinct categories of bodily prowess 'identified by the intersection of the athlete's socio-economic status with the degree of physical commitment required to achieve the ideal body'.[44] These competing conceptions of manliness may conveniently be labelled aristocratic, bourgeois, proletarian, and peasant respectively, with a large degree of overlap between the last two categories in a society that was only recently and very partially industrialized. As Terret explains, they may also be broadly equated with the mindsets of the relevant social groupings:

> For the aristocracy, 'man' was defined by grace, style and the elegance of his demeanour, values cultivated by careful grooming and the academic arts. In the eyes of the bourgeoisie the ideal man was individualistic and thrived in activities where intense effort was given full expression through achievements and record-making performances. On the one hand the lower classes of society favoured an ideal of self-control, formalized by medical doctors and developed in schools, which dominated school and military physical education regimens, and the field of medicine. On the other, the lower classes fostered an ideal of physical strength expressed by more traditional symbols of masculinity found either in gymnastic exercises or in the practice of acrobatics, wrestling and tightrope walking.[45]

While the athletic ideal types privileged by the lower orders would remain relatively stable in this period – and particularly the valorization of physical strength that characterized the peasantry, which still constituted 80 per cent of the total French population – the models of masculinity favoured by the upper echelons of French society were subjected to serious strain. This questioning of prevailing aristocratic and middle-class models of physical excellence had its roots in the defeat of 1870, and was fuelled by the wide-ranging social changes that accompanied urbanization, industrialization, and the Third Republic's own drive for political unification. As previously noted, the crisis of masculine confidence that resulted was epitomized by a preoccupation with 'decadence' on the part of the leading classes of the nation. This malaise was conceived of in physical, moral, and political terms, and was to give fresh impetus to the recently introduced athletic sports.

Central to the expansion of the new games was the dominant position in bourgeois culture that had been attained by medical practitioners by the mid-nineteenth century. As a recent American study of French leisure habits in this period has made clear, 'by [the *belle époque*], the professionalization of medicine was an accomplished fact, just as medicine's spread as a social authority had achieved vast dimensions. [. . .] Webbed together with overarching concepts like rationality, anticlericalism, respectability, and science, which together stood for something like an emerging bourgeois worldview, medicalization was an effective and appealing mode of order.'[46] More specifically, the prevailing hygienicist (and even eugenicist) discourse explicitly linked bodily fitness with social order and national advancement. Indeed, the 1870 defeat itself was now explained as the result of the lack of physical fitness of the French 'race'. Exploiting both their elevated status as scientists and networks of influence that notably included freemasonry, medical practitioners were to exert considerable influence on government policy at this time. So, for instance, seven physicians sat in 1888 on an official committee established to make recommendations regarding the introduction of physical exercise – and particularly the recently imported athletic sports – into the national educational curriculum. Others played a leading role in the establishment of the first mass sporting organizations. One such pioneer was a Dr Michaux, the founder, in 1903, and first president of the Fédération Gymnastique et Sportive des Patronages de France (FGSPF), a Catholic organization that sought to use a network of sports-based youth-clubs to preserve the Church's influence at this difficult time.[47] Others included Marcellin Berthelot, a member of the Academy of Medicine and a former Minister of Public Instruction, who – aided by no less a figure than the future prime minister and 'tiger' of the Great War, Dr Georges Clémenceau – presided over the Ligue Nationale de l'Education Physique (LNEP), formed in 1888.[48] Of particular significance for the development of French rugby, as we shall see in Chapter 2, was the establishment on the same model, also in 1888, of the first major sporting organization outside Paris, Dr Philippe Tissié's Bordeaux-based Ligue Girondine de l'Education Physique (LGEP).[49] For these and other such medical men 'patriotic and sanitary concerns turned them into militant missionaries of sport'.[50] Physical education, which drew equally on the official ideologies of public hygiene and state-schooling, was thus destined to become a privileged vector for the dissemination of the new games and the ideas that informed them.

Rugby was well placed to present itself as both a physical and a moral hygiene, and thus to tap profitably into the fears of a bourgeoisie obsessed with degeneracy and its avoidance. The chaste athleticism evoked by the rugby-playing Pierre Mac Orlan, for instance, in his 1918 work, *La Clique du Café Brebis*, would thus appeal to those living in fear of masculine dissipation in all its forms. Moreover, as Mac Orlan puts it in this novel: 'We had discovered the importance of our muscles at a very young age. This was the foundation of what we did on the Marne and all the rest.'[51] That women were to be excluded from participation in the new sports, and thus from their much vaunted physical, moral, and especially patriotic benefits, was never seriously questioned at the time; indeed, this exclusion was the ultimate proof of the new games' suitability for the renewal of the (male) youth of the nation. The distinctive forms of sociability offered by the new games would thus be reserved for men on grounds that ranged from the preservation of public decency to the claim by eminent medical authorities that the female body was unsuited to physical exercise. The prevailing myth of 'feminine nature' was thus unquestioningly assimilated by these first French sportsmen, who consequently reproduced the dominant social construction of the sexes in their practices and their discourse.[52] Indeed, the new opportunities for self-expression and self-discovery offered to French males by the imported athletic sports would, from the outset, be predicated on the denial of comparable opportunities to women. With only minor modifications, such as the involvement of a number of women in the 'touch-rugby' game of *barette* – which enjoyed a brief vogue as a genteel alternative (both for males and females) to the full-contact game[53] – this would continue to hold true as rugby was now discovered, and remade in its own image, by provincial France, and particularly the south-west.

However, before the cultural centre of the new games moved out of the capital – never to return, or at least not until very recently, and then only very partially – Paris was to impose its stamp indelibly on the national relationship with the new game. As has been previously suggested, the particular attractiveness to the French liberal bourgeoisie of rugby football and the other sporting manifestations of Victorian Britain's self-confidence had its origins in this class's acute appreciation of the economic, industrial, and commercial might of their nearest neighbour's burgeoning colonial Empire.[54] Indeed, it was Coubertin himself who had urged his compatriots to 'use sport for colonial ends', as well as to 'strengthen the muscles of Marianne', or at least those of her sons.[55] Yet for all their avowed admiration of the British way of playing, the pioneers of rugby in France were, from the outset, determined to practise the new games in their own manner. Indeed, in the early days, French *rugbymen* were basically athletes who swapped the track of the summer months for the rugby field in winter, and their personal and collective commitment to the specificity of the new game did not go very much beyond this switch of location. Rather then accepting the game's most basic principles of collective endeavour and self-sacrifice for the greater good – precisely the ethos that had recommended the game to the British public schools in the first place – the game's French pioneers saw it, above all, as a way of asserting the bodily prowess and social distinction of the individual. Christian Pociello has analysed this early development in terms both of the morphology and the class origins of these first French players. As students whose primary sporting interest was in running and jumping, and as either aristocrats or members of the *haute bourgeoisie*, they were ill disposed to both the physicality and the anonymity of rugby's forward-play, in particular. Indeed, some players went so far as to refuse to participate in the union game's most distinctive feature, the scrummage, or otherwise to compromise their dignity on the field, for instance by tackling opponents below the waist. In a game characterized first and foremost by physical contact, they sought precisely to avoid getting to grips with their fellow players, using feints and side-steps to preserve their splendid isolation on the pitch, valuing above all the solo dash for the opposition's try-line. As Pociello points out, this early preference for mobility rather than power, for individuality rather than collectivity, and for intelligence rather than force was to lay the foundations for an authentic national style, quickly identified and celebrated by spectators and the sporting press alike.[56] Thierry Terret usefully develops these arguments, underlining the doubly hybrid (aristocratic and bourgeois, new and old), and inherently fragile, concept of dynamic masculinity that underpinned the whole performance:

> Between 1882 and 1892, when rugby first became a recognized sport, the players developed a non-violent and spectacular style of play by combining the aristocratic demand for elegance with the bourgeois emphasis on individual performance. Rugby thus provided the opportunity to demonstrate the qualities of dexterity, speed and quick decision-making that were the prerogatives of the upper classes. In contrast, strength was a value that was neither admired nor sought after. [. . .] True tackles were rare. [. . .] . . . the French rugby player had not yet broken with the dandy of the *belle époque*. When men wished to impress, they were likely to choose elegance over masculine strength.[57]

It was this socially acceptable form of masculine effort, then, that allowed cultured young Parisian men to engage in the new game. However, as the account in *L'Illustration* of the 1892 mismatch between Stade Français and Rosslyn Park will have suggested, the Parisian emphasis on elegance did not make for success in international competition. The weakness of the first French clubs in playing terms was quickly revealed as leading English sides began to visit Paris. Rosslyn Park were followed by Oxford University in 1893, with the Racing Club taking the opportunity to introduce the visiting students to the delights of the Moulin Rouge, where they too appreciated the spectacle provided by entertainers such as 'La Goulue', 'Valentin le Désossé', and the other stars of a music-hall golden age most famously celebrated by Toulouse-Lautrec.[58] Potter and Duthen point out that 'a combined Stade Français and Racing Club team, full of pluck, went to London in 1893 "for matches with the Civil Service F.C. at Richmond and Park House F.C. at Blackheath, losing both, but the first very narrowly". . .'.[59] By 1902, French club XVs had also played in Ireland, Scotland and Wales.[60] Most of them with a similar lack of success, although Stade Français had managed the exploit of defeating a weakened Rosslyn Park side, by 16–0, on a repeat visit to Paris in 1894.[61]

However, perhaps the most significant date to note at this early stage is 1900, when the latest of the *expositions universelles* or world fairs to be held in Paris took place (following those of 1855, 1867, 1878, and 1889). These major events celebrated commerce, technological and scientific achievements, and also the arts, as well as providing a showcase for the French colonial empire. They were therefore of considerable cultural significance, and the public impact of the 1900 fair inevitably dwarfed the second edition of Coubertin's fledgling Olympic Games, which, after their revival in Athens in 1896, were held in Paris to coincide with the universal exhibition. Nevertheless, under the auspices of the USFSA, the competition did, at least, take place, with rugby featuring by special invitation. A combined French side made up entirely of Parisian players thus took the field against representative sides from Frankfurt in Germany and Moseley in England, in matches held in front of some five thousand spectators at the velodrome stadium in the Bois de Vincennes in the altogether less fashionable eastern suburbs of the city. With victories in both matches, including no less than seven tries scored against an under-strength Moseley side, the French emerged as the clear victors in the hastily arranged three-way international competition. *L'Auto*, the leading sporting journal of the day – which, just three years later, under its inspirational editor Henri Desgrange, would launch the great Tour de France cycle race for patriotic as well as commercial reasons – was predictably enthusiastic in its coverage of this success; while Coubertin personally decreed that gold medals should be struck for every member of the winning side.[62] Yet this literally glittering Olympic success was the beginning of the end for Parisian dominance of French rugby, as the new game's centre of gravity now shifted rapidly, and irreversibly, to the south-west.

Notes

1. Edmond Renoir, 'Un match de foot-ball', 1892, reproduced in E. Baschet (ed.), *L'Illustration, Histoire d'un siècle, 1843–1944: VII. Années 1892–1898* (Paris, Le Livre de Paris, 1988), pp. 36–7.
2. Eugen Weber, 'Gymnastics and sports in *Fin-de-Siècle* France: opium of the classes?', *The American Historical Review*, 76/1, February 1971, pp.

70–98, at pp. 86–9. See also Richard Escot and Jacques Rivière, *Un siècle de rugby* (Paris, Calmann-Lévy, 1997), p. 45.

3. Other forms include American, Gaelic, and Australian Rules football, as well as the thirteen-a-side code of rugby league, which split from rugby union in 1896.

4. On 'invented traditions' in European sport more generally see Eric Hobsbawm, 'Mass-producing traditions: Europe, 1870–1914' in Eric Hobsbawm and Terence Ranger (eds), *The Invention of Tradition* (Cambridge, Cambridge University Press, 1983), pp. 263–307.

5. Reproduced in Sean Smith, *The Union Game: A Rugby History* (London, BBC, 1999), p. 18.

6. See Gareth Williams, 'From William Webb Ellis to World Cup – the social history of rugby union', in the same author's *1905 and All That: Essays on Rugby Football, Sport and Welsh Society* (Llandysul, Gomer Press, 1991), pp.8–48.

7. See Edmund Van Esbeck, *The Story of Irish Rugby* (London, Stanley Paul, 1986), p. 4.

8. For an incisive account of the social origins of rugby football, see Eric Dunning and Kenneth Sheard, *Barbarians, Gentlemen and Players: A Sociological Study of the Development of Rugby Football* (Oxford, Martin Robertson, 1979).

9. Jill Forbes and Michael Kelly, *French Cultural Studies: An Introduction* (Oxford, Oxford University Press, 1995), p. 12.

10. Ibid.

11. Hervé Le Bras, cited by Fernand Braudel, *The Identity of France: II. People and Production* (trans. Siân Reynolds; London, Collins, 1990), p. 542.

12. Weber, 'Gymnastics and sports', pp. 70–98. See also Theodore Zeldin, *France, 1848–1945: II. Intellect, Taste and Anxiety* (Oxford, Clarendon Press, 1977); Pierre Arnaud (ed.), *Les Athlètes de la République: gymnastique, sport et idéologie républicaine 1870–1914* (Toulouse, Privat, 1987); Pierre Arnaud (ed.), *Le Militaire, l'écolier, le gymnaste: Naissance de l'éducation physique en France (1869–1889)* (Lyons, Presses Universitaires de Lyon, 1991); Eugen Weber, *Peasants into Frenchmen: The Modernization of Rural France, 1870–1914* (London, Chatto & Windus, 1977); Eugen Weber, 'Pierre de Coubertin and the introduction of organized sport', in the same author's *My France: Politics, Culture, Myth* (Cambridge, MA, Belknap/Harvard University Press, 1991), pp. 207–25.

13. Braudel, *The Identity of France*, II, p. 671.

14. Weber, 'Gymnastics and sports', pp. 70–98; Richard Holt, *Sport and Society in Modern France* (London, Macmillan, 1981). See also Ronald

Hubscher *et al.*, *L'Histoire en mouvements: Le sport dans la société française (XIXe–XXe siècle)* (Paris, Armand Colin, 1992), pp. 93–108, where emphasis is placed on the Republican credentials of the wave of *associationisme* that followed the liberalization of the law on the formation of sports clubs and other groups (including particularly political associations) in 1901.

15. Jean-Pierre Callède, *L'Esprit sportif: Essai sur le développement associatif de la culture sportive* (Bordeaux, P. U. de Bordeaux, 1987), p. 169.
16. Weber, 'Gymnastics and sports', pp. 70–98. For a developed Marxist critique of sport see Jean-Marie Brohm, *Critiques du Sport* (Paris, Bourgeois, 1976).
17. However, neither Coubertin's personal influence nor that of the USFSA went unchallenged; far from it. See Holt, *Sport and Society*, pp. 64–5, on competing political groupings such as the Ligue Nationale de l'Education Physique (LNEP), formed in 1888, which had a markedly different ideological agenda (both less socially exclusive and more critical of Great Britain) as the basis for its encouragement of a revival of traditional French sports. Prominent supporters of the Ligue included Georges Clémenceau, Marcellin Berthelot, and Jean Macé. The efforts made to promote authentically French athletic sports by the flamboyant Paschal Grousset – former liberal journalist, *communard*, and political exile, and future Radical-Socialist deputy and defender of Dreyfus – should also be considered in this light (ibid.). See also Chapter 2.
18. This term is commonly used to suggest the spirit of aristocratic elitism associated with the early days of modern sport's development in America, and particularly the amateur ethos of the Corinthian Yacht Club.
19. Holt, *Sport and Society*, pp. 63–4.
20. Ibid., p. 64.
21. Leo Charney and Vanessa R. Schwartz (eds), *Cinema and the Invention of Modern Life* (Berkeley, CA, University of California Press, 1995), p. 1.
22. See Charles Rearick, *Pleasures of the Belle Epoque* (London and New Haven, CT, Yale University Press, 1985).
23. See Ferran Canyameres, *L'Homme de la Belle Epoque* (Paris, Les Editions Universelles, 1946) for a biography of Joseph Oller.
24. Weber, 'Gymnastics and sports', p. 84.
25. Ibid., p. 85.
26. See Jean-Pierre Bodis, 'Le rugby en France jusqu'à la seconde guerre mondiale: aspects politiques et sociaux', *Revue de Pau et du Béarn*, no.17, 1990, pp. 217–18, for a critical view of the standard accounts of the origins and activities of this club. Jean Lacouture, *Voyous et gentlemen: Une histoire du rugby* (Paris, Gallimard, 1993), p. 31, suggests that it was

with this club that the writer Pierre Mac Orlan would later embark on his own rugby-playing career.

27. Jean Lacouture, *Le Rugby, c'est un monde* (Paris, Seuil, 1979), pp. 31–2.
28. Escot and Rivière, *Un siècle de rugby*, p. 20.
29. Bodis, 'Le rugby en France', pp. 218–20. The influence of Ernest Renan and, especially, Hippolyte Taine might also be noted in this regard.
30. Bodis, 'Le rugby en France', pp. 220–1; Hubscher *et al.*, *L'Histoire en mouvements*, pp. 72–5; Holt, *Sport and Society*, pp. 62–8.
31. Alex Potter and Georges Duthen, *The Rise of French Rugby* (London, Bailey & Swinfen, 1961), p. 39.
32. Bodis, 'Le rugby en France', p. 220.
33. Williams, *1905 and All That*, p. 43.
34. Henri Garcia, *La Fabuleuse histoire du rugby* (Paris, ODIL, 1973), p. 933. The standard (i.e. reverse numerical) order of players from full-back (no. 15) to loose-head prop (no. 1) is adopted here, as is the familiar division of the members of the team according to their position on the field of play: full-back; three-quarters; half-backs; back-row forwards; second-row forwards; front-row forwards.
35. Bodis, 'Le rugby en France', pp. 221–3.
36. See Hubscher *et al.*, *L'Histoire en mouvements*, pp. 145–9.
37. Bodis, 'Le rugby en France', p. 223. See also Christian Pociello, *Le Rugby ou la guerre des styles* (Paris, A. M. Métailié, 1983), p. 37.
38. Holt, *Sport and Society*, pp. 62–8.
39. Pascal Ory, 'Naissance des loisirs' in Yves Lequin, *Histoire des Français: XIXe–XXe siècles: III. Les Citoyens et la démocratie* (Paris, A. Colin, 1984), pp. 264–72; p. 268 for the specific reference.
40. Holt, *Sport and Society*, p. 66.
41. Escot and Rivière, *Un siècle de rugby*, p. 29. Bodis, 'Le rugby en France', p. 223, dates the first clear reference to this famous trophy to 1912, but also notes that Georges Pastre has claimed that it is older than this. Intriguingly, the 'Brennus Shield' may also refer to the Gallic leader Brennus, who sacked Rome in 390 or 387 BC (and perhaps also his namesake who invaded Greece in 279 BC): an example of Gaulish triumphalism substantially antedating Astérix (see Chapter 7). I am indebted to David Phelps for this observation.
42. See Sébastien Darbon, *Rugby d'ici: Une manière d'être au monde*, (Paris, Editions Autrement, 1999), pp. 207–13; Lacouture, *Voyous et gentlemen*, pp. 136–45.
43. Lacouture, *Le Rugby*, pp. 35–6; cf. Henri Garcia, *Seigneurs et forçats du rugby: un siècle d'ovale en France* (Paris, Calmann-Lévy, 1994), p. 38. For a recent anthology drawing on over a century of French writing

on rugby football see Françoise, Lionel, and Serge Laget, *Rugby en toutes lettres* (Biarritz, Atlantica, 1999).

44. Thierry Terret, 'Learning to be a man: French rugby and masculinity' in Timothy J. L. Chandler and John Nauright, *Making the Rugby World: Race, Gender, Commerce* (London, Frank Cass, 1999), pp. 63–87, at p. 66.

45. Terret, 'French rugby and masculinity', p. 66. See also Robert Nye, *Masculinity and Male Codes of Honour in Modern France* (Oxford, Oxford University Press, 1993).

46. Douglas Peter Mackaman, *Leisure Settings: Bourgeois Culture, Medicine, and the Spa in Modern France* (Chicago, University of Chicago Press, 1998), pp. 4–5. Cf. Ruth Harris, *Murderers and Madness: Medicine, Law and Society in the Fin de Siècle* (Cambridge, MA, Harvard University Press, 1989), p. 11; cited by Forbes and Kelly, *French Cultural Studies*, p. 41. See also Robert Nye, *Crime, Madness, and Politics in Modern France: The Medical Concept of National Decline* (Princeton, NJ, Princeton University Press, 1984).

47. This point is developed in Chapter 2.

48. See Holt, *Sport and Society*, pp. 64–5.

49. Hubscher *et al.*, *L'Histoire en mouvements*, pp. 31–2; see also Note 19 above.

50. Weber, 'Gymnastics and sports', p. 87.

51. Pierre Mac Orlan, *La Clique du Café Brebis* (Paris, Renaissance du Livre, 1918; Paris, NRF/Gallimard, 1951 and 1991), p. 81. The whole of this chapter, on 'Les sports et Sylvie', is worthy of attention. Part of this material is also very usefully analysed by Terret, 'French rugby and masculinity', pp. 68–9.

52. Hubscher *et al.*, *L'Histoire en mouvements*, pp. 101–4.

53. Lacouture, *Voyous et gentlemen*, pp. 46–7; cf. Terret, 'French rugby and masculinity', pp. 76–7.

54. Pociello, *Le Rugby ou la guerre des styles*, p. 37.

55. Pierre de Coubertin, *Essais de psychologie sportive* (Grenoble, Jérôme Millon, 1992), p. 181. The memorable expression 'fortifier les muscles de Marianne' is that of Pierre Chambat; cited by Hubscher *et al.*, *L'Histoire en mouvements*, p. 26.

56. Pociello, *Le Rugby ou la guerre des styles*, pp. 36–42.

57. Terret, 'French rugby and masculinity', pp. 67–8.

58. Escot and Rivière, *Un siècle de rugby*, p. 31.

59. Potter and Duthen, *The Rise of French Rugby*, p. 40.

60. Ibid.

61. Escot and Rivière, *Un siècle de rugby*, p. 31.

62. Ibid., p. 35. *L'Auto*, also known as *L'Auto-Vélo*, was the direct predecessor of the modern French sporting instititution, *L'Equipe*. The title of the newspaper changed as a result of the former publication's too visible sympathy for the collaborationist cause during the German occupation of France in the Second World War. See Marianne Amar, *Nés pour courir: La Quatrième République face au sport* (Grenoble, P. U. de Grenoble, 1987), pp. 37–41.

− 2 −

The Expansion into the Provinces

France's first, and exclusively Parisian, clubs were to be followed by others in the provinces as rugby and the other athletic sports spread across the country in the 1890s. Everywhere a key role was played in the early phases of the new games' implantation by expatriate Britons and local *lycéens*. University students and teachers trained at the leading *écoles normales* were similarly influential in the diffusion of rugby in particular, with important educational centres – notably Bordeaux and Toulouse, but also Nantes in the north-west and Lyons in the south-east – being won over to the game.[1] The emergence of the south-west as the leading provincial centre was primarily due to the proselytizing dynamism of Dr Philippe Tissié and his Bordeaux-based Ligue Girondine de l'Education Physique (LGEP), founded in 1888 on the model of Paschal Grousset's militantly Republican Ligue Nationale de l'Education Physique (LNEP).[2] The academic authorities of the new Republic had made the creation through education of a unitary national culture – the transformation of 'peasants into Frenchmen', in Eugen Weber's memorable phrase[3] – its primary social and ideological objective, and the LGDP's influence with the local representatives of the state was to prove crucial in this regard:

> [Tissié's] energy, his influence, and that of the Ligue he founded, gained the support of the regional rectorate. As a result, the directives of the Ministry of Education, largely ignored in other areas, were applied in Aquitaine, where most secondary and a great many elementary schools made sports and games part of the regular curriculum. Offspring of modest homes, familiarized with running and games in primary school, could be found practising sports in associations of their own or in the Stade Bordelais, whose foundation in 1889 was a direct result of the enthusiasm generated by the Ligue.[4]

Thus it was that the first regional committee of Coubertin's USFSA was also established in Bordeaux, in 1893, to be followed four years later by those of Toulouse and Lyons. Stade Bordelais would go on to win seven national rugby championships between 1899 and 1911, drawing crowds approaching 30,000. As these attendance figures indicate, the pre-1914 development of the game in the Gironde was accompanied by a dramatic increase in its appeal as a spectator sport, which would, in turn, encourage the process of rugby's democratization and popularization in the south-west region as a whole. This diffusion can be traced with remarkable accuracy along the valley of the Garonne, which links Bordeaux and Toulouse, and then into the lesser administrative centres and even villages of this overwhelmingly rural part of France.[5] In Dr Philippe Tissié French rugby had found its most influential advocate, and in the south-west it was to find its spiritual home.

Both the national railway network and, for the privileged few, the new technology of the internal combustion engine were significantly increasing personal mobility at this time, and thus encouraged the process of sporting diffusion. Such developments as the creation of the Touring Club de France and the *Guides Michelin* in 1890 were obvious markers of this shift in habits, at least as far as the social elite was concerned, as was the foundation of the Automobile Club de France in 1895. Those who had come into contact with rugby in Paris, or through contacts with those educated in Paris, now began to play the new game in new places. The head start that rugby effectively had on football – and that was to last until the Great War – thus meant that it became the first of the modern team games to reach the French provinces, and in the case of the region to the south and west of the Loire it was able to establish an effective hegemony that would endure until the present day. The presence in Bordeaux, the centre of France's wine trade, of a large British colony was a major factor in the game's rapid expansion, with new clubs being set up on a regular basis. However, at least as important was the evangelizing zeal of Tissié and his supporters. In fact, the LGEP's intention was to promote supposedly traditional French alternatives to the new English sports, which in the case of rugby involved a markedly less violent handling game called *barette*, which permitted only 'touch-tackling', and was thus even deemed suitable to be played by women.[6] Yet, paradoxically, the impact of such patriotic initiatives was actually to promote the imported games. The *lycée*-based competitions that the LGEP organized – which were 'named *lendits* in imitation of mediaeval student festivals'[7] – soon gave way to characteristically modern varieties of sporting events, while their brief exposure to *barette* only left *lycéens* with a taste for a handling game that the partisans of rugby in its 'full-contact' form were only too willing to satisfy.[8] At this time, school teams typically adopted a flower as their emblem, such as *Les Muguets* [the lilies of the valley] from Bordeaux, *Les Coquelicots* [the poppies] from Pau, and *Les Violettes* [the violets] from Toulouse. The *lycéens* of Tarbes and Bayonne, for their part, preferred a reference to the chain of mountains that constitute the south-west's natural boundary with Spain: calling themselves *La Pyrénéenne* and *Les Montagnards* respectively. The apparent gentility of this nomenclature should not be allowed to disguise the role played by these and other schoolboy teams in the establishment of major clubs. The link between *La Pyrénéenne* and the great Stadoceste Tarbais (champions of France in 1920 and 1973), for instance, is well documented.[9]

It was as a member-association or *section* of Tissié's Bordeaux-based *ligue* that the Stade Bordelais club had first been established in 1889. Its foundation was a historic moment, in that this was the first all-French sports club of any kind to be set up outside Paris. Also significant was the rapid expansion of interest in rugby in the city, as evidenced by the establishment of a large number of rival clubs. Bodis has noted the existence around the turn of the century not only of Stade Bordelais, but also of the Bordeaux Université Club (which merged with Stade Bordelais in 1901), the Burdigala association, Les Volontaires – a name with military and *revanchard* nationalist overtones, more typical of the patriotic gymnastic and shooting clubs of the period – the Stade Athlétique Bordelais, and the Section Bordelaise.[10] This last club's name is an overt marker of its membership of Tissié's organization, as is that of a much more important association, the Section Paloise, founded in Pau in 1902 at the height of the game's expansion further into the south-west and still among the national elite. However, for the time being, it was Bordeaux that would come to dominate the national rugby scene at the expense of the Parisian pioneers.[11] The initial basis of Stade Bordelais's strength was its ability to recruit players and administrators from within the local bourgeoisie. Particularly significant from this point of view were the radical *notables*, who sought to further the Republican cause by using established anticlerical networks to promote rugby, specifically in opposition to the Catholic *patronages* and their sponsorship of association football (this point is developed in Chapter 3).

It is necessary to say something here of the antagonisms that brought Catholicism into conflict with the French state in the lead up to the dis-establishment of the Church in 1905, and, indeed, until the *Union Sacrée* was forced upon a deeply divided French nation by the approach of the First World War. Following the encyclical *Rerum Novarum* of 1891, which launched Pope Leo XIII's project of building a 'social Catholicism', sport in general and football in particular would constitute privileged sites for the ideological conflict between Church and state.[12] Central to this process was the battle for primacy between the secular USFSA and the Church's rival body, the FGSPF. The phenomenal recruitment of the *patronages* [Catholic youth clubs] in other regions of France – most obviously such strongholds of traditionalism as Brittany – was not generally matched in the south-west, which has a long tradition of political radicalism and resistance to centralized authority of all kinds. The FGSPF's decision to concentrate on encouraging football, specifically in opposition to rugby, meant that the latter game now became even more attractive to those who sought to oppose the Church and all its works.[13] Anticlerical opinion was thus drawn to Tissié's league, which proclaimed its own political affiliation in its adopted motto: 'For the Fatherland, through the Home, the School, and the Barracks'.[14] The linkage between the new sports associations and the great institutions of the Third Republic meant that many of the rugby clubs subsequently established throughout the region would be founded by schoolmasters and soldiers. Like the gymnasts before them, rugby players would thus be hailed as 'the athletes of the Republic'.[15]

On 23 April 1899, on the Sainte-Germaine pitch in Bordeaux, in front of some 3,000 enthusiastic spectators, Stade Bordelais beat Stade Français 5–3 to became champions of France for the first time – only the third club to do so after the Racing Club de France and Stade Français, and the first outside Paris. The clear contrast in aspirations flagged by the three clubs' names – between the national pretensions of the clubs based in the capital, and the regional, and even municipal, vocation of their conqueror from the Gironde – was a sign of things to come. For the presence in the victorious Bordeaux side of Englishmen like Cartwright and Harding[16] should not be allowed to disguise the significance of a sporting victory that was perceived at the time and subsequently as a much broader symbolic defeat inflicted on the French capital by its south-western provinces. Christian Pociello has drawn attention to the reporting of this first provincial victory by the local press, including particularly *La Petite Gironde*. This paper was typical of the rise of the popular press at this time, which went hand-in-hand with the development of sport as a mass-market commercial spectacle, and which would see the emergence of a specialized sporting press at both the national and regional level, such as *L'Auto*, based in Paris, and the local *Bordeaux-Sport*. In what has since become a standard feature of the reporting of the new game in France and elsewhere, the paper looked to military metaphors to celebrate the event. Hailing the courage of the local players in what was presented as an epic combat, the paper went on to set out a list of regionalist grievances against Paris, including particularly the failure of selectors based in the capital to pick Bordeaux players for the national side.[17] This was a distinctly paradoxical development given the loudly proclaimed patriotism of Tissié's LGEP and its supporters among the local Republican notability. However, it would prove to be anything but a temporary aberration. Daniel Herrero is one of many commentators on French rugby to have considered this aspect of the game's abiding appeal in the south-west:

The South-West is profoundly rural and rebellious. It was with the schoolmaster, and in the teacher-training colleges, that [rugby's] resonance would be strongest. The principal agent of social equilibrium in the [region's] villages, the schoolmaster adopted the game, conscious as he was of its educational virtues.

The South is vindictive and dominated by peasant values. The South is a land of expressiveness, openness, and generosity. The South loves festivity [*la fête*]. The South-West in its historic rebellion against the abusive power of the North seized upon the game of rugby football as its means of expression and its space for joy.[18]

The Stade Bordelais team thus entered the mythic pantheon of the *Midi*, becoming heroes in a struggle against the colonizing northern invader that could be traced back to the time of the Romans, but which had been thrown into sharp relief by the very events that had given rise to the modern French nation-state: 'rugby gave the south-west the opportunity to confront Parisian domination openly, to compete on its own soil against the capital which, since the Revolution of 1789, had never stopped pitting its centralist and authoritarian Jacobin tradition against the decentralist Girondist position that was particularly strong in Bordeaux'.[19]

In this pre-war period, in which rugby was still largely the preserve of the privileged classes, the game consequently became a focus for the aspirations of provincial elites, with Bordeaux and Toulouse to the fore in the expression of a south-western regional identity. Indeed, a mutual hostility to the militantly centralizing Paris of the Third Republic would even allow the south-west's two biggest cities to see beyond their habitual promotion of self-interest: 'At the beginning of the century the Parisian "enemy" allowed regional teams to overcome parochial rivalries.'[20] However, the durability of such regional solidarity could certainly not be taken for granted, as the stoning by Toulouse supporters of a train carrying Bordeaux fans in 1915 made clear.[21] Indeed, it was precisely the development of intense rivalries between south-western clubs themselves that was to characterize the development of French rugby in the inter-war period. At this stage, nevertheless, it was provincial resistance to Parisian political and cultural hegemony that was most obviously articulated through rugby football. This theme was soon picked up and amplified by the burgeoning popular press, with *Le Journal des sports*, for instance, proclaiming on 10 April 1909 that 'Bordeaux and Toulouse will avenge . . . all the provinces for the great injustices they have too long endured and for the unjustified humiliations that Paris believes it can inflict.'[22]

The year 1904 was to mark the beginning of Stade Bordelais's golden age: a period that would see the club never out of the championship final over a period of eight years, in spite of the constant emergence of new clubs at this time. Moreover, the club was rarely beaten in this period, becoming champions for four years in succession from 1904 to 1907, and then again in 1909 and 1911. Just as significantly, the club's success began to attract significant numbers of paying spectators – now numbered in their tens of thousands – in this pre-war period, both in Bordeaux and further afield.[23] Other markers of the club's growing social significance at this time included the appearance of its players in advertisements, such as those produced by the Nouvelles Galeries to mark the opening of their new Bordeaux department store in 1911.[24] Such commercial developments were destined to have major implications for the evolution of a game first adopted by a social elite for the defence of its own, narrowly conceived, class interests. The changes in question would make their most dramatic appearance in the period after the Great War. However, in the meantime, as France, like the other Western powers, became embroiled in the build-up to a seemingly inescapable conflict, it was the passage of the baton of French rugby-playing excellence from Bordeaux to clubs situated even deeper in the south-west that was worthy of note. From this point of view, the 1909 championship final was of particular significance, in that it brought together sides from Bordeaux and Toulouse, and was thus the first wholly provincial final, from which the capital was excluded. In 1912, Stade Toulousain would beat the *doyen* of French clubs, Racing Club de France, 8–6, to become champion in its own right. Watched by 15,000 home supporters at the Pont-Jumeaux stadium, paying a record amount to gain admission (25,000 francs), the victorious side included players who were destined to become major influences on the development of the French game, such as Adolphe Jauréguy and Philippe Struxiano. In 1913, at Colombes in Paris, 20,000 spectators – including many travelling supporters and south-western 'exiles', and paying a new record of 28,000 francs in gate-money[25] – were treated to a particularly emphatic demonstration of the far south-west's dominance when Aviron Bayonnais demolished the Parisian SCUF club 31–8.[26] Inspired by their Welsh fly-half and coach, Owen Roe, the Bayonne club would set a standard for French clubs to follow in subsequent decades. Where the Basque club led, the Catalans of AS Perpignan were not slow to follow, and, in 1914, they became champions themselves, narrowly defeating the Stadoceste club from Tarbes, a town neatly situated between Bayonne and Perpignan on France's Pyrenean frontier with Spain. This last pre-war final would thus point the way forward to the south-western hegemony of the modern era; while the championship itself would be suspended for the duration of the hostilities, to be replaced by the optimistically named Coupe de l'Espérance [the Hope Cup] for junior players too young for military service.

If the British presence in the Garonne region was primarily the result of Bordeaux's long-standing wine trade with Great Britain, then that in Pau and the Bayonne–Biarritz area had more to do with their enviable climate: the former, with its clear skies and pure mountain air, as a centre for the treatment of various ailments;[27] the latter as a *chic* holiday location and place of genteel retirement. It is thus significant that Pau should have had the first golf club in France. Established in 1856, the club would have an 'Anglo-Saxon' as its captain every year until the Great War. Biarritz, widely referred to at this time as *un pays d'Anglais* [an English colony], would become only the second French town to have a golf club in 1886.[28] Holt notes that 'at Pau the local *lycéens* first learned to play rugby through contact with visiting English public schoolboys'.[29] The prestigious Section Paloise would be set up in 1902 and Biarritz Olympique in 1907, just three years after the establishment of its near neighbour, the famous Aviron Bayonnais. Originally a rowing club, as its name indicates, the association's conversion to rugby would be the first stage in a process that would see Bayonne become the undisputed exponents of France's finest rugby within a decade. Pau and Bayonne were to lead the way for French rugby clubs, not only by drawing on the knowledge and talent of locally based expatriate Britons, but also by actively seeking out technical expertise in Britain itself. A Welsh student named Crockwell had introduced a more open style of play to the Pau club in 1907. He would be followed by a former Blackheath and Harlequins player, Tom Potter, who was to exert a considerable influence as captain and trainer of the Section Paloise from 1912 to 1914. In Bayonne, meanwhile, club officials involved in maritime trade took advantage of business links to invite players like Alfred Russell, from the Glasgow Academicals club, and Harry Owen Roe, from Penarth, to act as technical advisers to the Aviron Bayonnais. In particular, the impact of Roe's methods as player and coach would be such as to ensure Bayonne's complete domination of the national championship in 1913.[30]

Thus Stade Bordelais acted as a model and as a catalyst for the spread of the union game throughout the south-west. Between 1899 and 1914 the Bordeaux club's spectacular success provided the inspiration for the rapid emergence of clubs that would go on to become the French game's most celebrated exponents. In fact, such was the significance of this period that virtually every major French club that now exists was established at this time. Stade Bordelais was also of importance in that it supplied a number of the players – such as Jauréguy and Stuxiano – who became the first to represent their country in matches against the British and Irish, together with sides from the British Empire, starting with New Zealand in 1906. The French national XV began playing against the four 'home unions' in this same year, although its matches would not be included in the calculations for the annual international championship – the future Five Nations tournament – until 1910. Despite the fact that French sides were initially outclassed, the popularity of these encounters increased very rapidly, as was reflected in the number of spectators attending international matches at the main grounds, the Parc des Princes and Stade de Colombes, in Paris: 5,000 for England in 1908; 8,000 for Wales in 1909 and Scotland in 1910; 10,000 for Ireland in 1910; 20,000 for Wales in 1911; 25,000 for Scotland in 1913 and Wales in 1914.[31] The ability of French players to learn from the defeats inflicted in these first encounters was revealed as early as 1911, when *le XV de France* recorded its first international victory, against Scotland, in Paris, by the narrowest of margins (16–15). The failure to repeat the feat in the same fixture two years later led to the infamous '*affaire* Baxter', in which the English referee was attacked by angry French supporters, who invaded the pitch and subsequently went on the rampage through the capital. Partly comprehensible in terms of the ultra-nationalism of the period, this episode was also a hint at the troubles that lay ahead for French rugby, as was the decision of the Scottish Rugby Union to break off relations *sine die*.[32]

If Stade Bordelais were the first south-western side to inflict defeats on the Parisian foe, they would not be the most influential in the longer term. That role would fall to Stade Toulousain, who won the first of their national championships in 1912 and their fourteenth in 1997. Paul Voivenel, the leading chronicler of French rugby's early development, and subsequently an important administrator of the game, was among the first to note how the club came to be known as *la Vierge Rouge* [the Red Virgin]. This striking nickname resulted from the fact that the Toulouse side had not lost a single game, home or away, competitive match or friendly, in the 1912 season.[33] As depicted in postcards specially produced to commemorate the team's success, 'Zézette', as the club's imaginary heroine was soon nicknamed, might be placed in a long line of chaste feminine icons that includes the Virgin Mary, Joan of Arc, Marianne, and the Revolutionary figure of Liberty. Pierre Duboscq sees her rather as a south-western version of the Roman goddess Minerva, a warrior princess leading the local micro-society into battle against the forces of a centralizing Republic. The patriotic vision of Coubertin's USFSA, encapsulated in the slogan 'Ludus pro patria', was thus in the process of being replaced by an alternative sporting paradigm in the south-west – 'Ludus pro loco', as Duboscq puts it – as regional identity politics began to inflect the increasingly popular game in new ways.[34] Indeed, the first decade of the twentieth century, in which Toulouse was at the centre of a second wave of French rugby growth, was a period in which the game became established as an integral part of the region's culture, appealing to an increasingly knowledgeable, and, crucially, socially more diverse audience. The mythification of the 'inviolate' 1912 Stade Toulousain side is consequently seen by Pech and Thomas as part of a process of popularization that appealed to the familiar rituals and rhythms of the Church as rugby established itself in the south-west as a 'quasi-religion'.[35] Moreover, the new Sunday rite of the rugby match attracted both independent-minded Catholics who could see beyond the football-playing *patronages* and the anticlerical majority of a region in which the Radical tradition was still strong. From the staunch Catholicism of the Basque country in the far west of the region to the rural socialism (and even the communism in the inter-war years) of the Limousin, on its northern fringes, south-western rugby could offer a support for or an alternative to established dominical modes of sociability, as required. The appearance at this time of a new caste of officially designated referees to take proper charge of proceedings – held in locations that were themselves increasingly sacralized as shrines to the new cult of the oval ball – was also to reinforce this link with older modes of patriarchally structured authority.[36]

If the Garonne river was the primary artery for the new sport's diffusion – 'like a wind whipping up and channeling rugby's spread like wildfire, [from Bordeaux] towards Agen, Toulouse, and Carcassonne, before the flames went on to take hold in Perpignan'[37] – it was not the only one. Both the sociologist Christian Pociello and the geographer Jean-Pierre Augustin have mapped rugby's spread throughout the south-west, and have conclusively demonstrated that the foundations of the region's hegemony after the Great War were laid at this time.[38] As the sport spread into the countryside, it ceased to be the preserve of an urban elite, and became instead a source of amusement, but also, increasingly, of prestige, for local centres, smaller towns, and even villages. It was at this time, in fact, that rugby took root in the *bourg* [a 'settlement, something between a large village and a small town, always the site of a market'], as opposed to the city, and became imbued with the value-systems of the *pays* ['within France used of districts or regions with their own identity'][39] as distinct from those of the Republican nation-state or *patrie*. As Pociello puts it: 'It was the principal towns of the south, human reservoirs and university centres, that initially, and logically, provided a base for the phenomenon (Bordeaux, Toulouse . . .). But, as it lost its student-based character, rugby migrated from the residential districts to the working-class suburbs, before becoming a typical feature of the small or medium-sized town.'[40] Others, following Robert Barran, have gone even further, arguing that the real basis of French rugby's strength after the First World War, and until the very recent past, was actually *le rugby des villages*.[41] The apparent difference of opinion may be semantic as much as anything else, with the key terms in which the relevant locations are described – *village, bourg, bourgade* – clearly overlapping to a certain extent. The really important thing, as we shall see in more detail in Chapter 3, was that this moral and material investment in rugby football by relatively small south-western communities was to result in some very old, and often unpalatable, wine finding its way into the new bottles of the union game.

The Great War, when it finally came, would hit the south-west hard, in spite of the region's obvious physical separation from the main battle fronts in the north-east of the country. Young men would be mobilized as elsewhere, with the patriotically minded players of the new athletic sports fated to pay a disproportionately heavy toll in terms of deaths and injuries on the battlefield. The number of French deaths resulting from the hostilities was to be in the region of 1.4 million, or approximately 3.5 per cent of the total population, with the highest loss of life recorded in the military districts of Rennes (in Brittany) and Limoges (in the south-west), where more than 19 per cent of those mobilized were killed. Bodis has calculated that the figure for French international rugby players killed in the conflict is even higher, at 21 per cent, or 23 out of the total 111 'capped' players, not including an American and two British nationals, who had all played for the *XV de France*, and who also perished in the conflict. Moreover, this contingent of south-western rugby players – which obviously included not only the international stars but also the much more numerous club players of the region – was still dominated by the liberal professional classes, with the result that a disproportionate number of members of the local intellectual elites were lost between 1914 and 1918.[42] This fact is striking enough in itself; but the Great War's impact on the rugby-playing communities of the south-west may best be illustrated by reference to a single, highly symbolic game, played just prior to the outbreak of hostilities.

The 1913 championship final had seen the Basques of the Aviron Bayonnais club, led by their Welsh *fils adoptif*, Owen Roe, triumph over the SCUF of Paris, in a convincing demonstration of the power and artistry of *la manière bayonnaise*. The young Paul Voivenel personally observed the emergence of what he calls 'the dazzling glory of Bayonne', providing some valuable detail regarding the broader social resonance of this particular club and its widely appreciated style of play:

> . . . on 20 April 1913, at Colombes, and in front of more than twenty thousand excited spectators, the AB, in the final, triumphed over the SCUF, the favourites, by 31 points (7 tries, 5 goals) to 8 points (2 tries, 1 goal).
>
> Unknown three years earlier, the new champions had demonstrated to an astonished crowd what has been called 'the fireworks of the Bayonne method'.

The immense stadium was packed. All the Southerners living in Paris were crowded together. There was singing in the sunshine. *It was at this time that supporters started wearing the colours of their respective teams.*[43]

Claude Duhau's history of the Aviron Bayonnais in its 'heroic period' provides further insights into the team's local cultural resonance at this time. Of these, the most appealing is perhaps the role played by 'the famous "Figaro" of Bayonne', Edmond Perron, the singing barber of no. 5 Rue Thiers, and a prolific composer of waltzes, mazurkas, quadrilles, and so forth, who composed and published the 'Marche de l'AB' in 1909.[44] This club song was thus a forerunner of Maurice Chevalier's more famous 'Marche du Rugby', with lyrics and score by Jean and Lucien Boyer, which played to packed houses at the Théâtre des Nouveautés in Paris in 1924, and which was composed to celebrate Stade Toulousain's three consecutive championship wins (1922–4).[45]

In 1914, the Aviron Bayonnais side got as far as the quarter-finals, where the talented Basques had to travel to play the equally gifted Catalans of Perpignan. For Voivenel, as for the Catalan poet Albert Bausil,[46] what followed was quite simply the finest game of rugby ever played, or *le Match-Roi* as Voivenel terms it, and thus the epitome of a game that in France is routinely – and usually unquestioningly – referred to as *le sport-roi*.[47] In his contemporary newspaper account of the game, Voivenel explains the beauty of this particular encounter in a style that would point the way forward for a self-consciously literary school of sports journalism that has no obvious equivalent in the English-language press, although there are parallels in Italy and elsewhere in Europe. In extracts such as the following, which undoubtedly influenced later writers such as Antoine Blondin and Jean Lacouture, Voivenel demonstrates the justice of Blondin's assertion that sports journalism should not necessarily be considered a minor genre.[48] His explanation of the appeal of the match is worthy of quotation at some length, not only for stylistic reasons – in so far as these may properly be appreciated in a translation – but also for the light it casts on the ethnic stereotyping that underlies French rugby's mythologizing of the game's centrality in the cultural life of the carefully delineated *pays* of the south-west:

> Let me talk you through it – not as a technician, for I have ceased to be one at the present time – but rather as a simple spectator who lets his imagination wander wherever his sensations may lead him. Journalists who, as in a medical examination, press and poke at a match, analysing it all the while, are in the exact position of a literary critic who *studies* a work too much really to *feel* it.
>
> On Sunday I watched a battle in which my side's colours were not at stake. I was indifferent to the outcome. My impressions are thus free of any bias, and I

am sure that I have only recorded moods and feelings inspired by the *game* alone, by its symbolism and, let us dare to say it, by its *art*.

Two races clashed: Basques and Catalans. That both teams contained athletes who were from outside these regions [*étrangers aux pays*] had not the slightest importance, for these outsiders were embraced and incorporated, 'digested' as it were, and had quickly become part of the collective *soul*.

Basques and Catalans! You know all the sporting poetry that is already attached to those two names.

On one side, the representatives of a land where the Ocean lives a more tumultuous existence, where the greenery is powerful and dark, where the pines huddle together in interminable forests, where the pretty villas climb up the rough slopes, and where the skies are pale blue with hints of silver; – and on the other the men from wildest Roussillon, where the colours are deeper, and where autumn is sumptuous. There, pelota players, supple, stocky, elastic, with a feline agility, the brothers of [Pierre Loti's fictional smuggler] Ramuntcho, dressed in the colours of their sky and their foaming waves; here, taller lads, with wiry legs and broad shoulders, decked out in purple and gold that emphasize the rich colours of their province, the land of garnet-coloured grapes that their poets liken to drops of blood.

Basques and Catalans![49]

Thus presented, Voivenel's south-west is not far removed from the sacralized Lorraine of Maurice Barrès and other such right-wing literary defenders of the *patrie* as the latest war with Germany loomed. Indeed, the values articulated here, and particularly the interweaving of sport-inflected concepts of place and race, were readily to be recuperated by the belligerent nationalism that preceded and informed the Great War. Moreover, three decades later, in an even more sinister development, these same ideas would be adopted by the reactionary 'old guard' that sought to impose an authoritarian 'new order' on a defeated French nation under the collaborationist Vichy administration. As we shall see in Chapter 5, Voivenel and a Perpignan fly-half of the 1920s, Joseph Pascot, would be at the heart of such developments.

For the time being, let us concentrate on the fact that it was not simply the quality of the play resulting from this clash of south-western *pays* that made the 1914 game stand out from all the others, nor yet the closeness of the result, which remained a draw after no less than four periods of extra time (Perpignan narrowly won the replay in Bayonne a few days later). Rather, the abiding greatness of this apparently interminable 'battle of the titans' came from the spiritual quality that developed as the exhausted players stumbled towards its eventual close, and which Voivenel narrates in the present tense:

The crowd has stopped shouting. Their excitement has given way to a gravity that is striking. It is as if the dark sky laden with clouds is weighing down on their heads. People become religious and fanatical support is replaced by a form of unconscious mysticism.[50]

Given the moment in French history at which it occurred, this feeling of foreboding was fully justified. Indeed, it leads us to consider the author's longer-term reasons for deciding that this game could never be equalled. For it was in the particular light cast by his own subsequent service as a medical officer in the Great War that Voivenel was to reassert the game's abiding greatness:

There has never been another match to compare with it in the history of Rugby.
And you will understand why I do not appreciate people bandying this term about.
In our championship there is only one *Match-Roi*.
The sacrifice of our heroes forbids us from ever identifying a second.[51]

For no fewer than fifteen of the thirty players who appeared on the pitch that day were to die in the 1914–18 conflict.[52] It was this level of sacrifice by French *rugbymen*, including his close friend, the international player Alfred Mayssonnié, that would lead Voivenel to campaign for a monument to commemorate the athletes who perished.[53] Amazingly, mobilized players would actually organize rugby matches at the front in the early days of the conflict. However, this initial optimism was soon replaced by harsher realities, as the soldier Henri Amand records:

I played my last match in 1915 in the Champagne region, near the front. We got changed in our trench. I played alongside [the Stade Français and French international player] Géo André, but the game was soon interrupted. The Germans put up an air-burst shell over the pitch and nobody wanted to hang around after that.[54]

Notes

1. Jean-Pierre Bodis, *Histoire mondiale du rugby* (Toulouse, Bibliothèque Historique Privat, 1987), pp. 143–5. For an account of the failure of rugby football to establish itself durably in other regions of France, and specifically Brittany in the north-west and Lyons in the south-east, see Philip Dine, 'Sporting assimilation and cultural confusion in Brittany' in Grant Jarvie (ed.), *Sport in the Making of Celtic Cultures* (London and

Leicester, Cassell and Leicester University Press, 1999), pp. 112–30, and the same author's 'The historical development of rugby in south-east France: *En marge de l'Ovalie?*' in Maurice Roche (ed.), *Sport, Popular Culture and Identity* (Aachen, Meyer & Meyer Verlag), pp. 211–24. Also on the south-east, see Jean Nicaud, *Cent ans de rugby régional* (Bourg-en-Bresse, Les Editions de la Taillanderie, 1992), and Daniel-Guy Gardian, *100 ans au FCL: 1893–1993* (Caluire, FC Lyon, 1993). Also of interest from this point of view (on the period after the First World War, when France's 'lost provinces' in the east were regained) is Francis Braesch and Hervé Bride, *Vous ne plaquerez pas l'Alsace et la Lorraine* (Colmar, Editions d'Alsace, 1980).

2. See Chapter 2, n. 19.
3. Eugen Weber, *Peasants into Frenchmen: The Modernization of Rural France, 1870–1914* (London, Chatto & Windus, 1977).
4. Eugen Weber, 'Gymnastics and sports in *Fin-de-Siècle* France: opium of the classes?', *The American Historical Review*, 76/1, February 1971, pp. 70–98; p. 87 for the quotation.
5. Christian Pociello, *Le Rugby ou la guerre des styles* (Paris, A. M. Métailié, 1983), pp. 47–54; Jean-Pierre Augustin, 'L'étonnante implantation du rugby dans le Midi', *Midi*, no. 4, 1987, pp. 9–11.
6. Jean Lacouture, *Voyous et gentlemen: Une histoire du rugby* (Paris, Galli-mard, 1993), pp. 46–7; cf. Thierry Terret, 'Learning to be a man: French rugby and masculinity' in Timothy J. L. Chandler and John Nauright, *Making the Rugby World: Race, Gender, Commerce* (London, Frank Cass, 1999), pp. 76–7.
7. Richard Holt, *Sport and Society in Modern France* (London, Macmillan, 1981), p. 65.
8. Augustin, 'Rugby dans le Midi', p. 7; Jean-Pierre Bodis, 'Le rugby en France jusqu'à la seconde guerre mondiale: aspects politiques et sociaux', *Revue de Pau et du Béarn*, no. 17 (1990), pp. 217–44, at p. 224.
9. Jean-Paul Rey, *Tarbes, le rugby en rouge et blanc* (Paris, Solar, 1973), pp. 55–6; cf. Holt, *Sport and Society*, pp. 68–9.
10. Bodis, 'Le rugby en France', pp. 223–4; cf. Terret, 'French rugby and masculinity', p. 63.
11. See Jean-Pierre Callède, *Histoire du sport en France: du Stade Bordelais au SBUC, 1889–1939* (Bordeaux, Editions de la Maison des Sciences de l'Homme d'Aquitaine, 1993); also Jean-Pierre Augustin and Alain Garrigou, *Le Rugby démêlé: Essai sur les Associations Sportives, le Pouvoir et les Notables* (Bordeaux, Le Mascaret, 1985), pp. 32–7 et seq.
12. Holt, *Sport and Society*, pp. 190–211.
13. See Jean-Pierre Augustin, 'Formes de ballons et formes de croyances',

Les Cahiers de l'animation, 2/40, 1983; also the same author's 'Les patronages du Sud-Ouest: la socialisation politique et le mouvement sportif, 1870–1914' in Pierre Arnaud and Jean Camy (eds), *La Naissance du mouvement sportif associatif en France: sociabilités et formes de pratiques sportives* (Lyons, P. U. de Lyon, 1986); B. Dubreuil, 'La naissance du sport catholique', in A. Ehrenberg, 'Aimez-vous les stades?: Les origines historiques des politiques sportives en France (1870–1930)', special number of *Recherches*, no. 43, April 1980, pp. 221–51.

14. Augustin, 'Rugby dans le Midi', p. 6.
15. Alex Potter and Georges Duthen note that 'With few exceptions the fifty-six teams in Division I of France's National Championship were founded between 1895 and 1910. University and college students, some of them urged on by professors, were the chief pioneers. In garrison towns they were often joined by troops': *The Rise of French Rugby* (London, Bailey & Swinfen, 1961), p. 40. See also Pierre Arnaud (ed.), *Les Athlètes de la République: gymnastique, sport et idéologie républicaine 1870–1914* (Toulouse, Privat, 1987) and the same editor's *Le Militaire, l'écolier, le gymnaste: Naissance de l'éducation physique en France (1869–1889)* (Lyons, P. U. de Lyon, 1991).
16. On the role of British players in Bordeaux see Jean-Pierre Augustin and Jean-Pierre Bodis, *Rugby en Aquitaine: histoire d'une rencontre* (Bordeaux, Centre Régional des Lettres d'Aquitaine and Editions Aubéron, 1994), pp. 34–7, including particularly the section on W. L. Morgan, the great Welsh player known as 'Billy Bordeaux'.
17. Pociello, *Le Rugby ou la guerre des styles*, pp. 46–7.
18. Daniel Herrero, *Passion ovale* (Monaco and Paris, Editions du Rocher, 1990), p. 138. See also Robert Barran, *Le Rugby des villages* (Paris, Les Editeurs Français Réunis, 1974), pp. 131–8, 'Olivier Saisset, l'instituteur des Cévennes'.
19. Terret, 'French rugby and masculinity', p. 64.
20. Ibid., pp. 71–2.
21. Sean Smith, *The Union Game: A Rugby History* (London, BBC, 1999), pp. 191–2.
22. Cited by Terret, 'French rugby and masculinity', p. 72. However, the Bordeaux club's violent encounter with the Racing Club in Paris in 1904 also pointed the way forward to rather less savoury developments in the south-western game: see Richard Escot and Jacques Rivière, *Un siècle de rugby* (Paris, Calmann-Lévy, 1997), p. 37.
23. Henri Garcia, *La Fabuleuse histoire du rugby* (Paris, ODIL, 1973), pp. 935–6.
24. Augustin, 'Rugby dans le Midi', p. 4.

25. Garcia, *La Fabuleuse histoire du rugby*, pp. 206–8.
26. See Augustin and Bodis, *Rugby en Aquitaine*, p. 33, on Bayonne's early vision of 'total' rugby.
27. Those coming to the town to convalesce would later famously include the novelist André Gide.
28. Ronald Hubscher *et al.*, *L'Histoire en mouvements: Le sport dans la société française (XIXe–XXe siècle)* (Paris, Armand Colin, 1992), p. 62.
29. Holt, *Sport and Society*, p. 68.
30. Augustin, 'Rugby dans le Midi', pp. 7–8.
31. Bodis, 'Le rugby en France', pp. 230–2. On the establishment and development of the main Paris grounds as sporting *lieux de mémoire* [memorial sites] see especially Florence Pizzorni Itié (ed.), *Les Yeux du Stade: Colombes, temple du Sport* (Paris, Editions de l'Albaron, 1993). It should be noted that the modern Stade de France at Saint-Denis in the Paris suburbs should not to be confused with the Stade Français club, who themselves play at the older Jean Bouin stadium adjacent to the Parc des Princes.
32. See Holt, *Sport and Society*, p. 137. See also Philip Dine, 'The tradition of violence in French sport' in Renate Günther and Jan Windebank (eds), *Violence and Conflict in Modern France* (Sheffield, Sheffield Academic Press, 1995), pp. 245–60.
33. Paul Voivenel, *Mon beau rugby: L'Esprit du Sport* (Toulouse, Editions Midi-Olympique, 1962), p. 58.
34. Pierre Duboscq (ed.), *Rugby, parabole du monde* (Paris, L'Harmattan, 1998), pp. 312–13.
35. Rémy Pech and Jack Thomas, 'La Naissance du rugby populaire à Toulouse (1893–1914)' in Pierre Arnaud and Jean Camy (eds), *La Naissance du mouvement sportif associatif en France: sociabilités et formes de pratiques sportives* (Lyons, P. U. de Lyon, 1986), pp. 97–126, at pp. 108–9. Terret, 'French rugby and masculinity', p. 72, comments similarly that 'The final that Toulouse won in 1912 against the Racing Club led to a virtual deification of the team: a red statue of the Virgin Mary wearing the local colours was set up to thank the players and their supporters.'
36. Pech and Thomas, 'La Naissance du rugby populaire', p. 109. On sport as a substitute for organized religion, see especially Alain Ehrenberg, *Le Culte de la performance* (Paris, Calmann-Lévy, 1991).
37. Pociello, *Le Rugby ou la guerre des styles*, p. 53.
38. Ibid., pp. 47–54; Augustin, 'Rugby dans le Midi', pp. 9–11.
39. Glossary provided by Siân Reynolds in her translation of Fernand Braudel, *The Identity of France: I. History and Environment* (London, Collins,

1988), pp. 405 and 409; cf. Weber, *Peasants into Frenchmen*, pp. 45–6, 67 and 98, on the distinction between *pays* and *patrie*.

40. Pociello, *Le Rugby ou la guerre des styles*, pp. 53–4.
41. See, for instance, André Quilis in Duboscq, *Rugby, parabole du monde*, p. 81; cf. Barran, *Le Rugby des villages*.
42. Bodis, 'Le rugby en France', p. 234.
43. Voivenel, *Mon beau rugby*, p. 72.
44. Claude Duhau, *Histoire de l'Aviron Bayonnais: I. L'époque héroïque, 1904–1914*, (Bayonne, Editions Christian Mendibourne, 1968, reprinted 1983), pp.44–5.
45. Escot and Rivière, *Un siècle de rugby*, p. 67.
46. Bodis, 'Le rugby en France', pp. 237–8, notes that Bausil, who also established a regionalist newspaper, *Le Cri catalan* (later *Le Coq catalan*), has been regarded as the 'spiritual father' of Charles Trenet, the popular singer who, from the 1940s onwards, offered audiences a reassuring image of a traditionalist France in songs such as 'La Mer' and, especially, 'Douce France'. See also Pech and Thomas, 'La Naissance du rugby populaire', p. 110, regarding Bausil, Voivenel, and other journalistic proselytizers of rugby in the south-west.
47. Voivenel, *Mon beau rugby*, p. 78. These terms are not straightforward to translate, but may be rendered as 'the king of matches' and 'the king of sports'.
48. See Yvan Audouard, *Monsieur Jadis est de retour: Antoine Blondin* (Paris, La Table Ronde, 1994), p. 172. See also the work on the Tour de France of the investigative journalist Albert Londres in the 1920s, which revealed a world that was as unknown to the broader French public as his more celebrated exposés (such as that on the penal colony of Devil's Island). Republished as *Tour de France, tour de souffrance* (Paris, Le Serpent à Plumes, 1996).
49. Voivenel, *Mon beau rugby*, p. 81.
50. Ibid., p. 83.
51. Ibid., p. 78.
52. Ibid., pp. 78 and 80.
53. See Chapter 5. On French memorials to the Great War, see Jay M. Winter, *Sites of Memory, Sites of Mourning: The Great War in European Cultural History* (Cambridge, Cambridge University Press, 1995), pp. 78–116.
54. Cited by Henri Garcia, *Seigneurs et forçats du rugby: un siècle d'ovale en France* (Paris, Calmann-Lévy, 1994), p. 38. See also ibid., p. 44, on Géo André as a player for club and country.

PART II

Rugby Goes to War, 1914–1945

− 3 −

Identity and Brutality in the South-West

French sport as a whole would not only recover surprisingly quickly in the wake of the First World War, but would also be subject to a major expansion in the numbers of both players and spectators. This new enthusiasm was manifested in various ways, including the establishment in 1922 of a new 'provisional service for physical education and sports' in the Ministry of Education, and the vocal, if highly idealized, advocacy of athletic sports on the part of intellectuals such as Henry de Montherlant and Jean Giraudoux. For Giraudoux, the rugby side was nothing less than a model for society: 'The rugby team requires fifteen men, of whom eight should be strong and active, two should be nimble and quick-witted, four should be tall, graceful, and swift, and the last one should be a model of calm and coolness under pressure: this is also the ideal ratio for society.'[1] Montherlant for his part noted that 'It would seem to be infinitely more important for little Frenchmen to become aware of the poetry to be found in a whole afternoon spent playing with a ball, than in struggling to uncover . . . the poetry that may or may not reside in a given verse by Racine'.[2] This was an artistic tendency that reached a crescendo with the Paris Olympics of 1924, which aroused widespread public interest, and where rugby significantly featured as an official sport. However, the pandemonium that resulted when the French were defeated by the United States in the final[3] is suggestive of the deeper and darker forces that were at play as interest in the game boomed in this period, and also helps to explain why rugby never again featured as an Olympic sport.

Rugby additionally saw its popularity reflected in contexts as diverse as the radio, which broadcast its first live match commentary in 1923; the music-hall, where Maurice Chevalier sang 'La Marche du Rugby'; the cinema, in the form of a 1928 film entitled *La Grande Passion*; and even men's fashion, with the general adoption across France of the *béret basque* made famous by the Aviron Bayonnais club. However, in the dramatically changed social order of post-1918 France, sport would be a focus not only for new pleasures, but also for new conflicts, and rugby in particular would reflect these changed national and, crucially, local preoccupations. For in what follows, attention will be focused above all on the leading role played by rugby football in the evolution of relations between the French nation-state's political and cultural centre, in Paris, and its south-western periphery. It will be argued, in fact, that the newly adopted game constituted one of the principal vectors for the expression of a variety of regional aspirations in this period, and thus represented an important theatre for the playing-out of an age-old drama of contested identities.

Maurice Agulhon is just one of many influential French commentators on his country's historical struggle to maintain its political unity in the face of its constituent regions' remarkable cultural diversity. The pioneering work of Eugen Weber in this field has been noted previously.[4] More recently, Hervé Le Bras and Emmanuel Todd have sought to explain what they call 'the invention of France';[5] while Fernand Braudel, that specialist in the 'deep structures' of French identity, has stressed that 'Yes, France is certainly diverse. And that diversity is visible, lasting and *structural*.'[6] However, it is Agulhon who has perhaps most crisply stated the central feature of French society's evolution between the First World War and the present day: 'To put it plainly, and at the risk of oversimplifying, it is possible to say that in 1914 the French were *united* in a national consciousness, but *diverse* in their cultural practices, whereas nowadays they are *diverse and divided* as regards the national dimension, but *more united* in their cultural practices.'[7] There could thus in 1918 be no doubting the patriotism of south-western *rugbymen*, who had given so many of their own to the national cause on the battlefields of the Great War. However, in the inter-war years the union game would offer a privileged site for the cultural expression of an enduring south-western identity in the face of radical social change; as, indeed, it would again after 1945. At the heart of these developments would be the relationship between the towns and the countryside, and the story of rugby's development would thus be played out against the backdrop of what Braudel describes as 'the spectacle that overshadows all others, in the France of the past and even today, [that] is the collapse of a peasant society'.[8] This point will be developed when we come to consider the cultural specificity of rugby football as played in the south-west of France.

Although the French national championship, like the Five Nations tournament, did not recommence until 1920, a number of important matches took place in France even before the hostilities had ended. As early as 9 April 1917, a team made up of New Zealand military personnel and wearing the famous strip of the All Blacks took on a representative side of French soldiers, also kitted out in their national colours, at the Vincennes municipal stadium, in eastern Paris. The French were heavily defeated (40–0), but for their full-back, Bechade from the Périgueux club, the encounter was to prove truly tragic: he was killed the following day as he made his way back to the front to rejoin his unit.[9] This first sporting encounter between representative sides drawn from the allied forces based in France was followed by several others as the war finally drew to a close. These military celebrations of victory reached their climax in the 'Inter-Allied Games', organized along Olympic lines in June 1919. Hosted by the American General Pershing, and mainly held in a purpose-built stadium in the Bois de Vincennes, the event included a rugby tournament, although only teams from France, the United States, and Romania participated, with the French winning a horribly violent final against the Americans (8–3).[10] For Allan Henri Muhr, an American citizen who had established himself in Paris, where he became an important figure in French rugby, both as a player and administrator, such brutality was wholly unacceptable. A stalwart of the Racing Club, Muhr had been picked to play for the French national side in its first ever international match in 1906, against New Zealand, and was very much one of the old school. However, as a volunteer ambulance-man during the Great War, Muhr probably knew what he was talking about when he said of the 1919 clash that 'It [was] the best that anyone could do without a knife or a revolver.'[11] Such brutality on the pitch, and also not infrequently off it, was to be a characterizing feature of French rugby throughout the 1920s, and would ultimately lead both to internal schism and international isolation in the 1930s.

More generally, *les années folles*, the 'mad years' from 1919 to 1929, were marked in France by a determination to embrace modernity as an antidote to the social and psychological trauma occasioned by the Great War. This enthusiasm for the new was by no means confined to the traditionally legitimated cultural forms, such as literature, music, painting, and the other 'high' arts. On the contrary, as Forbes and Kelly have pointed out: 'If the 1920s is an extraordinary decade of productivity and experimentation in all forms of high culture, it is also the scene for an unprecedented organization and expansion of popular culture, often the result of the availability of new technologies.'[12] Foremost among these new technologies was radio, with the stations established in Paris and the main provincial centres providing a staple diet of 'news and sports coverage, often in collaboration with powerful daily newspapers'.[13] Moreover, 'If French popular culture in the 1920s benefited from enhanced technology and organization in all fields, nowhere was this more visible than in sport.'[14] With the first regional radio stations created in Bordeaux and Toulouse in 1925, rugby in its south-western stronghold thus became one of many sports to benefit from this media-led expansion of interest. In organizational terms, a key moment occurred in

1920 when the Fédération Française de Rugby (FFR) gained its independence from Coubertin's socially elitist USFSA, as part of a wider fragmentation of French sport's administrative structures that had already seen the establishment of the Fédération Française de Football (FFF) the previous year. Under the presidency of Octave Léry, the fledgling FFR was to back up this display of organizational robustness with demonstrations of the emerging power of French rugby, both on and off the pitch.

The first Five Nations' match to take place after the war was itself remarkable for the number of war-wounded players who took the field that day. The France–Scotland game at the Parc des Princes on 1 January 1920 was narrowly won by the visitors (5–0), but would more memorably become known as *le match des borgnes*, due to the fact that no less than five of those on the pitch had lost an eye in the war: Thierry and Lubin-Lebrère on the French side; Hume, Laing, and Wemyss for the Scots.[15] The French side's creditable performance was itself a sign of things to come, as were the record crowds attracted by this and the other matches of the 1920 campaign.[16] Winning away for the first time in Ireland, France went on to take joint second place in 1921 – its best ever result – while the final points tally of 33 for and 32 against was the first time that a positive balance had been achieved. A turning-point had thus been arrived at in the national team's fortunes, based on the solid foundations that had been established in the French club game in its adopted heartland of the south-west.

Central to this development was the latest vintage of *la Vierge Rouge* of Stade Toulousain, which achieved successive championship victories in 1922–23–24 and then again in 1926–27. The club's 1923 victory was the first game to be broadcast live in its entirety by the Société Française Radio-Electrique (Radiola). The leading sports daily *L'Auto* hailed the event, inviting its readers to 'praise the progress which means that sportsmen in the provinces will be able to follow the main events of this great final as and when they occur'.[17] A precedent was thus set that would help to explain the dramatic expansion of public interest in rugby throughout the south-west that was to occur in the 1920s. Henri Garcia has usefully summed up the centrality of Toulouse to the game's exponential growth at this time:

> Never has rugby given rise to so much fervour in France as it did in the years after the Great War, in the 'mad years' when everyone displayed so much fervour for living. The world of the oval ball saw an unprecedented expansion in this period. From 260 clubs in 1920, the number increased to 880 in 1923, of which 139 were in the Pyrenees, 106 in the Languedoc, and 95 in the Périgord–Agenais region. Toulouse was thus the epicentre of a real explosion, and it is no surprise that *la Ville Rose* [the Pink City, as brick-built Toulouse is often known] should have become the Mecca of [French] rugby.[18]

The city's leading role in French rugby's expansion in this period was reflected not only in the dominance of the Stade Toulousain club on the field, but also in developments off it. No less than thirty-nine clubs were in existence in Toulouse in the inter-war years.[19] It was this wave of popular enthusiasm that explains the launching of France's first, and still most important, national rugby journal – the weekly *Midi-Olympique* – in the city in 1929.[20] However, as recent statistical research by Pech and Thomas makes clear, the real impact of this rapid expansion, both in terms of participation and as a spectator sport, was felt not in the cities, but in the countryside. With Toulouse as the centre, the union game spread into the smaller administrative centres, market-towns, and even villages of the region, in the process permanently transforming the social significance of 'the adopted game'.[21]

Rugby now entered the mainstream of local culture, with the fortunes of sides throughout the south-west becoming a focus for passionate interest on the part of whole communities. As Augustin has noted, by the mid-1920s, there was scarcely a *commune* in the region that did not have its own rugby team, and the game thus ceased to be 'an instrument of national socialization, becoming instead an instrument of local socialization'.[22] For in this only lately and very partially urbanized and industrialized region more than in any other, the traditional peasant values of the *pays* still held sway; that is to say the essential frame of reference was the immediate neighbourhood and the local community. Part of this enduring peasant value-system was the network of immemorial inter-communal enmities that now came to be perpetuated on the rugby field. Thus, in the south-west, rugby, in its rapidly democratized form, rather than its original elitist one, was to give rise to extreme violence in the inter-war period, both on and off the pitch, thereby setting entire communities against each other. For as rugby became rural, its meaning changed: 'In the past, it had been a diversion, a gratuitous and disinterested activity; henceforth it became a means of self-affirmation, and part of a quest for identity.'[23] This new function may be understood in terms of rural continuities and changes in the wake of the Great War, which would together lead to a crisis of traditional values in the south-west, and especially of local constructions of masculinity.

The first aspect of this process that needs to be considered is 'the transformation of rugby clubs from a type of aristocratic sociability around the turn of the century to a type of communitarian sociability' in the 1920s.[24] After 1918, as Jean-Pierre Augustin has pointed out, there was 'an ideological and political revolution . . . in the countryside of the *Midi*':

> The traditional land-owning elites were progressively replaced by new Radical *notables*, who relied for support on Republican and anticlerical networks. The

role of local schoolmasters thus became considerable in so far as their militant activity both helped the new *notables* to establish themselves firmly and encouraged the communitarian sociability that was developing around the rugby clubs.[25]

Examples consequently abound of the leading role played by village schoolmasters in the spread of rugby at this time and subsequently.[26] In the process of its school-based diffusion throughout the south-west, the sport was permanently detached from the principles of elitist amateurism and athletic gratuity that had informed its early development both in Paris and Bordeaux. What emerged to fill that ideological vacuum was not simply the militant Republicanism of the schoolmasters, but rather a complex network of *particularismes*: a patchwork of distinct micro-identities, each underpinned by a strongly developed sense of belonging to a given locality, be it *bourg* or *pays*. This ancient vision of the world was both internally coherent and externally robust, and at its heart was the primacy of the group over the individual: that is to say, an emphasis on common goals and collective effort as central to the organic solidarity of the traditionally structured village as it is to the efficient organization of any team on the rugby field. Where the Parisian pioneers had shown the value of individual brilliance – something that would never be wholly forgotten on the hard, fast grounds of the French south-west[27] – the provinces now committed themselves to a more consciously instrumental, and consequently much darker, conception of the union game.

As we noted in our general introduction, the ethnographer Sébastien Darbon has suggested that rugby football is characterized, at the most basic, structural, level, by a permanent battle-front [*une ligne de front permanente*].[28] In considering rugby in this way, Darbon follows the sociologist Christian Pociello, who argues at some length that violence, rather than being an aberration, is essential to rugby, which he considers to be nothing less than 'a war by another name' [*une guerre euphémisée*].[29] Moreover, Pociello has talked about the evolution of French rugby in terms of 'a war of styles', with three main tendencies visible over time: *le rugby-panache*, *le rugby de tranchées*, and *le rugby de décisions*.[30] These ideal types of play overlap both historically and geographically, and examples of each – or, at least, combinations in which one or other of the three themes is more or less clearly dominant – may still be found today in any area of rugby-playing France. However, it as a model of the game's historical evolution that Pociello's schema is most appealing. For the first appearance of *le rugby-panache* – the attacking game of individual flair – coincides with the 'heroic age' of the game's pioneers in France, and is thus linked to the 'Corinthian' ethos of Paris and Bordeaux. In contrast, the highly technical, and even technocratic, 'rugby of decision-making' is a much more recent development (although hinted at in the insights of some of the game's earlier practitioners), and is usually associated with the rise of a group of physical education teachers, who first became successful players and then influential coaches from the later 1960s onwards. However, it is the south-west's development in the 1920s of a conception of rugby football as a form of 'trench warfare' that principally concerns us here. It is perhaps not going too far to argue for a causal link between the communal trauma of the Great War, which had so recently ended, and the emergence of a style of play that was to attach a wholly unprecedented significance to the bitter defence of the smallest scrap of local territory. That this process would involve actual fatalities in the later 1920s is an indication of the intensity that rugby-based rivalries would develop in the south-west.

French rugby's valorization of local solidarity in this period was accompanied by a hostility to outsiders that was as easily focused on the national capital as it was on the next village. For as the game was popularized and democratized it became a focus for a catalogue of southern grievances against the north in general and Paris in particular. Rugby thus mobilized anti-Parisian sentiments that could spring from immediate material circumstances or have their roots in communal folk-memories, or both. The primary fault-line involved here was none other than the ancient north–south divide that has undermined French cultural unity since the country's prehistory. As Braudel puts it: 'while there has at the highest level been a single French "civilization" . . . there have at the same time been for centuries, within France, at least two great underlying civilizations at loggerheads, each with a linguistic realm: the northern civilization of *oïl*, eventually victorious, and the southern civilization of *oc*, fated to become on the whole a near-colony, crushed by the north and its material prosperity'.[31] The Languedoc, broadly defined, may have been politically, economically, and culturally dominated by the north since time out of mind, but scope nevertheless remained for resistance, both real and symbolic. The Languedoc wine-growers' revolt of 1907 was just the most recent example of a tradition of southern resistance that went back to the medieval *jacqueries* and beyond. The catastrophic phylloxera crisis of 1865–1890 was likewise a powerful folk-memory in a region that in many places had become a wine-growing monoculture in response to the new railway network's opening up of northern markets in the mid-nineteenth century.[32] Ancient grievances ranging from the subjugation of the Cathars by the Albigensian crusades of the thirteenth century, through the fate of the Protestant Huguenots, to the legacy of *le Midi rouge* of 1848 and 1871 could all be linked to more recent causes of resentment against Paris; as indeed they would remain features of the rhetoric of militant southern regionalism up to the present day.[33] What is more, all of these ancient wrongs could be symbolically righted on the rugby pitch, where the south-west was in the process of establishing its abiding hegemony.

The newly arrived game of rugby football was also able to draw on cultural continuities by tapping into a distinctly southern tradition of conviviality and festivity. This was precisely what the sociologist Pierre Sansot sought to underline by giving his study of the union game the title *Le Rugby est une fête*; a title that Jean Gachassin, perhaps the finest exponent of *le rugby-panache*, also chose for his autobiography.[34] The ethnographer Sébastien Darbon has characterized the south-western *culture du rugby* as based, on the one hand, on 'a certain conception of the group', itself reliant on internal solidarity and external closure, and on the other, on 'the taste for violence, a relationship with food and drink that some would consider excessive, and a pronounced valorization of the epic narrative'.[35] It is the overlap between violence, the pleasures of the table, and story-telling that most directly concerns us here. This interweaving of cultural strands is most visible in the commonalities that exist (as regards participation and administration, as well as modes of representation) between rugby in the south-west of France and a variety of activities based on hunting and other blood-sports.[36] The most obvious of these is *la tauromachie* [bull-fighting], as many supporters of rugby in the winter switch their allegiance to the *corrida* in the summer months. Also of importance from this point of view are shooting and fishing associations, and, perhaps above all, the village-based groups responsible for the maintenance and operation of local *palombières*, complex and often very extensive systems of hides and decoys used for the hunting of passing flocks of wood-pigeons. All of these activities are associated with the ritualized enjoyment of carefully delineated varieties of food and drink. The masculine conviviality of south-western rugby is, therefore, by no means confined to the (often excessive) post-match drinking and associated merry-making (typically including the singing of obscene songs) that frequently characterize rugby cultures elsewhere. That is not to say that the French *troisième mi-temps* – literally 'the third half', after the two halves of the match just ended – does not include these elements, but rather to note that they are only part of a much broader network of sociability, and one in which women and children play a somewhat more significant role than is typically the case elsewhere.

The role of the *amicales*, or local supporters' associations, is an important one from this point of view, with their principal function being to raise funds for celebratory meals at key moments in the rugby calendar, as well as organizing post-match receptions. As Darbon puts it in his detailed ethno-graphic study of the Tyrosse club, perhaps the most successful example of *le rugby des villages*: 'Thus is established a strange circulation of food and drink, which, in a never-ending cycle, feeds the club's tills so as better to feed the players, drawing into this infernal dance the town's inhabitants, who are happy to show their support for rugby while having a good time, and local traders who are only too well aware of their business interests, but who may also be fervent supporters in their own right.'[37] Darbon draws particular attention to the *fêtes de Tyrosse*, held in July each year, and famous throughout the south-west. Combining varieties of bull-running and bull-fighting with music and dancing – rather like a more modest version of the celebrated San Firmin festival in the Spanish Basque city of Pamplona, the basis of Ernest Hemingway's novel *Fiesta* (1927)[38] – this week of activities is an important annual source of revenue for the local rugby club. The *pièce de résistance* on the menu of the Tyrosse *amicale*'s banquet on this occasion is always *daube de taureau* [bull stew], further underlining the close association in the local micro-culture of *la tauromachie*, festive eating and drinking, and rugby football.[39] The rhetorical link between all three will be considered further when we examine the literary and televisual representation of the game in Chapter 7. However, we shall refer briefly in the final section of this chapter to the close link between violence and the epic narrative in south-western rugby culture. For if the union game became after the Great War a medium for the expression of traditional rural virtues and antagonisms, it would also provide a wholly new space for the construction of collective memories.[40]

In the event, French rugby football would fall victim to its own success in the later 1920s, when the *amateurisme marron* or 'shamateurism' that had characterized the sport's development throughout the decade combined with a new national championship structure based on qualification in regional pools to give rise to a number of shocking incidents usually lumped together in the local, Spanish-inflected, vernacular as *le rugby de muerte*: that is to say, the rugby of death.[41] The classic example of this phenomenon is provided by the unfortunate events surrounding the rise of the Quillan club under the patronage of a local hat-manufacturer, Jean Bourrel. In the manner typical of the entrepreneurial class that increasingly dominated the local organization of rugby in the south-west, this businessman was able by means of offers of advantageous employment in his factory to poach players from the leading clubs of the region. (Others have since used and abused their positions to similar effect, with the ability of local mayors in particular to offer municipally funded sinecures to talented recruits being at least as important as industrial or commercial enticements after 1945.) These 'mercenaries' were brought to Quillan, a tiny *bourg* in the predominantly wine-growing Aude *département*, with the result that rank outsiders were transformed into the champions of France in 1929. Such was the intensity of the rivalry between the Quillan club and Perpignan, the long-established Catalan club from which the bulk of the team, including three internationals, had been tempted away, that the 1927 away fixture resulted in the death from injuries inflicted on the pitch of one of the Quillan players, the hooker Gaston Rivière. This was by no means an isolated incident, and examples abound of extremely violent confrontations between these and other clubs in the region at this time, of which the most notorious were Carcassonne–Toulouse 1927, Lézignan–Béziers 1929, and, slightly further afield, Pau–Agen 1930.[42] Nor was the mayhem limited to domestic fixtures, with the brutal 1930 France–Wales encounter in Paris being an important case in point. Such an extension of rugby-based hostilities indicates that a tradition of sporting violence rooted in age-old local rivalries had, by 1930, been very significantly intensified in response to the pressures of illicit professionalism in the south-west. Indeed, brutality had been institutionalized to such a degree that it gave rise to an authentically *méridional* rugby-playing ethos. This harsh code was effectively transferred to the national and then the international stage as players, and, increasingly, supporters, travelled from the French game's heartland for matches in Paris and abroad. Its effects were to prove extremely difficult to eradicate in subsequent decades.

Beaten finalists in 1928 and 1930, Quillan's single championship triumph came at the expense of their great local rivals, Lézignan. At the 1929 final at Stade Toulousain's Ponts-Jumeaux stadium, the 20,000 assembled spectators thus witnessed the narrow victory (11–8) of a *bourg* of 3,000 inhabitants over another *bourg* of 6,000 souls from just down the road in the same Aude *département*.[43] Dominated throughout by fighting between the two sets of players, this was *le rugby des villages* with a vengeance. While the violence that was an inherent part of this intense local rivalry was widely condemned at the time, and has been critically dissected by historians and sociologists ever since, there is ample evidence to suggest that the traditional south-western enjoyment of ritualized violence is alive and well in the sport. For, as Thierry Terret reminds us, 'another symbol of the south-west was the "*castagne*", a Gascon noun meaning "fight" which has a large number of declensions and metaphors that clearly reveal the cultural importance of fighting . . . [in a] part of the country [that] was already well-known for its machismo'.[44] The emergence of the western part of the Languedoc, and particularly the Aude *département*, as a force to be reckoned with in the national championship, is closely bound up not only with a new class of enterprising and socially ambitious *notables* like Jean Bourrel, who looked to the game as a way of enhancing their local standing,[45] but also with a number of outstanding players. Of these the most memorable is undoubtedly the redoubtable Jean 'Le Sultan' Sébédio. A Basque from the fishing port of Saint-Jean-de-Luz, Sébédio was an excellent *pelota* player as well as a hugely talented rugby forward. A member of the French national team either side of the Great War – indeed, he was the first working-class player to be selected for *le XV de France*[46] – Sébédio was celebrated as *une force de la nature*, being immensely strong despite his only medium size. Having played for both Tarbes and Biarritz before the war, he was mobilized and fought in the Syrian campaign (where he earned his nickname), before embarking on what was effectively a second playing career with Béziers briefly, and then famously with Carcassonne.

It was as a trainer that Sébédio took the Lézignan side to the 1929 final with Quillan, in spite of a training regime that was unusual to say the least: 'Having already lost a good deal of his vitality as a result of frighteningly excessive drinking, he cultivated his persona by sitting in the middle of the pitch with a long whip and a wide sombrero, making his players run round him like circus horses.'[47] Sébédio's incarnation in his own person of the structural linkage between drink and rugby in the Aude and the rest of the Languedoc is particularly striking, with other centres for both activities established in Narbonne, in Béziers, and, indeed, throughout the ancient *provincia narbonensis*, where the Romans had first planted vines.[48] However, it was Sébédio's close association with violence, and particularly his ability to intimidate visiting players and referees, that is, paradoxically, most fondly remembered by French rugby's chroniclers. So, in his colourful collection of portraits of *Seigneurs et forçats du rugby* [Lords and Slaves of Rugby], Henri Garcia tells with relish how visiting supporters descending from trains at Lézignan under the Sultan's reign were greeted with the cry 'Lézignan! Lézignan la Matraque! Tout le monde descend!' ['Lézignan! Lézignan the Cosh! Everyone out!'].[49] Garcia also enjoys telling how Sébédio kept a human skeleton hanging in the referee's changing room, with a whistle stuck between its jaws, and would inform the concerned official casually that it was 'nothing to worry about, just the last referee to give a penalty against Lézignan'.[50] However, it is as one of the stars of Garcia's picaresque *Contes du rugby* that 'the Sultan' really comes into his own. Depicted in his heyday as a player with the Association Sportive Carcassonnaise, Sébédio is as memorable a figure in the bar-room as he is on the pitch. Whether engaging in terrifying post-match drinking competitions with predictably cowed opponents, or refusing to accept the decisions of intimidated match officials, Sébédio is depicted as a genuinely fearsome figure, but also, crucially, an admirable and even a lovable one:

> The Sultan feared no man, either on the pitch or at the bar. Jean Sébédio was an
> exceptional being. He could play in virtually every position in the team, such

was his strength, speed, agility, and skill. All those who knew him are unanimous in asserting that they have rarely seen a player of his calibre.

[. . .]

Such a man was worth his weight in gold to a team, but for referees, he was a nightmare. In Carcassonne, on the pitch at the Pépinière ground, the Sultan was the only master after God and a long way ahead of the referee.[51]

The undisputed master in his *fief*, Sébédio epitomizes the *méridional* cult of the strong-man. Moreover, he is very much a patriarch in its original sense, the head of the clan or tribe, and as such an iconic figure in the culture of the south-west.[52]

One of the most remarkable of the many insights into the deep structures of French social life provided by cultural anthropologists such as Hervé Le Bras and Emmanuel Todd is the revelation of the abiding hold of family structures on the respective mentalities of the north and south of France: 'The division, still visible today, between the [southern] extended family zone and the [northern] nuclear family zone corresponds in general terms to a series of other contrasts identifiable throughout French history: language, literacy, living standards, forms of property ownership and urbanization, and religious and political attitudes.'[53] The particular variety of extended family that characterizes the *Midi* is the patriarchal or community type, which is a horizontally structured system – based on the patriarch and all his children, married and unmarried – and which may be so extended as to 'give rise to whole clans or local communities'.[54] What is more, its zone of influence corresponds uncannily to that of rugby football's diffusion in the south-west of France. This demographic bedrock may be the foundation for French rugby's regular rhetorical appeal to the theme of *la grande famille du rugby* [the great rugby family], and also its very marked tendency to produce dynasties.[55]

However, for all his *légende*, his regularly recounted and embellished feats, 'Sultan' Sébédio was destined to end his colourful life on a less than impressive note. The seemingly all-powerful patriarch of Carcassonne and Lézignan died an alcoholic, weighing only 50 kilograms [8 stones], in 1951,[56] thus providing a powerful illustration of the internal contradictions of the south-western *culture du rugby* that he had done so much to shape. In this respect, his life and death were symptomatic of the wider crisis undergone by southern male identities at this time: 'It is reasonable to believe that rugby served as a way for a male peasant to affirm his virtues at a time when they were being called into question. [. . .] Rugby was a way peasant men could overcome their inferiority complex and take advantage of the morphological and muscular capital they had developed through work.'[57] Yet, as the case of Sébédio reveals, symbolic victories achieved on the field would often come only at a heavy personal cost off it. What is more, the social elites that had dominated French rugby in its early days would shortly cooperate with the forces of sporting conservatism in the British Isles and the British Empire in an attempt to put an end to the uncontested dominion in the south-west of 'the Sultan' and all those he represented. The 1930s would thus be a period of crises and compromises as French rugby's old guard sought to claw back the advances made by a game that 'had outstripped its exclusive origins, had been taken over by the working classes and had touched the remotest corners of the provinces'.[58] As for the distinctively patriarchal style of rugby in the south-west, that was to achieve its fullest expression not on the pitch, in spite of Sébédio's best efforts, but rather in the administrative structures of the FFR. More specifically, it would produce a string of authoritarian presidents, such as René Crabos, a star of the 1920s, and the federation's president between 1952 and 1964, and, above all, his successor from 1968 to 1991, the dictatorial Albert Ferrasse.

Notes

1. Jean Giraudoux, *Le Sport* (Paris, Grasset, 1928); cited in Sébastien Darbon, *Rugby d'ici: Une manière d'être au monde*, (Paris, Editions Autrement, 1999), p. 48.
2. Henry de Montherlant, *Le paradis à l'ombre des épées* and *Les onze devant la porte dorée*; cited by Jean-Pierre Augustin and Alain Garrigou, *Le Rugby démêlé: Essai sur les Associations Sportives, le Pouvoir et les Notables* (Bordeaux, Le Mascaret, 1985), p. 68. Also of significance in this movement were such diverse figures as Blaise Cendrars, Jean Cocteau, Jules Supervielle, and Max Jacob, all of whom came together around 'Géo-Charles', pseudonym of the poet Charles Guyot; see René Bourgeois, *Géo-Charles: Un poète de la vie moderne* (Echirolles, Editions Galerie-Musée Géo-Charles, 1985), pp. 30–42.
3. Sean Smith, *The Union Game: A Rugby History* (London, BBC, 1999), p. 193; Thierry Terret, 'Learning to be a man: French rugby and masculinity' in Timothy J. L. Chandler and John Nauright, *Making the Rugby World: Race, Gender, Commerce* (London, Frank Cass, 1999), pp. 79–80.
4. Eugen Weber, *Peasants into Frenchmen: The Modernization of Rural France, 1870–1914* (London, Chatto & Windus, 1977).
5. Hervé Le Bras and Emmanuel Todd, *L'Invention de la France: atlas anthropologique et politique* (Paris, Livre de Poche, 1981); see also Hervé Le Bras, *Les Trois France* (Paris, Editions Odile Jacob, 1986 and 1995);

also Emmanuel Todd, *The Making of Modern France: Ideology, Politics and Culture* (trans. Anthony and Betty Forster; Oxford, Blackwell, 1991).

6. Fernand Braudel, *The Identity of France: II. People and Production* (trans. Siân Reynolds; London, Collins, 1990), p. 669.

7. Maurice Agulhon, 'La fabrication de la France, problèmes et controverses' in Martine Segalen (ed.), *L'Autre et le semblable: Regards sur l'ethnologie des sociétés contemporaines* (Paris, Presses du CNRS, 1989), pp. 109–20; p. 120 for the quotation.

8. Braudel, *The Identity of France*, II, p. 674.

9. Henri Garcia, *Seigneurs et forçats du rugby: un siècle d'ovale en France* (Paris, Calmann-Lévy, 1994), p. 38.

10. Ibid.; cf. Richard Escot and Jacques Rivière, *Un siècle de rugby* (Paris, Calmann-Lévy, 1997), p. 55.

11. Muhr would take up a similar role with the Red Cross in the Second World War. Following the entry of the United States into the war in 1942, Muhr was arrested by the Gestapo and deported to the Neuengamme concentration camp near Hamburg, where he died. Garcia, *Seigneurs et forçats*, p. 34.

12. Jill Forbes and Michael Kelly, *French Cultural Studies: An Introduction* (Oxford, Oxford University Press, 1995), p. 65.

13. Ibid.

14. Ibid., p. 66.

15. Garcia, *Seigneurs et forçats*, p. 41.

16. Henri Garcia, *La Fabuleuse histoire du rugby* (Paris, ODIL, 1973), pp. 225–8 and 232–4.

17. Ibid., pp. 245–6.

18. Garcia, *Seigneurs et forçats*, p. 48; see Jean-Pierre Bodis, 'Le rugby en France jusqu'à la seconde guerre mondiale: aspects politiques et sociaux', *Revue de Pau et du Béarn*, no. 17 (1990), pp. 217–44, at pp. 234–5, for additional statistics regarding rugby's phenomenal development at this time, and most spectacularly in the Languedoc.

19. Bodis, 'Le rugby en France', pp. 235–7.

20. Rémy Pech and Jack Thomas in Pierre Duboscq (ed.), *Rugby, parabole du monde* (Paris, L'Harmattan, 1998) p. 202.

21. Ibid., pp. 200–1. The term 'the adopted game' is taken from Smith, *The Union Game*, pp. 184–231.

22. Jean-Pierre Augustin, 'L'étonnante implantation du rugby dans le Midi', *Midi*, no. 4, 1987, p. 11.

23. Bodis, 'Le rugby en France', p. 237.

24. Jean-Pierre Augustin and Jean-Pierre Bodis, *Rugby en Aquitaine: histoire d'une rencontre* (Bordeaux, Centre Régional des Lettres d'Aquitaine and Editions Aubéron, 1994), p. 90.

25. Augustin, 'Rugby dans le Midi', p. 11.

26. See, for instance, Renaud de Laborderie, *Le Rugby dans le sang* (Paris, Calmann-Lévy, 1968), pp. 15–17; cited in Sébastien Darbon, *Rugby, mode de vie: Ethographie d'un club, Saint-Vincent-de-Tyrosse* (Paris, Editions Jean-Michel Place, 1995), pp. 32–3. See also Duboscq, *Rugby, parabole du monde*, p. 202.

27. Augustin and Bodis, *Rugby en Aquitaine*, p. 36.

28. Darbon, *Rugby d'ici*, pp. 37–8.

29. Christian Pociello, *Le Rugby ou la guerre des styles* (Paris, A. M. Métailié, 1983), pp. 101–66.

30. Ibid., p. 276. See also Alain Garrigou, 'Le travail, la fête et l'athlétisme: les enjeux des styles de jeu' in Société Française de Sociologie du Sport, *Sport et changement social* (Talence, Maison des Sciences de l'Homme d'Aquitaine, 1987), pp. 147–55.

31. Fernand Braudel, *The Identity of France: I. History and Environment* (trans. Siân Reynolds; London, Collins, 1988), p.85. The historical distinction between the languages, and lands, of *oïl* and *oc* (based on their distinctive ways of saying 'yes') is what gives rise to the modern region of Languedoc in the south-west.

32. Braudel, *The Identity of France*, I, pp. 335–6.

33. See Robert Gildea, *France Since 1945* (Oxford, Oxford University Press, 1996), pp.131–2.

34. Jean Gachassin (with E. Cazes), *Le Rugby est une fête* (Paris, Solar, 1969); Pierre Sansot, *Le Rugby est une fête* (Paris, Plon, 1990); see also Pierre Sansot, 'Le rugby et les nouvelles pratiques sportives' in Collective, *L'Univers du rugby: Actes du Colloque de Larrazet* (Montauban, Edicopie, 1988), pp. 63–74.

35. Darbon, *Rugby d'ici*, pp. 40–4.

36. See Pociello, *Le Rugby ou la guerre des styles*, pp. 63–70, on the reference to bull-fighting in Jean Lacouture's journalism. The *corrida* is also a regular theme in the television commentaries of Pierre Albaladejo, who, following Roger Couderc's death in 1984, formed a successful partnership with Pierre Salviac.

37. Darbon, *Rugby, mode de vie*, p. 107. It is no coincidence that Robert Barran also opens his tour of a number of exemplary village-based clubs by visiting Tyrosse: Robert Barran, *Le Rugby des villages* (Paris, Les Editeurs Français Réunis, 1974), pp. 55–9. It has been calculated that this small town on the main road between Dax and Bayonne has the highest ratio of rugby-players, and particularly international rugby players, *per capita* of any commune in France; see Augustin and Bodis, *Rugby en Aquitaine*, pp. 151–2.

38. Henry de Montherlant's own youthful infatuation with bull-fighting is fictionalized in his novel *Les Bestiaires* (Paris, Gallimard, 1954).
39. Darbon, *Rugby, mode de vie*, p. 106; cf. Pociello, *Le Rugby ou la guerre des styles*, pp. 63–70; Terret, 'French rugby and masculinity', p.73; Rémy Pech and Jack Thomas, 'La Naissance du rugby populaire à Toulouse (1893–1914)' in Pierre Arnaud and Jean Camy (eds), *La Naissance du mouvement sportif associatif en France: sociabilités et formes de pratiques sportives* (Lyons, Presses Universitaires de Lyon, 1986), pp. 99–100.
40. Augustin, 'Rugby dans le Midi', p. 11.
41. This term would seem to have first been coined by Paul Voivenel, in an influential article written in 1927, and subsequently included in his *Mon beau rugby: L'Esprit du Sport* (Toulouse, Editions Midi-Olympique, 1962), pp.108–14.
42. René Barnoud, *Quel drôle de ballon!: Mêlées et démêlés* (Lyons, A. Rey, n.d. [1978?]), p. 54, notes that very similar incidents were also typical of rugby in the south-east at this time.
43. Alex Potter and Georges Duthen, *The Rise of French Rugby* (London, Bailey & Swinfen, 1961), p. 56. Mike Rylance, *The Forbidden Game: The Untold Story of French Rugby League* (Brighouse, League Publications, 1999), pp. 11–12, gives the populations as 2,500 and 5,000 respectively in his detailed account of the match; see also Duboscq, *Rugby, parabole du monde*, p. 169, among the many accounts of this notorious match.
44. Terret, 'French rugby and masculinity', pp. 73–4; cf. Pierre Bourdieu, *La Distinction: critique sociale du jugement* (Paris, Minuit, 1979), pp. 231 and 234–5.
45. See Bodis, 'Le rugby en France', p. 239.
46. Rylance, *The Forbidden Game*, p. 11.
47. Garcia, *Seigneurs et forçats*, p. 47.
48. Braudel, *The Identity of France*, II, pp. 318–19. See also 'A Lézignan-Corbières: La Vigne au secours du rugby' in Barran, *Le Rugby des villages*, pp. 143–51.
49. Garcia, *Seigneurs et forçats*, p. 53. There is also a play on the word *descendre* here, giving the sense 'All fall down!'.
50. Ibid., p.47.
51. Henri Garcia, *Les Contes du rugby* (Paris, La Table Ronde, 1961), pp. 63–5.
52. See Pociello, *Le Rugby ou la guerre des styles*, pp. 70–4, on the peasant family.
53. Braudel, *The Identity of France*, I, p.105.

54. Le Bras and Todd cited in Braudel, *The Identity of France*, I, p. 104; cf. Patrick Le Galès, 'The regions' in Malcolm Cook and Grace Davie (eds), *Modern France: Society in Transition* (London, Routledge, 1998), pp. 91–112, at p. 104.
55. See Darbon, *Rugby, mode de vie*, p. 32, n. 1.
56. Garcia, *Seigneurs et forçats*, p. 47.
57. Terret, 'French rugby and masculinity', p. 73.
58. Rylance, *The Forbidden Game*, p. 11.

− 4 −

French Rugby in the Wilderness

The 1930s were destined to be French rugby's wilderness years: a period marked by internal schism and international isolation. The resulting weakness of the union game in its south-western heartland would leave it vulnerable to challenges from other regions and even from other sports, including particularly the newly imported game of rugby league. At the same time, rugby became the focus for the expression of broader social antagonisms, as France prepared unwillingly for yet another war against Germany. It is this complex tale of strife both on and off the pitch that must now be examined in order to allow us to make sense of French rugby's subsequent, and altogether remarkable, development in the even darker years of the Nazi occupation. As we saw in the preceding chapter, the precocious profession-alism and endemic violence that together characterized the French game in the later 1920s had their origins in the transformation of a marker of elitist social distinction into a site of popular cultural investment: they were the results, in short, of the replacement of Parisian *rugby-chic* by south-western *rugby-choc*.[1] The FFR's decision as of the 1921–22 season to organize the national championship on the basis of a system of qualification from regional pools had significantly intensified the competition between neighbouring towns and villages in the Languedoc. It thus fanned the flames of disorder, and rendered almost inevitable the crisis that overtook French rugby in the early 1930s:

> The crisis of 1931 clearly illustrates the transformation, since the beginning of the century, of [French] rugby clubs from a type of aristocratic sociability to a type of communitarian sociability. According to the former model, sport is more akin to a game, and is played by groups belonging to the same class (in terms of both age and social origin); its idealism is clearly stated, 'the most important thing is to take part'. According to the latter model, sport is more akin to a rite; what unites individuals is no longer the fact of belonging to the same class, but rather that of belonging to a locality and its community; it is a local ethos. The most important thing now is to win, and thus to enable all those who participate in the sport (the players, but also administrators and spectators) to be on the winning side.[2]

In this localized construction of rugby football, all is fair if it leads to success, including particularly the systematic recourse to violence both on and off the pitch, the payment of players, and the poaching of talent from other clubs. Thus, in the 1930s, French rugby's distinctive micro-politics of identity became ever more tightly entwined with both local commercial interests and a range of national political conflicts. Some of these, such as Church–state tensions, were familiar territory; others, such as the struggles between employers and organized labour, were, in contrast, very much products of their time. Often, old and new antagonisms would come together in unexpected and powerfully corrosive combinations that affected all aspects of local social organization, including particularly the region's dominant sport.

Given the depressed economic circumstances of the 1930s, it is not surprising that the fiercely competitive rugby played in south-western *départements* like the Tarn and the Ariège at this time should have had particularly clear links with employment. Thus, the textile industry in towns like Castres, Mazamet, and Lavelanet would be an important factor in the recruitment of talented players to their rugby clubs, as would leather-working in Graulhet, the glassworks in Albi, and the mines of Carmaux.[3] As Rémy Pech and Jack Thomas have demonstrated, Carmaux provides perhaps the clearest evidence of rugby's role as a vector for social and political conflict in this highly charged period. To understand events in Carmaux in the 1930s, it is necessary to go back to the 1892 local elections, which saw Jean-Baptiste Calvignac, one of the founding fathers of French trade unionism, elected as the town's mayor. Supported by miners from the local coalfield, and additionally by those employed in the town's glass industry, Calvignac also received significant backing from no less a figure than Jean Jaurès, the father of modern French socialism, who was himself elected as the local *député* in 1893. Ranged against Calvignac and his socialist municipal authority were the local employers (led by the Marquis de Solages, the owner of the mining company), the administrative authorities, including particularly the police, and the Church. Calvignac's electoral success instantly changed the balance of practical and symbolic forces within the town: 'From this moment on, an implacable struggle was engaged between two camps that were ferociously opposed in virtually every domain.'[4] This social and political dualism extended to the fashion for gymnastics that swept the country in the later nineteenth and early twentieth centuries, with local clubs being established along the now familiar dividing lines.[5] However, it was on the rugby field that this communal strife was to take its most original form, in a sporting variation on the theme of Gabriel Chevalier's celebrated novel *Clochemerle* (1934) that, in spite of its comic moments, was deadly serious.[6]

As part of the rapid expansion of French rugby in the wake of the Great War, the Tarn *département* emerged as a new area of strength, with major centres appearing in Albi, Castres, Graulhet, and Mazamet. The Football-Club Carmausin (FCC) was the first club to be established in the town. Founded in 1919, the club moved to a new municipal stadium in January 1921, and began to attract large crowds to the matches that saw it quickly prove itself to be a regional and, indeed, a national force. However, the creation later that year of a rugby section by the Etoile Carmausine – which was backed by the Compagnie des Mines, and had hitherto played only association football under the auspices of the Catholic FGSPF – was an obvious challenge to the FCC, and a clear indication that the ideological rivalries of the pre-war period had not been forgotten. For its part, the immediate construction of a rival stadium with a grandstand for 500 spectators, and changing rooms complete with hot showers – an almost unheard-of luxury in French rugby at this time – was proof of the mining company's commitment to the sporting expression of its political message.[7] Renamed Olympique de Carmaux (OC) in 1924, the new club soon began to compete with the FCC both on and off the pitch. The relatively rare direct encounters between the clubs saw victories for the FCC in 1922, and for the OC in 1927 and 1928. The significance of these results was marked, on the one hand, by the holding of a celebration ball at the local trade union offices, and, on the other – at least according to the socialist newspaper *Le Cri du Tarn* – by the singing of a 'Te Deum' at the town's Saint-Privat church. However, at the level of symbolism and rhetoric, the competition between the two was permanent and intense. Under their respective presidents, the conservative businessman Emile Falgueyrettes at the OC, and the veteran socialist mayor himself, Jean-Baptiste Calvignac, at the FCC, a war of words was conducted by the two clubs in the pages of an equally partisan local press.[8]

Although the FCC was the stronger side between 1922 and 1926, a devastating raid on the club's best players by the mine-owners' team prior to the 1927–28 season left it seriously weakened, with the OC henceforth the more powerful club. The outrage expressed by the *Cri du Tarn* at this flagrant example of poaching in the Quillan manner may readily be imagined. Having long been accused of giving the best jobs and privileged conditions to OC players and of similarly penalizing those miners determined to continue playing for the workers' club, the employers now used their economic muscle to oblige their employees to perform for them on the rugby pitch just as they already laboured for them in the galleries of the mine.[9] The expression habitually used to encourage French rugby forwards to 'get stuck in' to the opposition – *Allez au charbon!*, literally 'Get to the coalface!' – could nowhere have been more appropriate than in the Carmaux of the later 1920s. Yet, ironically, the company team's apparent triumph was to prove short-lived, with the OC club closing down its rugby section in October 1933, although it continued its involvement with soccer and basketball. The Compagnie des Mines attempted to present this closure in the best possible political light, claiming that various socialist-inspired plots to prevent the OC from gaining promotion had made the decision necessary, adding that the move also reflected a 'wish to bring to an end the incessant bickering' between the clubs. More pragmatically, in this period of financial crisis, the employers may have wished to concentrate their limited resources on the rising sport of association football. The *modus vivendi* of the later 1930s would give way in 1940 to a Vichy-promoted fusion of the two clubs in the interests of communal solidarity in the country's hour of need. In the euphoria of the Liberation – which would also see the nationalization of the mines – the unification of the old rivals in the new, and very significantly named, Union Sportive Carmausine would be further cemented, thus paving the way for the mining town's finest sporting hour, namely the USC's crowning as national champions in 1951.[10]

If the case of Carmaux dramatically illustrates the significant investment made by local economic and political actors in rugby football in the 1930s, that of Clermont-Ferrand reveals how national developments could impact on this most localized of sports. The 'capital city' of the Massif Central, Clermont-Ferrand had become synonymous with the tyre-manufacturing dynasty of Marcel Michelin, and his AS Montferrand club was just as much a works side as had been the notorious US Quillan of the hatmaker Jean Bourrel. Indeed, the FFR had actually intervened in the 1920s to change the name of the club, established in 1911, from AS Michelin to AS Montferrand.[11] Beaten finalists in both 1936 and 1937, Montferrand were involved in what was to prove the most politically charged of all French championship finals. The match played at the Ponts-Jumeaux stadium in Toulouse on 10 May 1936 came exactly a week after the election that had brought to power the joint socialist and communist administration of the Popular Front. Montferrand's defeat (6–3), in front of 25,000 spectators and with a nationwide radio audience, came at the hands of Narbonne, the town that had just elected the Prime Minister Léon Blum as its *député* [Member of Parliament]. This result may well have been read at the time, as Jean-Pierre Bodis suggests, as the victory over the forces of capitalism of 'the radiant socialism' of the *Front Populaire*.[12] The fact that Francis Vals, the Narbonne winger who scored the winning try, should have gone on to a glittering political career with the French socialist party (SFIO), would seem to bear out this hypothesis.[13] However, the real threat to French rugby in the 1930s came not from outside the game, but from within. Specifically, the commercially sponsored brutality of the sport as practised in the later 1920s provoked a split between the idealistic amateurs who had first introduced rugby to France and its more pragmatic players and administrators. The resulting schism was seized upon in turn by the British rugby unions as a justification for severing relations with their increasingly troublesome neighbour. Two fatalities served to crystallize traditionalist resistance to recent developments in the French game, one on the field of play, the other, paradoxically, in the skies.

Yves du Manoir, born in 1904 into an aristocratic Parisian family, was educated at the *lycée* Saint-Louis before going on to the Ecole Polytechnique, the first and still the most prestigious of France's highly selective *grandes écoles*, where he was paired with the future member of the Académie Française, Louis Armand. Graduating with excellent grades in all subjects, du Manoir opted for a career as a pilot in France's fledgling air force. An outside-half with the Racing Club, he also played eight times for France between 1925 and 1927, but, unexpectedly, was not selected for the home match against Scotland on 2 January 1928. On that day, he was consequently engaged instead on a training flight over central France when he died, in mysterious circumstances, in a crash.[14] For Robert Bernstein, a senior official with the Racing Club at the time, and for many among the game's traditionalists, du Manoir was 'the best and the most charming, the bravest and the kindest of players'.[15] His untimely death was commemorated by the Racing Club and the FFR in two ways: by the commissioning of a statue of the player to be erected at the Colombes stadium; and, in 1931, by the establishment of a new tournament, the 'Challenge Yves du Manoir'. This was to be the Parisian traditionalists' riposte to a national championship increasingly dominated by the ferocious *rugby de villages* of the Languedoc: 'a competition based on honest rugby, clean rugby, a rugby in which the spirit must be allied with the body, in all the richness of sport and friendship'.[16] By supporting such a competition, the FFR could present itself as doing its best to encourage fair play and associated sporting values.[17] It could thus be seen to be responding to the increasingly vocal criticism of south-western *rugby de muerte*, such as that of du Manoir's predecessor in the RCF and national sides, Géo André. A hugely talented all-rounder, André had won a silver medal in the high-jump in the 1908 (London) Olympics. Such was his prestige, in fact, that he was chosen to take the Olympic vow at the 1924 games in Paris. However, it was in his capacity as a journalist for *Le Miroir des Sports* that he had reported on the 1925 championship final between Jean Sébédio's Carcassonne and future Quillan stalwart Eugène Ribère's Perpignan:

I have no hesitation in declaring this game a match of brutes. Rarely have we witnessed such an eruption of the most intense passions. On the terraces, there were battles; and on the pitch, there was a battle royal. With the players excited by the cries of the spectators, and their brains overheated by the sun, the game was played in the most vicious possible spirit. [. . .] Played in this way, rugby is more like the ancient games of the Roman circuses.[18]

Such comments carried considerable weight in French rugby's traditionalist circles, as did those of Alain du Manoir, brother of the unfortunate Yves, who was one of many to criticize the 'anti-sporting, anti-educational, anti-moral attitude' of French rugby as practised in the 1920s and 1930s.[19]

The second rugby-related fatality of note in this connection might well have appeared to bear out the criticisms levelled at the French game by Géo André, Alain du Manoir, and others, including, ominously, the British rugby unions. The death in May 1930 of Michel Pradié, an eighteen-year-old schoolboy with the Agen club, following a late tackle by Jean Taillantou, an international player on the opposing Pau team, was to result in a court case and even questions in the French parliament:

Although malicious intent was never satisfactorily established in the judicial enquiry which followed, Taillantou was fined and sentenced to a suspended three-month prison sentence. Nor did the [French Rugby] Federation escape criticism. Rugby's governing body, as well as the Comité National des Sports which oversaw sport in France, were both held responsible for the events of that tragic day and made to give assurances regarding their future control of matches.[20]

The outrage in the face of such developments of those aristocratic amateurs who had pioneered the introduction of French rugby barely three decades earlier soon made itself plain. A clear division occurred within the French rugby establishment in January 1931, when a new body, the Union Française de Rugby Amateur (UFRA), split from the FFR in a last-ditch attempt at traditionalist resistance to ultimately unstoppable pressures within the game. In an early indication of the interest that would shortly be taken by the French state in the organization of sport, the under-secretary of state with responsibility for physical education, M. Tricard-Graveron, attempted to reconcile the two sides, but to no avail.[21]

Jean-Pierre Bodis has suggested that the UFRA's loudly declared wish to safeguard the hallowed principle of amateurism may have been under-pinned by the undeclared wish of these leading clubs to maintain their virtually total control over the gate receipts generated by their respective teams.[22] However, there can also be little doubt that this move was at least as much an attempt to return to the 'golden age' of French rugby's elitist amateurism in its early days.[23] Although fourteen of the oldest and most prestigious French clubs were involved, the venture was to prove short-lived, with the UFRA clubs effectively returning to the FFR fold in May 1932. However, the initiative undoubtedly contributed to the severing of relations by the British and Irish unions, and those in the Dominions, at the beginning of the 1931–32 season, and also to a more general fragment-ation within French rugby. Henceforth, *le XV de France*, joint runners-up in the Five Nations championship in 1931, would be restricted to matches against Germany, Italy, and Romania. In sporting terms these fixtures were more or less meaningless, although France's 3–0 defeat by Germany in Frankfurt in March 1938, in front of 20,000 spectators, undoubtedly represented a new low point in the fortunes of the national side. However, in symbolic terms, French rugby's willingness to be involved in regular fixtures with such increasingly unappealing opponents – playing against Nazi Germany, in particular, at least once every season until May 1938 – may be considered to foreshadow the zeal with which the French rugby authorities were to associate themselves with the collaborationist Vichy regime following the fall of France a mere two years later.

International isolation was very keenly felt in French rugby circles in the period 1931–39. It was only in February 1940, in a gesture of reconciliation explained by the historical circumstances – and, of course, made practically possible by the calm before the storm associated with *la drôle de guerre* [the phoney war] – that a joint British side would come to Paris to play a French national team. Even then, this first visit for a decade was only made possible by the FFR's final acceptance at its 1939 annual congress in Marseilles of the requirement by the International Board, world rugby's governing body, that it should suspend its national championship, long perceived as the root cause of all the French game's ills. Moreover, arriving at this strictly limited and temporary understanding had required the application of pressure behind the scenes by both the French Ministry of Foreign Affairs and the British Foreign Office, with Anthony Eden's name, in particular, being mentioned in this context.[24] If the 38–3 scoreline provided one indication of the weak-ness of French rugby union after its years in the wilderness, another was the decline in the number of French clubs from 784 in 1930 to only 473 in 1939.[25] After this time, the onset of the Second World War would obviously preclude French sporting contacts with Britain and its Empire, and French rugby would turn inwards, with both negative and positive results.

Where the staunchly amateur (English) Rugby Football Union and the (English-dominated) International Board[26] had feared to tread, the Rugby Football League, which had replaced the breakaway Northern Rugby Union in 1922, was only too eager to make inroads. Profiting from the vacuum left in France by the suspension of international fixtures, demonstration matches were organized from 1933 onwards. Following unofficial contacts between British rugby league officials and dissident French rugby union administrators, the first 'propaganda' match between a British select side and an Australian one took place at the Stade Pershing in Paris in December 1933. The event was sponsored, typically of such innovations in the French context, by *L'Echo des Sports*, the great rival of *L'Auto*, and met with considerable journalistic and popular acclaim.[27] This clear opportunity for renewed international competition greatly facilitated the recruitment from 1934 on of leading French union players – particularly disqualified or suspended ones – to the new game; a campaign orchestrated by ex-international Jean Galia at Villeneuve-sur-Lot, near Agen, which rapidly became established as the nerve-centre of *le rugby à treize* [thirteen-a-side rugby].[28] Galia had enough players available by the spring of 1934 to arrange both the first French rugby league overseas tour, of the North of England, and then a series of demonstration fixtures between the French side and a Yorkshire select team in Paris, Villeneuve, Bordeaux, and Pau, as well as Lyons in the south-east. The outraged FFR responded by banning administrators, players, and even the pitches on which the outlawed league demonstrations had taken place. However, this heavy-handed reaction appears to have been miscalculated, as existing clubs switched and new ones sprang up with equal rapidity.[29] Although a number of major clubs were established outside the south-west, notably in the Lyons area in the southeast, it was in French rugby union's traditional heartland that the game really took off, with important centres for rugby league being established in Carcassonne, Perpignan, and Villeneuve in particular. Predictably, a key role was played in rugby league's diffusion, as with rugby union before it, by local *notables*; or at least by those who would like to be thought of as such. This included such men as the mysterious Joseph Pansera at the Lyon-Villeurbanne club, who was involved in the building trade and other less legitimate business, and was eventually shot dead by underworld rivals as a result of his arms-dealing activities.[30]

Yet the main attraction of the new game was felt in the south-west, with dramatic results. For it was at this time of internal schism and international isolation that the rugby union clubs of the south-east exerted their strongest influence on the French national championship: RC Toulon defeated the Lyon Olympique Universitaire club in the 1931 final; Lyon themselves went on to become champions for the following two seasons; while CS Vienne, just a few miles further down the Rhône, were champions in 1937, under the inspired leadership of a transplanted international star from the 1920s, the Basque Jean Etcheberry. As Augustin and Garrigou suggest: 'By weakening the clubs of the south-west, [the split between rugby union and rugby league] allowed clubs in eastern and central France to come into the limelight.'[31] This challenge to the hegemony of the south-west was also particularly marked in the southern zone of the Massif Central: thus an area in which, as Richard Holt has noted, 'modern sports were still virtually unknown . . . before 1914'[32] became an important centre of rugby strength. It is this fact that explains the new significance of clubs such as Carmaux and Montferrand discussed earlier. Now that we have examined these two clubs in order to illustrate the way in which broader social antagonisms were articulated through rugby football in the 1930s, it will be helpful next to consider an interesting counter-example from the region. For the case of Albi, located like Carmaux in the *département* of the Tarn, demonstrates that rugby union and rugby league were, after all, capable of peaceful coexistence at this time, and, moreover, that rugby football as a whole could help to reconcile mutually hostile segments of French society.

The town of Albi is today remembered as the historic centre of the Cathars, a medieval religious movement that sought to establish a 'pure' or 'perfect' version of Christianity, and thus to build heaven on earth in their south-western mountain strongholds. However, Catharism should certainly not be understood as an early precursor of the Protestant reformation: it was in reality a deeply pessimistic creed in ordinary human terms, which if carried to its logical conclusion would have resulted in the extinction of the believing population, since 'Perfects' were required to be celibate, or at least not to breed. Yet it was not the inherent self-destructiveness of the Cathars' creed that was to leave the most lasting impression on the south-west, but rather the bloody fate of these misguided believers at the hands of the latest wave of military invaders from the north. Predictably, these idealists encountered fierce opposition from the Paris-dominated, and widely corrupt, official Church, which culminated in the movement's brutal suppression by the Albigensian Crusade of 1208–1229.[33] The area's historic link to the Cathars is widely celebrated by its modern-day inhabitants, and Albi's association since the 1930s with rugby league provides a particular focus for such sentiments. In this it resembles Carcassonne, another abiding centre of *treiziste* enthusiasm, which, with its wonderfully restored fortifications – now protected as a World Heritage site – constitutes a permanent reminder of the Cathar connection and those turbulent times. Mike Rylance helpfully makes the case for this interpretation of French rugby's 'heretical tradition':

> Nowadays it isn't just the *treizistes* who wear the Cathar mantle. The whole of
> the population of a certain area of the south-west, with its epicentre around

Carcassonne, sees itself as part of the Cathar tradition. In some cases the name is simply taken for commercial reasons, as the various businesses connected to the tourist industry of the area will testify. But at another it's a means of establishing an identity which proclaims a separateness from the rest of France – especially from the north and Paris. It reveals an individuality which is bold enough to stand up for its own particular values and which from time to time defies the prevailing tone set by the capital.

Rugby league follows in the Cathar tradition because it demonstrates a similar mentality, which began as an alternative to the abuses of the ruling authority, the FFR, with its headquarters in Paris.[34]

While Rylance's concluding statement may broadly be justified, in the particular case of Albi, at least, it needs to be understood against an unusual background of tolerance, both between the two rugby codes, and, even more significantly, otherwise antagonistic social groups. Indeed, the development of rugby football in the Albi of the 1930s would seem to provide a relatively rare example of peaceful coexistence at this time, not only between the orthodox faith of rugby union and the dissident religion of rugby league, but also between secular Republicanism and Roman Catholicism.

The study by Martin Fontès of rugby's evolution in the town is itself unusual in that it takes an equal interest in both sports; a laudably ecumenical approach that is strikingly at odds with that generally displayed by writers on the two codes, whether in French or English.[35] From Fontès we learn that rugby first came to Albi in 1895, with the main rugby union club, the Sporting Club Albigeois, being established in 1907. However, it was the local rugby league side, the Racing Club Albigeois, which was to bring fame to the town in 1938, just five years after its creation. By defeating Villeneuve (8–3) in the final in Bordeaux, the Albi club became champions of France, and were welcomed back to the town by a large and enthusiastic crowd at the railway station. Players and administrators alike were then carried by supporters to a civic reception at the town hall, while the municipal band played as they progressed triumphantly through the streets. For the correspondent of the *Petite Gironde* newspaper: 'On this evening, when Albi was enjoying a moment of sporting glory without precedent, the people did not want to forget those who were the finest sons of the city.'[36] It is worth noting that the local *treizistes*, like the French rugby league authorities as a whole, had ensured that this great victory had been achieved without recourse to the dirty play that had disfigured rugby union: 'The committee of the Albi club . . . reminded their team that the paying public had a right to expect sanctions to be taken against over-aggressive players.'[37] Also of significance in this victory was the role played by Albi's Welsh coach, Tom

Parker, who was one of several imported trainers to play a role in the rapid rise of *le rugby à treize*.[38]

However, in spite of the conspicuous success of rugby league in Albi, relations between the thirteen-a-side code and its long-established rival were remarkably cordial, for the most part. So while Fontès may talk about the 'war' between the two forms of rugby, he is at pains to stress that, the occasional incident apart, peaceful coexistence was the norm in *Albi-la-sereine*. This is not to say that the rivalry between the two codes did not draw upon existing social cleavages, for, as he notes, 'conservatives, residents of the town-centre, and conformists seemed to prefer rugby union [while] innovators, those from the suburbs, and others were drawn to rugby league'.[39] More specifically, 'the union game had always attracted a majority of *notables* and doctors'.[40] However, in spite of some resistance on the part of their respective administrators, there was a remarkably regular movement of players between the codes, in both directions, together with a high degree of fraternization. Fontès provides photographs of mixed teams, made up of players drawn from both sides of the official divide, which were organized in the town in the 1930s, and comments as follows with regard to patterns of sociability at this time: 'The players from the two sides maintained excellent relations, celebrated their victories together in the cafés of the town, and went in for long and joyous post-match sessions!'[41]

One of the *notables* identified in this connection is '*l'Abbé* Pistre, "Rugby's Pope", [who] only ever wore a single rugby jersey: that of the SC Albi'.[42] This celebrated cleric is worthy of comment, not only as further evidence of rugby's crossing of the usual social boundaries in Albi, but also as the outstanding exception to the general rule regarding the Church hierarchy's hostility to rugby football. A native of Mazamet, Henri Pistre was ordained in Albi in 1923 – reputedly wearing his old SC Albi jersey under his *soutane* – and was to be associated with the *département* of the Tarn throughout his life. For Henri Garcia, he is 'le vicaire du rugby', a title that reflects not only his playing career, but also his important role in the 1930s as first-team trainer with the Castres Olympique club (champions of France in 1950), and, moreover, as the rugby correspondent for *Le Courrier Sportif du Tarn*. Indeed, the priest's practice, on the occasion of major matches, of saying Sunday vespers immediately after the main morning mass, so as to allow his congregation and himself to concentrate fully on the afternoon's sporting ritual and the inevitable post-match festivities, suggests a degree of devotion to rugby football that sometimes strained the conventional boundaries of his vocation.[43] That Pistre was not a wholly isolated case is suggested by the role that had been played by *le père* Didon at the Ecole Albert-le-Grand at Arcueil in the early days of rugby's development in

Paris.[44] By the same token, the dedication of a village church to the game in the 1960s, as Notre-Dame du Rugby, is evidence of rugby's ability to cross this particular ideological boundary in more recent times.[45]

Elsewhere, however, relations between *quinzistes* and *treizistes*, let alone Church and state, were by no means so cordial, and rugby's tensions would effectively foreshadow the dramatic events that were to occur in the game in response to the wider upheavals of the Second World War. These tensions focused especially on the recruitment of established union players by the new league clubs, and could tear apart local communities, and even families. The underlying cause for such strife was the widely held belief that French rugby union was being drained of its lifeblood by the haemorrhage of 'administrators, referees and top players', all of whom, to introduce another metaphor, 'had joined the one-way traffic heading in rugby league's direction'.[46] These players included such outstanding talents as the captain of the *XV de France*, Joseph Desclaux, his fellow international Max Rousié – held by many to be the best French player ever, irrespective of code – and emerging stars such as the hugely gifted Catalan Puig-Aubert, who would keep the torch of *le rugby à treize* alight through and after the dark days of the Second World War. The enthusiasm for league at this time was such that demonstration matches were played in areas outside rugby football's established areas of strength, such as Nantes, and even, remarkably, in the colonies, with a match being played between army regiments in Haiphong in French Indo-China (now Vietnam).[47] Paris became an area of significant *treiziste* activity, with the professional Paris XIII club rapidly being joined by student associations such as the Quartier Etudiant Club, and even the wonderfully named Arts Décoratifs XIII, as well as working-class associations such as the Treize Populaire Parisien. The dissidents of the QEC, based in the 'Latin Quarter' of the city, around the Sorbonne, had broken away from the venerable Paris University Club, and included among their members Louis Jacquinot, a future government minister, Francis Lopez, who would become better known as a singer under his stage-name of André Dassary, and the future journalist, and radio and television commentator on French rugby union matches, Loys Van Lee.[48]

However, the real strength of the new thirteen-a-side code was primarily measurable in other ways. By the time the FFR came to take stock of its desperate situation at its annual congress in Marseilles in 1939, the 891 union clubs of 1924, which had dropped to 784 in 1930, had plummeted to 471. The French rugby league, meanwhile, after only five years in existence, had no less than 434 affiliated associations.[49] Equally impressive were the respective gate receipts for the 1939 championship finals in the two codes, in which for the first time the *treizistes* took more money (230,000 francs) than the *quinzistes* (218,000 francs).[50] Such real and symbolic victories were accompanied by some outstanding performances on the pitch, which reached their climax with what Rylance calls the 'golden season' of 1938–39. This included particularly an away victory for the French national side over England (12–9), something their union counterparts had failed to accomplish in more than thirty years of trying: 'After only four full seasons the *treizistes* had achieved what the *quinzistes* had never managed since the beginning of international matches in 1906.'[51] It was scarcely any surprise that both the public and the press should have looked increasingly towards rugby league as the real force in French rugby football at this time.[52] Conservative elements in rugby union would take note of these developments, and their resentment against *le néo-rugby*, as league was also known, began to fester.[53] In the same way, many political reactionaries would witness, and condemn, the social experimentation of the leftist Popular Front (1936–38), biding their time until they were able to strike back.[54] In such influential figures on the union side as Jean Borotra, Joseph 'Jep' Pascot, and Dr Paul Voivenel, sporting conservatism and political reaction would come together in a particularly potent combination. International political and military developments would shortly conspire to present such men with the perfect opportunity to settle old scores.

Notes

1. These terms are suggested by Christian Pociello, *Le Rugby ou la guerre des styles* (Paris, A. M. Métailié, 1983), p. 42.
2. Jean-Pierre Augustin and Alain Garrigou, *Le Rugby démêlé: Essai sur les Associations Sportives, le Pouvoir et les Notables* (Bordeaux, Le Mascaret, 1985), pp. 75–6. Pierre Charreton, 'Sport et sociabilité mondaine dans la littérature française, 1880–1930', *Sport-Histoire*, no. 1, 1988, pp.111–12, notes that a more general shift in French sport from aristocratic to popular sociability is reflected in the sport-based literature of the 1930s.
3. See Louis Montels, *Graulhet: 80 ans de rugby* (Graulhet, Sporting Club Graulhétois, 1988); also the documentary film by Jean-Pascal Fontorbes and A.-M. Granié, *Le Rugby dans le cuir* (1985; 70 minutes). On Carmaux see Rolande Trempé, *Les Mineurs de Carmaux* (Paris, Editions Ouvrières, 1971).
4. Rémy Pech and Jack Thomas, 'Pratiques sportives et antagonismes sociaux: Le rugby à Carmaux, 1920–1933' in Société Française de Sociologie du Sport, *Sport et changement social*, (Talence, Maison des Sciences de L'Homme d'Aquitaine, 1987), pp. 217–27, at p. 217.

5. Ibid., pp. 218–19.

6. Gabriel Chevallier, *Clochemerle* (Paris, Presses Universitaires de France, 1934).

7. Pech and Thomas, 'Pratiques sportives et antagonismes sociaux', p. 219.

8. Ibid., pp. 221–2.

9. Ibid., pp. 223–5.

10. Ibid., p. 225.

11. Robert Barran, *Le Rugby des villages* (Paris, Les Editeurs Français Réunis, 1974), p. 96.

12. Jean-Pierre Bodis, 'Le rugby en France jusqu'à la seconde guerre mondiale: aspects politiques et sociaux', *Revue de Pau et du Béarn*, no. 17, 1990, pp. 217–44, at p. 242.

13. Ibid.

14. Henri Garcia, *Seigneurs et forçats du rugby: un siècle d'ovale en France* (Paris, Calmann-Lévy, 1994), p. 62; cf. Richard Escot and Jacques Rivière, *Un siècle de rugby* (Paris, Calmann-Lévy, 1997), p. 78.

15. Cited by Jean Mérillon, *Le Challenge Yves du Manoir* (Paris, Chiron, 1990), p. 5.

16. Ibid., p. 12.

17. Ibid., pp. 17–18.

18. Garcia, *Seigneurs et forçats du rugby*, pp. 44 and 52–3.

19. Mike Rylance, *The Forbidden Game: The Untold Story of French Rugby League* (Brighouse, League Publications, 1999), p. 117.

20. Ibid., p. 13; cf. Sean Smith, *The Union Game: A Rugby History* (London, BBC, 1999), p. 195.

21. Henri Garcia, *La Fabuleuse histoire du rugby* (Paris, ODIL, 1973), p. 264. See also Hervé Girette, 'De Jean Galia à Vichy: Les origines du XIII en France', *L'Indépendant* [Perpignan], 26 July 1995, unpaginated, regarding similar government interventions in 1934 and 1937.

22. Bodis, 'Le rugby en France', p. 241.

23. Ibid. On the enduring appeal of the myth of the golden age in French political philosophy see Raoul Girardet, *Mythes et mythologies politiques* (Paris, Seuil, 1986), pp. 97–138.

24. See Alex Potter and Georges Duthen, *The Rise of French Rugby* (London, Bailey & Swinfen, 1961), p. 58; Bodis, 'Le rugby en France', p. 244; Henri Garcia, *Rugby-Champagne* (Paris, La Table Ronde, 1960), pp. 38–9.

25. Potter and Duthen, *The Rise of French Rugby*, p. 58.

26. Created in 1887, this body would not admit a French representative until 1978.

27. Augustin and Garrigou, *Le Rugby démêlé*, p. 77.
28. In this, he was rather like Jacques Fouroux in recent years. See Chapter 9. On Galia's key role as a proselytizer for the thirteen-a-side game see especially Garcia, *Rugby-Champagne*, pp. 29–41; also Rylance, *The Forbidden Game*, pp. 27–83.
29. Augustin and Garrigou, *Le Rugby démêlé*, pp. 77–8.
30. Jean-Pierre Bodis, *Histoire mondiale du rugby* (Toulouse, Bibliothèque Historique Privat, 1987), p. 212; Rylance, *The Forbidden Game*, p. 100; René Barnoud, *Quel drôle de ballon!: Mêlées et démêlés* (Lyons, A. Rey, n.d. [1978?]), pp.92–5. On the role of *patrons* and *notables* more generally see Pociello, *Le Rugby ou la guerre des styles*, pp. 91–9; also Daniel Fabre, 'Les dessous de la mêlée: urnes et mascottes', *Autrement*, special number on 'Occitanie', no. 25, June 1980, pp. 121–6.
31. Augustin and Garrigou, *Le Rugby démêlé*, pp. 76–8.
32. Richard Holt, *Sport and Society in Modern France* (London, Macmillan, 1981), p. 69.
33. This period is recounted in Emmanuel Le Roy Ladurie's celebrated study of *Montaillou, village occitan de 1294 à 1324* (Paris, Gallimard, 1975), a serious work of historical scholarship that also enjoyed considerable popular success; *Montaillou: Cathars and Catholics in a French Village, 1294–1324* (trans. Barbara Bray; London, Scolar Press, 1978). For a useful introduction to this field see Malcolm Barber, *The Cathars in Languedoc* (London, Longman, 2000).
34. Rylance, *The Forbidden Game*, p. 160.
35. Martin Fontès, *Un siècle et plus de rugby en Albi: XV–XIII* (Aiguelèze, Association Connaissances et Traditions de France, 1997). Garcia, *Rugby-Champagne*, is also a rare example of a refusal to condone what has been described as rugby football's equivalent of *apartheid*. See also the account by a future Stade Toulousain captain of his thoroughly positive experiences as a league player with Albi XIII, in Robert Barran, *Du rugby et des hommes* (Paris, Albin Michel, 1971), pp. 27–30.
36. Fontès, *Un siècle et plus de rugby en Albi*, p. 127.
37. Rylance, *The Forbidden Game*, p. 115.
38. Ibid., p. 74.
39. Fontès, *Un siècle et plus de rugby en Albi*, pp. 253–5.
40. Ibid.
41. Ibid.
42. Ibid., p. 240.
43. Henri Garcia, *Les Contes du rugby* (Paris, La Table Ronde, 1961), pp. 197–215.
44. Bodis, 'Le rugby en France', pp. 220–1.

45. See Chapter 7, n. 44.
46. Rylance, *The Forbidden Game*, p. 115.
47. Ibid., p. 82.
48. Garcia, *Rugby-Champagne*, pp. 36–7; Rylance, *The Forbidden Game*, pp. 48 and 98. Through his role in popularizing the song that became the anthem of the Vichy regime, *Maréchal nous voilà!*, Lopez-Dassary, a product of the Biarritz club, would subsequently become notorious himself. See Jean Nicaud, *Cent ans de rugby régional* (Bourg-en-Bresse, Les Editions de la Taillanderie, 1992), p. 108.
49. Girette, 'De Jean Galia à Vichy'.
50. Bodis, *Histoire mondiale du rugby*, p. 215.
51. Rylance, *The Forbidden Game*, p. 112.
52. Bodis, 'Le rugby en France', p. 243.
53. The pro-union journalist Pierre About summed up the mood at the time with a pamphlet revealingly entitled 'La Guerre des Deux Rugbys' [The War of the Two Rugbys] (1938); cited by Rylance, *The Forbidden Game*, pp. 116–17.
54. Bodis, 'Le rugby en France', p. 243, suggests that there may actually have been a link between strong left-wing traditions in parts of the south-west, such as the Languedoc, and the particular success enjoyed by rugby league.

– 5 –

Maréchal nous voilà! – The Wartime Betrayal of *le rugby à treize*

Between 1931 and 1939, French rugby's years in the wilderness, the only international matches played by the national side had been against the increasingly unattractive triumvirate of Germany, Italy, and Romania. These matches were played under the auspices of a new organization, the Fédération Internationale de Rugby Amateur (FIRA), a title that clearly reflected its origins in the internal and external splits triggered by the 'shamateurism' that had characterized the French game in the 1920s. Established late in 1933, this alternative governing body for the increasingly disunited rugby world was predictably dominated by France, its only major rugby-playing nation. However, the list of member countries is most striking for other reasons:

> France became the most important member of the new organisation (the others, apart from Germany, being Belgium, Holland, Italy, Portugal, Romania, Spain and Catalonia). [. . .] . . . the moves which led to its establishment show the privileged relationship between rugby union's masters and a certain type of political régime. Of the founder members of FIRA, not only Germany and Italy were in thrall to fascism but similar political tendencies were or would be evident in most of the other countries too.[1]

Mike Rylance is almost certainly overstating his case here, particularly as regards the inclusion of Belgium, Holland, Spain, and, perhaps especially, Catalonia on this list of fascist or quasi-fascist regimes. These countries, and especially the Republican movements in Spain and Catalonia, might more properly be numbered among the principal opponents, and subsequent victims, of fascism rather than among its promoters. Moreover, it is quite possible that the main reason for the adherence of some of these countries' rugby establishments to FIRA was rather the absence of any viable altern-ative, and the relative exclusivity and insularity of the anglophone unions. Yet in the cases of Germany, Italy, and Romania, where rugby union was reasonably well established and had particularly strong links with the military, just as it did in France, the basic point made by Rylance remains a valid one. Subsequent developments within the French game would reveal this ideological linkage to be anything but arbitrary. Moreover, the enthusiastic response of the French rugby authorities to the changed circumstances of wartime would prove to be central to the development of the union game in the post-war period. Indeed, it now seems clear that it was in the dark days of the Occupation that the new wine was laid down that would mature into the celebrated *rugby-champagne* served up by French teams in the 1950s and 1960s. For a few observers, better informed than most, or at least with clearer memories, that heady sporting brew was, in consequence, destined always to retain a distinctly bitter aftertaste.

Issues of forgetfulness and remembering are thus central to this particular story, as they are to so much of recent French history. The French experience of the Second World War remains remarkable, both to foreign observers and to the French themselves, primarily as a result of the continuing competition between rival interpretations of the relevant historical events. After the national celebration of a mythified Resistance in the immediate post-war period, the French finally came in the 1970s to a more informed appreciation of the nature of their individual and collective responses to military defeat and occupation between 1940 and 1944.[2] This is a process that has continued in more recent years with the extensively reported trials of war criminals such as Klaus Barbie, Paul Touvier, René Bousquet, and, most recently, Maurice Papon, and even includes the ongoing debate regarding the extent of the former President of the Republic (1981–1995) François Mitterrand's involvement in wartime collaboration. Much that was previously forgotten or concealed has consequently been revealed, and a historical consensus now exists that combines the apparently competing narratives of resistance and collaboration into a far more complex, and proportionately more coherent, narrative. However, one particular social strand has for long been excluded from serious public scrutiny, despite the best efforts of a select band of academics, journalists, and a number of actual victims of this particular collective act of forgetfulness. The abiding significance of the omission is underlined by the decision of the French government late in 1998 to establish an official commission to investigate sports policy during the Occupation. The brainchild of the current (Communist) Minister for Youth and Sport, Marie-George Buffet, the commission is expected to report in 2001–2002.[3] It is highly likely that the eventual findings of the commission will be critical of the stance taken by French rugby union in this period, and it is that 'untold story' which will be explored, as far as the information currently available permits, in the remainder of this chapter.[4]

Maréchal nous voilà! – *Wartime Betrayal of* le rugby à treize

As the continuing preoccupation – even obsession – of the French with their experiences during the war years suggests, it is difficult to overstate the impact on French society of military defeat and occupation in June 1940. The fall of France was to be followed by an armistice that brought about the division of the traumatized country, leaving the Germans in control of the occupied northern zone, together with the Atlantic littoral, and the collaborationist administration of *Maréchal* Philippe Pétain in charge of the 'free' southern zone (which was itself occupied in November 1942). Led by this hero of the First World War, the Vichy-based regime immediately set about carrying out its own 'National Revolution', a fascistic project that replaced the familiar Republican motto of *Liberté, Egalité, Fraternité* with the slogan *Travail, Famille, Patrie* [Work, Family, Fatherland]. For all its ideological antipathy to the leftist coalition of the *Front Populaire* that had briefly governed in the immediate pre-war period (1936–8), the military and political 'old guard' that set about the task of installing Vichy's version of the 'new order' followed in the footsteps of their opponents in affirming the necessity of including sport in any project of national regeneration. Vichy thus became only the second French administration to recognize the importance of sport in modern society, and the first to seek a leading role for the state in its management and expansion. More specifically, sports were to be included in the 'return to the soil' that the collaborationist administration adopted as the guiding principle of its reactionary project. Implicit in this linkage was a hierarchy of sporting practices that would see traditional, regional, and, above all, amateur games given priority over more recently imported ones, and especially anything tainted by association with overt professionalism. This was to have major repercussions as far as rugby football was concerned. However, in order effectively to situate that specific aspect of popular culture, it is useful to look more broadly at the very particular character of French cultural life under the Occupation. A snapshot taken from another sporting context is particularly revealing in this respect.

On 5 April 1943, an Allied air raid on occupied Paris resulted in over 300 deaths, including seven fatalities at the Longchamp racecourse, where fourteen bombs fell on the day of the track's grand reopening. Amazingly, racing was only temporarily interrupted, resuming again for the Prix des Sablons, the day's big race, after just an hour and a half, although the horses' route round the track had to be modified to skirt bomb craters, and the lack of electricity meant that the *Pari Mutuel* totalisator betting facilities were somewhat disorganized. The *habitués* of Longchamp were thus able to get back to the real business of winning and losing at the races after a minor interruption by the Second World War. Such a reaction may strike us now as either admirable or contemptible, depending on our own prejudices, but must, in all events, be reckoned remarkable. It certainly does not sit easily with the received wisdom regarding what the French themselves still refer to as *les années noires*, the 'dark years' of the Occupation, with all that this period conventionally evokes in the way of fear and oppression, drudgery and shortages. The great historian of those undoubtedly painful times, Henri Amouroux, has wondered whether Parisian racegoers, upon learning of the full devastation and loss of life caused by the air raid, felt any remorse for taking more interest in bloodstock than in their compatriots' bloodshed. His view of their likely response tells us much that is germane to an understanding of French cultural life from 1940 to 1944:

> Life must go on. [*Il faut bien vivre.*] And life, under the Occupation, meant not only finding enough to fill one's stomach, but also endeavouring to be happy.
>
> In order to forget an unbearably dreary present, to forget, for just a few hours, the Occupation, the black market, and the uncertainties of the war, the French, who had run out of petrol for their cars and were saving their bicycle tyres for food-scavenging raids, still had the theatre, cinemas, race-tracks, libraries, and stadiums.
>
> They made the most of them . . .[5]

Thus, for Amouroux, a basic human impulse, the desire to escape the harshness, or at least the dullness, of daily life explains the paradoxical flowering of French culture under the Occupation. Viewed in this light, sport may be seen as just one aspect of a broader dynamism at this time, in both the 'high-cultural' and 'popular' spheres. As Forbes and Kelly have argued: 'Cultural activity under the Occupation was changed by the situation, but it certainly was not halted. Theatres were full, books sold in large quantities, and cinema audiences increased over the four years.'[6] The sporting boom that occurred in this period was not the exception, then, but the rule. However, as Amouroux himself hints, sporting activity was not merely perceived as a substitute for established modes of leisure rendered impossible by the circumstances. Crucially, it was also perceived as a means of national regeneration:

> Deprived of dances and long Sunday excursions, the young – and the not so young – rushed to the stadiums, which, at least as far as athletics was concerned, had never seen such crowds. All over France people were running, jumping, or playing football. Deprived of alcohol, the French discovered the joys of sport. Defeated by a German army that wore shorts, and that had not let the odd river get in its way, they discovered that the path to national rebirth ran along cinder tracks.[7]

It is this connection that accounts for the unprecedented moral and material investment made by the Vichy administration in sport and associated leisure activities.

While the Popular Front may have been the first French government to take leisure seriously, Vichy would actually establish the genuine centrality of sport in its project of national regeneration through the re-education in body, mind, and spirit of the youth of France. It did this through a combination of dramatically increased funding and new institutions backed up by strong legislation. The Commissariat Général à l'Education Générale et aux Sports (CGEGS) was created as early as 15 October 1940, with its head, Jean Borotra, the famous tennis star, responsible for an annual budget of nearly 2 billion francs, i.e. twenty times the amount made available in 1937 to Léo Lagrange, the equivalent minister under the Popular Front.[8] For Gilbert Garrier, Vichy's dramatically successful actions in the sporting domain were characteristic of the ambiguous and paradoxical nature of the *Etat français* as a whole: 'A set of measures intended to reassure the regime and its reactionary and elitist ideology contributed to the establishment of the liberated France of the Fourth Republic.'[9] Garrier follows Jean-Louis Gay-Lescot in pointing to the parallel between the rise in birth-rates in France after 1942 and the simultaneous development of physical activities, reading the renaissance of French sport under the Occupation as an expression of national resilience and even resistance:

> What is certain is that, consciously or not, for many French people between 1940 and the autumn of 1943, sport, rather than being a mere distraction from gloomy thoughts, was considered and practised as a manifestation of national identity and patriotic spirit. The formation of a robust youth became inseparable from the belief, gaining in confidence with every passing month, that France would one day be set free.[10]

However, this is a rather more comfortable image of French attitudes to sport at this time than would seem to be justified by the case of rugby union, particularly as regards its relations with its upstart rival, rugby league.

Central to Vichy's youth and sports policy had been the *Charte des Sports*, promulgated in December 1940, and accurately described by Gay-Lescot as 'a weapon of war'.[11] This 'Sports Charter' was the first government text relating directly to the organization of sport, which had hitherto been auto-nomous, and was to set a precedent for state intervention in the management of French sport in the post-war period.[12] However, in the particular context of the Occupation, this intervention would take the form of a very sinister settling of scores between rugby union, weakened by its international isolation throughout the 1930s, and the newly imported thirteen-a-side code of rugby league, which had mounted a serious and sustained challenge to union's hegemony since its introduction to France in 1933. At its last pre-war annual congress, in Marseilles on 24 June 1939, the FFR had been obliged to take stock of the damage done by its decade in the wilderness. From a high of 891 clubs in 1924, the FFR's membership had fallen to 471 by 1939. In comparison, the Ligue Française de Rugby à Treize (LFRT) had already gained 434 clubs as members in its first five years of existence.[13] It was this very visible threat to 'the exalted position enjoyed by the fifteen-a-side game' that would spell rugby league's doom in the dramatically changed circumstances of 1940: as the domestic political order was convulsed and Vichy embarked on its reactionary National Revolution, 'the level of support which rugby league could count on was always offset by the significantly greater proportion of opposition ranged against it'.[14] Like the 'Maurrasians and other right-wing ideologues in Vichy', the enemies of rugby league thus found themselves 'suddenly in a position to act upon the prejudices and aversions which they had long expressed in print. They did so with a vengeance.'[15] So while other professional sports, such as soccer and cycling, were to become targets of Vichy, with the numbers and activities of professional practitioners of both disciplines being significantly reduced, rugby league was to become the single sport targeted for total suppression.

The decree dissolving the LFRT, and moreover seizing its total assets, was signed by Pétain himself on 19 December 1941, and was just part of a forcible reunification of the avowedly amateur fifteen-a-side rugby code and its openly professional thirteen-a-side rival. The national championship, suspended in 1939, was also re-established, with the victors of knock-out competitions in the occupied and 'free' zones meeting in a final decider. Players previously tainted by association with rugby league were allowed and even encouraged to participate in the new championship. In addition, the various regional committees organized so-called *veillées du rugby*: rugby-excursions *cum* camping-trips designed as a way of promoting physical fitness and the inculcation of the values of the National Revolution. Under the vigorous stewardship of Lieutenant-Colonel Joseph 'Jep' Pascot, a former international player from the Perpignan club who replaced Borotra at the head of the CGEGS in 1942, French rugby union made remarkable advances.[16] Amazingly, in this period of hardship for the French nation as a whole – but wholly in line with the broader cultural dynamic that we have already noted – the union code saw its popularity leap, with 464 clubs in existence, representing over 16,000 playing members, by the 1942–3 season, and another 18 new clubs, each with over a hundred members, having been set up by the following year.[17]

Maréchal nous voilà! – *Wartime Betrayal of* le rugby à treize

The extent to which French rugby union players and, especially, administrators were complicit in Vichy's recuperation and promotion of their game for propagandist purposes is hinted at by a remarkable document produced by Borotra's ministry in March 1941. Entitled *Toulouse, capitale du rugby . . .*, this was one of a series of regionally focused promotional brochures aimed at the young. Of particular interest is the report on 'The Day of Remembrance' held in Toulouse on 2 November 1940, to honour the memory of all those who had fallen in the Great War, but especially sportsmen. With Borotra presiding, the solemn event was attended by national representatives of the FFR, together with representatives of all of its regional committees within the *zone libre*. The centre-piece of the event was Antoine Bourdelle's statue of Herakles, also known as 'The Archer', and described as the first and only 'Monument aux Sports' in France, or anywhere else come to that. Taking as his text the slogan 'be strong to be useful [to your country]' – with its clear echoes of the motto of Coubertin's defunct USFSA, *ludus pro patria* – Borotra himself emphasized Vichy's conception of the role to be played by sport and sportsmen in the project of national regeneration:

> Young people of our country, listen with us, your elders, to the final lesson given by our dead: SPORT, THIS MODERN CHIVALRY, MUST BE FOR FRANCE, NOT ONLY A SOURCE OF VIGOUR AND PHYSICAL STRENGTH, BUT ALSO A SCHOOL OF COURAGE, TENACITY, SELFLESSNESS, AND LOYALTY, A LIVING FAITH.
> That is the message that, from beyond the grave, is addressed to us today by our athletes who have given their lives for the Fatherland.[18]

Going even further, Dr Paul Voivenel, one of French rugby union's most respected spokesmen, stressed that 'Henceforth, we shall be working under the red, white and blue banner of the tricolour, religiously . . . united behind our Leader, MARSHAL PETAIN.'[19]

Such was the proselytizing zeal of the FFR, with the conspicuous support of the very highest echelons of the *Etat français*, that Gay-Lescot has singled out the wartime boom in rugby union's fortunes as the prime example of participatory sport's dramatic increase in popularity in this period.[20] However, the Vichy regime's systematic encouragement of amateur sport is not by itself enough to account for rugby union's spectacular recovery from its pre-war position of weakness, even given the relative lack of alternative forms of recreation during the Occupation. It may be that French rugby union's enforced isolation from the British Empire throughout the 1930s was perceived as a distinct advantage in the wake of the German victory. This was in marked contrast to rugby league, which had retained its strong links with the north of England and Australasia in the immediate pre-war period. However, of an altogether higher order of significance was the leading role taken by French rugby union's senior administrators in the direct suppression of the league code. Henri Garcia has memorably summed up the position:

> Catastrophes certainly seem to have suited the FFR. The onset of war had brought back an indispensable opponent [i.e. the British rugby unions]. The Occupation was to rid it of an undesirable and dangerous rival. In whose name, in the name of what, by what influences, what dark machinations, and in accordance with what principles did the Vichy government decide, on 29 December 1941, to issue a decree banning a single sport: rugby league?
>
> I know that the dust of time has covered up more than one injustice, but how can all those who love sport, as opposed to a ruling clique, forget this decree by the Vichy government?[21]

Garcia reproduces the decree in full, before asking a key question that has remained unanswered until now: 'Who played the role of Lady Macbeth? It's a mystery! But one thing is certain: that the war between the two rugby codes ended with an assassination.'[22] As with so many political killings, conspiracy theories abound, particularly, and unsurprisingly, among the supporters of the victimized sport, *le rugby à treize*. However, it would now seem to be beyond doubt that while Pétain himself may have wielded the knife – acting on the advice of his Secretary of State for National Education and Youth, Jérôme Carcopino, and, below him, the Commissioner for General Education and Sport, Jean Borotra – the real damage was done by two medical men, the recently appointed president of the FFR, Dr Albert Ginesty, and the influential president of its Pyrenees regional committee, Dr Paul Voivenel. It was this pair, together with Borotra's assistant and eventual replacement, Colonel Joseph 'Jep' Pascot, who led the whispering campaign that preceded Vichy's administrative 'murder' of French rugby league and gave the regime's action a spurious legitimacy. However, before we examine this network of complicity in detail, it is necessary to consider a little more closely the ideological attractions of rugby union for the collaborationist administration.

As previously noted, local sporting activities were particularly favoured at this time, both for ideological reasons, and more mundanely as a result of the severe limitations on travel within an occupied and partitioned France.[23] A virtue was thus made of necessity, to rugby union's lasting advantage. For, as we have seen, the French game had, in the inter-war years, become imbued with the distinctive regional flavour, and even the local fervour, that continue to characterize it today. It was precisely this close association of the game with the south-west, and particularly the daily life of its villages and small towns, that had given rise in the later 1920s to the intense local rivalries associated with *le rugby de muerte* (a term coined by Voivenel himself in a highly critical and subsequently very influential article first published in 1927).[24] Yet it was also this previously stigmatized mentality, a particular sporting variant on the familiar rural *esprit de clocher* [parochialism], that Voivenel now chose to champion, describing it by his preferred (and altogether more positive) term of *le campanilisme*.[25] In his regular pieces for *Midi-Olympique*, then as now the 'Bible' of French rugby union, Voivenel stressed that this local rootedness was the key both to past glories and, he fervently hoped, future success. The ghost at this particular sporting feast was, of course, the conspicuous recent impact of the union game's despised offspring, rugby league. The radically altered political landscape of 1940 would provide the perfect ideological and practical conditions in which the ideas of Voivenel and like-minded figures within the FFR's hierarchy would take root and grow.

Central to this process were the reality and the mythology of rural France, both of which were intimately associated with Vichy's claim to moral and political legitimacy in the wake of national catastrophe. For the new administration portrayed itself, first and foremost, as realistic: in its unflinching appreciation of the material circumstances in which the country now found itself; in its 'apolitical' freedom from the fanciful ideologies associated with previous administrations, and especially the leftist Popular Front; and, above all, in its closeness to the *pays réel* or 'real France'. This deeper, abiding, French nation was associated with the countryside and its peasant inhabitants, as opposed specifically to the urban industrial workers and their political representatives, who, together with a variety of other scapegoats – such as the Jews, freemasons, and immigrants – were deemed to bear the real burden of responsibility for the country's defeat and occupation. It was this decadent France that Vichy now looked to replace with a community founded on traditional, if not actually eternal, French values and structures. Vichy's National Revolution was thus profoundly reactionary, and all strands of opinion within the regime 'certainly shared Pétain's assumption about the continuing moral and social importance of a large rural sector'.[26] This was the core of Vichy's vision of the *retour à la terre* [return to the soil], which linked an excessive economic valorization of the nation's agricultural base with an almost mystical faith in the age-old wisdom of the sons and daughters of the French soil. Thus 'Vichy's attempt to forge a new national image of social groupings and national history placed the image of the peasant and rural folklore at the centre of its web of propaganda'.[27] A remarkable speech made by Pétain as early as 1935 – and in circumstances that would have a considerable bearing on the future sporting developments that most interest us here – shows that such thinking had been a considerable time in the making.

On 17 November 1935, Pétain, the celebrated defender of Verdun in 1916, travelled to the village of Capoulet-Junac in the south-western *département* of the Ariège to inaugurate a memorial to local men who had fallen in the Great War. That the great man, no less than a *Maréchal de France*, should deign to accept this small and remote municipality's invitation would be a source of enduring pride for the local *notable* directly responsible for the construction of the memorial, Capoulet-Junac's mayor, Dr Paul Voivenel. The bulk of Pétain's oration before the village's *monument aux morts*, subsequently known as the 'Le Discours au Paysan' [The Address to the Peasant], would be repeated by him after he became head of the *Etat français*, again in the south-west, in his 'Discours de Pau' of 20 April 1941. In his own celebration of *L'Ame de la France* [The Soul of France] (1941), Voivenel reproduces the whole of the 1935 version of the speech. The following extract will give something of its flavour:

> As evening falls on the newly sown fields, and as the flickering lamps in the cottages are lit one by one, the peasant, still bent under the weight of his efforts, casts a last glance over his field, as if it pains him to leave it. Yet the day has been a hard one. [. . .]
>
> [. . .] However, the labour of the peasant, unlike that of the industrial worker, does not always receive the rewards that it deserves, and these rewards are never immediate. Many months separate the tilling of the fields from the harvest, during which time one must live on hope. Nothing is certain in the fields. Work alone is not enough. [. . .] The town-dweller can live from day to day, but the farmer must make provisions, calculate, struggle. Disappointments have no effect on this man, who is driven by his innate sense of the job to be done and his passion for the soil. Whatever happens, he faces up to things, he stands firm. It was from this daily, and thus constantly renewed, miracle that France first sprang, a hard-working and thrifty nation, attached to its freedom. It was the peasant who forged the country through his heroic patience, it is he who ensures its economic and spiritual stability. The prodigious expansion of our material resources has not changed the source of our moral strength. This strength is imprinted all the more firmly on the peasant's heart in that he draws it directly from the very soil of the fatherland.[28]

Pétain continues in this vein at some length, moving from the elegiac to the rousingly patriotic as he recalls the role played by peasants in the defence of the national territory in the Great War. Once again, abnegation and resignation are the key to their strength, and thus that of the true French nation that they incarnate, just as they defend it:

> For to the intimate fusion of origins, personalities, and individuals that constitutes an army, the man of the soil brings an element of inestimable value: solidity. [...]
>
> During the war ... the peasant fought in the ranks, with the deeply held belief that he was defending his own land. The most terrible trials never dented his faith. As long as the enemy remained on French soil, he retained the fierce resolution to defeat him.[29]

The obvious irony of this sort of appeal in the changed circumstances of France after 1940 is not what directly concerns us here. Rather it is the abiding faith of Pétain, and his followers, in the French peasant and the value-systems of which he is supposedly the centre. These included particularly the patriarchal structures of authority that Pétain himself most clearly represented as the would-be 'father' of the French nation.

That Voivenel was a devoted Pétainist is beyond doubt. Indeed, his own comments in his 1941 volume in praise of 'our providential Head of State', 'the greatest Head of State that [France] has ever had', clearly demonstrate his political affinities; as does his explanation of the catastrophe of 1940 in terms of a gullible French nation's willingness to listen 'to people who were not of our race [and thus] did not share our blood group'.[30] The sinister irony of a medical man talking in such terms will need little underlining to a modern audience. It also hints at the psychological frailty of those who took it upon themselves to rebuild the French nation in their own image in 'a period that placed the mark of exclusion at the heart of its own self-definition'.[31] Thus, in the sporting context, as elsewhere, Vichy would from the outset demonstrate its 'determination to exclude from the *pays réel* large sections of the population': all those, in fact, who were deemed to be undesirable on either racial or ideological grounds, thus confirming that the 'organic community that the National Revolution sought to promote was also a homogeneous, purified community'.[32] The banning from competition of Alfred Nakache, the country's leading swimmer, on the basis of his Jewish family origins, is the most obvious example of this policy's impact on targeted individuals and groups; but Jewish rugby players like the Parisian Herzovitch were also attacked by the collaborationist press in the city.[33]

Less obvious than this far-right racial agenda, perhaps, is the special relevance of rugby to Vichy's reactionary project. This is hinted at in Voivenel's comment that 'to understand one's village is to understand

France'.[34] Indeed, this was the real strength, he believed, of Pétain's thinking, and one that chimed very closely with his own view of the game that – together with medicine, and the memory of his own service in the First World War – dominated his life and his prolific writing. As he put it in the postscript to the 1962 edition of his major work on rugby (first published in 1942): 'Rugby is linked to the soil. Its parochialism [*campanilisme*] is a form of patriotism.'[35] It was this unshakeable belief in the eternal virtues of the union game, and the corresponding hostility to its upstart league rival, that would lead Voivenel to become directly involved in Vichy's project of National Revolution. The broad ideological linkage between Vichy's 'return to the soil' and rugby union's rootedness in the still predominantly rural south-west was reinforced by the pragmatic advantages of an alliance: working with and through the collaborationist administration enabled the FFR to exert real influence; while the union game's *méridional* power-base, and its historic antipathy to the national capital, suited Vichy's 'defensive parochialism [which was] implicitly also aimed against Paris, where Pétain's writ did not run'.[36] Yet above and beyond this, there would seem to have been something in the very nature of the union game that predisposed it to appeal to the architects of the National Revolution, and *vice versa*: a structural linkage that underpinned rugby's willing participation in Vichy's promotion of 'rural values'. More specifically, it is the game's unique preoccupation with the defence of territory that has particularly endeared it to rural French communities, with whom it shares an obsession with maintaining control of *le pré carré* [literally 'the square or enclosed field', one's own land]. More-over, for veterans of the Great War, such as Pétain and Voivenel, in which the defence of the tiniest portions of national territory had routinely demanded enormous human sacrifice, the ethos of a game that had itself been transformed under French conditions into a variety of 'trench warfare' may have been particularly attractive.

Certainly, the ability of leading FFR officials like Voivenel and Ginesty to work with Vichy's administrators was never in doubt. It was Pétain's first minister for sport, Jean Borotra, 'the bounding Basque', and member of the glamorous tennis-playing 'musketeers' who had brought France international success in the 1926 Davis Cup,[37] who set the ball rolling. Borotra was hostile from the outset to professional sport, which he and many others at Vichy readily associated with the physical and moral degeneration that the regime blamed for the catastrophe of 1940. Moreover, Borotra also had a strong personal investment in rugby union: like his immediate superior, the then Minister for the Family and Youth, fellow Basque and president of the national pelota federation, Jean Ybarnégaray, Borotra had strong associations with the Aviron Bayonnais rugby union club, which had been particularly badly hit by defections to rugby league.[38] To coincide with the publication in September 1940 of a document that amounted to a first draft of Vichy's 'Sports Charter', Borotra's ministry embarked on a series of consultations with the major sporting federations. Borotra dealt personally with Dr Albert Ginesty, the newly elected president of the FFR, and, acting on his advice, invited Dr Paul Voivenel to prepare a report on the current position of both rugby union and rugby league, with a view to reorganizing the two games. Voivenel duly reported on 4 October 1940. Although reproduced in full, and discussed with considerable pride, in the 1942 first edition of Voivenel's *Mon beau rugby*, this document was, not surprisingly, omitted from the second edition in 1962.

There were three main strands to the critique of rugby league that Voivenel presented as the core of his report, which – although he himself never made the point – mapped neatly on to Vichy's motto of *Travail, Famille, Patrie*. He began by attacking the game's professionalism, not only in the usual sense of the possibilities it offered for personal monetary gain, but also in terms of the intense training schedules that it imposed on players, even those who wished to remain amateurs, which effectively precluded normal professional activity: Voivenel argued that, because of these demands, rugby league should be regarded as inherently *un métier* [a job] rather than *un jeu* [a game], even where it was not played for money.[39] The claim to legitimacy of rugby league was dismissed by the simple expedient of denying its existence as a sport in its own right: the game was not actually a new one, Voivenel contended, but merely a deformed and polluted version of the 'classic' union game. Voivenel expressed this view in terms clearly intended to appeal to the sporting preferences and prejudices of his Vichyite readership: 'A modification of the rules, a slight reduction in the number of players is no more a justification for breaking away than lowering the net or having more players would be in tennis, or the fact of playing with bare hands or the *chistera* is in pelota.'[40] However, concluded Voivenel, even if these major criticisms of rugby league did not apply, it would still be necessary to get rid of the game in the national interest: 'the *necessity of cohesion* alone is, in all fairness [*en toute justice*], enough to impose its disappearance'.[41] This would be a view with which the guardians of the National Revolution would readily sympathize, as Mike Rylance explains:

What Voivenel by this report and other union conspirators by their intrigues were now doing was to give the [French Rugby] Federation, which was on its uppers both morally and financially, a quite undeserved second chance to reform, wiping out the memory of all those events of the past twenty years which had shown that this body was incapable of fulfilling its responsibilities and quite out of touch with developments in both sport and society in general. At the same time Federation officials and sympathisers were preparing to destroy the rival who had won both the moral battle and popular support.[42]

The end for rugby league would not be long in coming. The report having received Borotra's approval, a follow-up meeting took place on 17 October 1940 between Voivenel, Ginesty, and Marcel Laborde, the French rugby league's embattled president, together with Borotra's then deputy and future successor, Pascot.[43] Not only was Pascot actively involved both in the suppression of rugby league and the promotion of the rival fifteen-a-side code, but he would also seem to have been the moving spirit behind much of Vichy's sports policy even before he took over full responsibility in 1942. The committee that he chaired would now be responsible for managing the reunification of the two codes, as was announced immediately by Pascot on national radio, and officially decreed by Pétain a year later on 19 December 1941.

Rugby was thus forcibly reunited, and the union game was encouraged, along with a wide range of sports and open-air activities deemed to further the cause of national regeneration. The exploits of Marcel Cerdan in the boxing ring, Maurice Herzog in the mountains, and Jean-Yves Cousteau under the sea thus came to exemplify a new national determination and self-confidence in the sporting domain that would carry over almost seamlessly into the post-war period, as would the mountaineering-based literature of Pierre Frison-Roche, whose *Premier de cordée* was a great publishing success, and was also filmed in 1943 by Louis Daquin. As Gay-Lescot notes, the inspiration behind this popularization of the mountains and their symbolism was straightforwardly Pétainist rather than resistentialist.[44] Pascot himself would contribute to the broader cultural influence of French sport in 1944 with a new edition of his *Six maillots de rugby*, a celebration of his playing career first published in 1926, and now including a preface by Voivenel.[45] For his part, Pascot's foremost literary admirer, Paul Souchon, produced a collection of poems entitled *Les Chants du stade* in 1943, which, as well as a general 'Ode to Sport' and a celebration of 'The Joys of Sunday', includes particularly a poem entitled 'Pyrenean Rugby', which is specifically dedicated to Pascot, and which clearly echoes the rurally located nationalism of both Voivenel and Pétain in its opening stanza:

> Let the goalposts be raised,
> Triumphantly, at the bottom of the meadow,
> Rugby, like a fatherland,
> Summons the children of the South.[46]

The artistic quality (or the lack of it) of such cultural products is not the issue here, but rather the reflection in 'high' cultural forms of a resurgent 'popular' sporting culture at this time. The national rugby championship was re-established in the autumn of 1942, with the final being contested by the victors of the occupied and 'free' zones, before reverting to its familiar format from 1943 onwards. A key role was played in these wartime championship finals by returning players from rugby league, such as the great Puig-Aubert, a superbly talented attacking full-back who contributed significantly to the success of Pascot's own Perpignan club in 1944. Also revealed for the first time were a new generation of talented youngsters who would go on to shine in the post-war period, including notably Jean Prat from Lourdes, who played on the losing side in the 1945 final. Normal sporting life, or at least something like it, was thus restored, with 28,000 paying spectators attending the championship final at the Parc des Princes in Paris on 21 March 1943, and another 35,000 the following year's match on 26 March 1944.[47] Whether or not participation in these and other sporting activities – as player, administrator, or supporter – amounts to complicity with collaborationist objectives is, inevitably, a moot point, and one that extends to all areas of cultural life under the Occupation. A select band of rugby players, drawn from both codes, just like an equally limited number of courageous individuals in other areas of French sport and society, decided to engage actively in the fight against the Nazi invaders and their collaborationist supporters: *treizistes* and *quinzistes* were thus reunited, symbolically at least, in defence of the nation.[48] However, many more on the union side would be only too happy to continue to profit from Vichy's wartime betrayal of *le rugby à treize*.

Notes

1. Mike Rylance, *The Forbidden Game: The Untold Story of French Rugby League* (Brighouse, League Publications, 1999), pp. 144–5. Rylance notes revealingly that the official language of the new organization was German.
2. Central to this process was the filmic representation of the multi-faceted reality of French collaboration – first in Marcel Ophuls's epoch-making documentary *Le Chagrin et la pitié* (1971), and then in fictions such as Louis Malle's *Lacombe Lucien* (1974) – which was to open the floodgates to revelations about the darker and less easily avowed aspects of the war years. See Jill Forbes and Michael Kelly, *French Cultural Studies: An Introduction* (Oxford, Oxford University Press, 1995), pp. 90–1. An important role was also played at this time by non-French historians of

the Occupation, led by Robert O. Paxton, in his *Vichy France: Old Guard and New Order 1940–1944* (New York, Alfred A. Knopf and London, Barrie & Jenkins, 1972). See also W. D. Halls, *The Youth of Vichy France* (Oxford, Clarendon Press, 1981).

3. See Benoît Hopquin, 'Le sport français s'interroge sur son attitude sous Vichy' and 'Le rugby à XIII, victime de la vindicte du régime', *Le Monde*, 11 December 1998, p. 25.

4. The term 'untold story' is suggested by the subtitle of Rylance, *The Forbidden Game*.

5. Henri Amouroux, *La Vie des Français sous l'Occupation* (Paris, Fayard, 1961 and 1990), p. 460.

6. Forbes and Kelly, *French Cultural Studies*, p. 81. See also Jean-Pierre Rioux (ed.), *La Vie culturelle sous Vichy* (Paris, Editions Complexe, 1990).

7. Amouroux, *La Vie des Français sous l'Occupation*, p. 473; see also pp. 473–7.

8. Gilbert Garrier in Ronald Hubscher *et al.*, *L'Histoire en mouvements: Le sport dans la société française (XIXe–XXe siècle)* (Paris, Armand Colin, 1992), pp. 188–98. See also Pierre Mauroy, *Léo Lagrange* (Paris, Denoël, 1997), p. 69.

9. Garrier in Hubscher *et al.*, *L'Histoire en mouvements*, p. 198. See also Philip Dine, 'Sport and the State in contemporary France: from *la Charte des Sports* to decentralisation', *Modern & Contemporary France*, vol. 6, no. 3, 1998, pp. 301–11.

10. Garrier in Hubscher *et al.*, *L'Histoire en mouvements*, p. 198; more generally, and on the underlying reasons, see Jean-Louis Gay-Lescot, *Sport et éducation sous Vichy, 1940–1944* (Lyons, P. U. de Lyon, 1991), p. 52.

11. Gay-Lescot, *Sport et éducation sous Vichy*, p. 31.

12. See the report by the 'Sport For All' Clearing House (CDDS/Council of Europe), *Sports Structures in Europe: Situation in the Countries of the Committee for the Development of Sport of the Council of Europe*, 1993, F.2, pp. 1–4.

13. Figures given in Hervé Girette, 'De Jean Galia à Vichy: Les origines du XIII en France', *L'Indépendant* [Perpignan], 26 July 1995, unpaginated.

14. Rylance, *The Forbidden Game*, pp. 145–6.

15. Andrew Shennan, *Rethinking France: Plans for Renewal, 1940–1946* (Oxford, Clarendon, 1989), p. 26.

16. Borotra's wartime record has been the subject of considerable debate. A recent biography gives a good introduction to the issues raised: Daniel Amson, *Borotra: De Wimbledon à Vichy* (Paris, Tallandier, 1999).

17. Gay-Lescot, *Sport et éducation sous Vichy*, p. 170.
18. Commissariat Général à l'Education Générale et aux Sports, *Toulouse, capitale du rugby . . .*, *Les Cahiers de la France Sportive*, no. 3, March 1941, unpaginated. (Emphasis in the original.)
19. Ibid.
20. Gay-Lescot, *Sport et éducation sous Vichy*, p. 170.
21. Henri Garcia, *Rugby-Champagne* (Paris, La Table Ronde, 1960), p. 39.
22. Ibid., p. 41.
23. Gay-Lescot, *Sport et éducation sous Vichy*, pp. 166–76.
24. Paul Voivenel, *Mon beau rugby: L'Esprit du Sport* (Toulouse, Editions de l'Héraklès, 1942; Toulouse, Editions Midi Olympique, 1962), 1962, pp. 108–14.
25. This term suggests a village world centred on the Church, with the *campanile* [bell-tower] serving as a focal point for social exchanges in much the same way as the parish-pump might have done in other contexts.
26. Shennan, *Rethinking France*, p. 25.
27. Forbes and Kelly, *French Cultural Studies*, p. 86.
28. Paul Voivenel, *L'Ame de la France* (Toulouse, Editions de l'Héraklès, 1941), pp. ii–iii.
29. Ibid., pp. iii–iv.
30. Ibid., pp. 1, 9, 10.
31. Forbes and Kelly, *French Cultural Studies*, p. 91.
32. Shennan, *Rethinking France*, p. 25.
33. Gay-Lescot, *Sport et éducation sous Vichy*, pp. 182 and 208. Nakache was subsequently sent to a concentration camp, but survived.
34. Voivenel, *Mon beau rugby*, 1942, p. 26.
35. Voivenel, *Mon beau rugby*, 1962, p. 279.
36. Forbes and Kelly, *French Cultural Studies*, p. 87.
37. The other members of the winning team were Jacques Brugnon, Henri Cochet, and René Lacoste, whose 'Crocodile' nickname would later become the logo for his very successful sportswear company.
38. Rylance, *The Forbidden Game*, p. 128.
39. Voivenel, *Mon beau rugby*, 1942, pp. 220–33.
40. Ibid., p. 224.
41. Ibid., p. 225. Emphasis in the original.
42. Rylance, *The Forbidden Game*, p. 133.
43. This is Voivenel's date for the meeting and Pascot's announcement. Rylance places it slightly earlier on 13 October 1940: *The Forbidden Game*, p. 134.
44. Gay-Lescot, *Sport et éducation sous Vichy*, pp. 173–4.

45. Jep Pascot, *Six maillots de rugby* (Paris, Aux Horizons de France, 1944).
46. Paul Souchon, *Les Chants du stade* (Paris, Editions Tallandier and Commissariat Générale à l'Education Général et aux Sports, 1943).
47. Figures taken from Henri Garcia, *La Fabuleuse histoire du rugby* (Paris, ODIL, 1973), pp. 941–2.
48. René Barnoud, Robert Barran, and, of course, Jacques Chaban-Delmas are among the *rugbymen* to have distinguished themselves by their participation in Resistance activity. However, according to Gay-Lescot, *Sport et éducation sous Vichy*, p. 195, such figures were very much in the minority. See also Bernard Busson, *Héros du sport, Héros de France* (Paris, Editions d'Art Athos, 1947), and, more generally, H. R. Kedward and Roger Austin (eds), *Vichy France and the Resistance: Culture and Ideology* (London, Croom Helm, 1985).

PART III

Uncorking *le rugby-champagne, 1945–1968*

– 6 –

The Second Miracle of Lourdes[1]

The Liberation of France brought, amongst everything else, the lifting of the ban imposed on French rugby league by the collaborationist Vichy administration. As part of the wider pattern of reprisals that went to make up the *épuration*, or 'purging', of France as the Germans retreated, a number of union clubs were attacked and damaged by *treizistes*. These included particularly the facilities belonging to AS Perpignan, the reigning champions of France and also the home club of the disgraced sports minister Joseph Pascot.[2] In the immediate post-war period a number of other significant developments took place, such as the decision in 1946 by the Football Club de Lyon to go over completely to the thirteen–a–side code. Although short-lived and not conspicuously successful, this move by the oldest and most socially exclusive union club in the south-east – champions of France in 1910, and previously ardent campaigners against professionalism as members of the breakaway UFRA in the early 1930s – was indicative of league's appeal after 1945, for the immediate post-war period was, paradoxically, to be a golden age for *les treizistes*. This renaissance may have been due, at least in part, to the wartime ban itself.[3] After the Liberation, the league game was, in its own way, able to benefit from a national wave of sympathy for the victims of the Second World War that, among other things, saw the once outlawed French Communist Party (PCF) become the country's largest political grouping. Moreover, as a still very new sporting discipline, the game may have been able to exploit the fascination with novelty that characterized the frenetically modernizing France of *les trente glorieuses*, the period of unprecedented economic expansion and social restructuring from 1945 to 1975.

Yet the *treizistes* had to fight hard even to achieve official recognition by the state-run Comité National des Sports, headed now by Alfred Eluère, who also happened to be the president of the FFR. The sport was finally able to gain admittance only by agreeing not to call itself 'rugby' at all, that term being reserved for the union game:

And so rugby league was forced to be known by the nondescript title of *jeu à treize*, the thirteen-a-side game, in contravention of the law allowing a federation a free choice of name. Not until 1993 did French rugby league finally earn the right to call itself the Fédération Française de Rugby à XIII. A neat twist to this already convoluted story – a reinvention of history worthy of certain former communist régimes – was that the newly named Fédération Française de Jeu à XIII could not now claim any reparation for the funds and property taken by Vichy because it had not existed at that time.[4]

The fact that the FFR had been able to preserve its privileged position – as 'the official, state-recognised form of rugby'[5] – even after its enthusiastic collaboration with the Vichy administration was largely the result of the reluctance of the new national authorities to engage with the issue of what might be termed 'cultural collaboration', other than in the most extreme cases, such as that of the author Robert Brasillach.[6] French sport's voluntary amnesia began soon after the Liberation, with Vichy's athletes and administrators having to face little in the way of official sanctions. So not only did Pascot, following a half-hearted trial, escape with merely a token sentence, but rugby union itself was officially rehabilitated without hesitation. This lack of any effective purge of Vichyite structures and personnel has led Marianne Amar to talk of 'une épuration introuvable' [a non-existent purge] in the sporting sphere.[7]

This particular example of the deeper continuities underlying the visible changes in the post-war French polity meant that virtually the whole system of sports administration established under Vichy remained in place after the Liberation, and thus provided the essential framework within which the state would seek to manage French sport for decades to come. Such a failure of collective memory was the essential precondition for the dazzling display of political pragmatism that would now occur, as the once collaborationist union code, hitherto 'the "national" sport of a France whose northern boundary is marked by a line drawn from the Charente to the Jura',[8] would shortly be adopted as the national sport of France *tout court*, largely as a result of the efforts of the post-war state, and especially the Gaullist Fifth Republic. Moreover, French rugby union's administrators would make sure that the game's enhanced public prominence would whenever possible be used to reduce the influence of its principal rival: 'The cultivation of the media, politicians and civil servants – anyone, in fact, likely to be able to put pressure on rugby league – all were means by which to grind the enemy down.'[9] The long-term success of this strategy may be judged by the marginal existence to which French rugby league has nowadays been reduced. Yet, temporarily at least, *les treizistes* were able to overcome all the obstacles placed in their way by the defenders of rugby union. It was in the international arena that the thirteen-a-side game was best able to demonstrate its appeal to a France still traumatized by defeat and occupation, and in need of a focus for national self-esteem. The French rugby union side, which might have performed this function, had been starved of serious international competition between 1931 and 1945, and, no doubt in consequence, proved incapable of beating foreign opponents with any consistency in the decade that followed the Liberation. However, in marked contrast, the country's league representatives, led by the great Puig-Aubert, rapidly achieved a degree of success that obliged many doubters at home to reconsider the thirteen-a-side code. After defeating Great Britain at Wembley in the spring of 1949, and a British Empire select side in Bordeaux at the end of the same season, Puig-Aubert's team was to have its finest hour in the 1951 tour of Australia, where the French recorded their first series win. The squad that had left Marseilles very anonymously returned to a welcome fit for the sporting heroes that they had now become:

> Upsetting all the odds, the French didn't just beat the Aussies, they did so in a style that left the opposition looking clueless. Inspired, always inventive, France piled up 35 points to 14 in the Third Test in Sydney to humiliate the Australians with a 2–1 victory in the series. Thousands lined the streets of Marseille as the team returned home to an American-style ticker-tape welcome. The inimitable Puig-Aubert, who had been offered a massive contract to play in Sydney, was voted France's sportsman of the year.[10]

In this light, 1954 may be seen to constitute a watershed in the development of rugby football in France. To begin with, it was in that year that, thanks to the energy and ambition of the administrator Paul Barrière, the first rugby league World Cup took place; no less than 34 years before rugby union came up with its own version. With the French putting up 25 million francs to guarantee the competition's finances, the encounters between France, Great Britain, Australia, and New Zealand took place over a fortnight, with the final held at the Parc des Princes in Paris. The matches, played across the country, met with an enthusiastic popular response, culminating in the final game that saw Great Britain narrowly beat France. Bodis may be overstating the case somewhat when he suggests that a victory might have enabled rugby league to catch up with rugby union in France;[11] but there can be little doubt that defeat meant that an opportunity had been missed to present a resounding national advertisement for what was still very much a minority sport. French rugby union was to exploit this opening to the full. For it was in the 1950s that its own golden age really began, with

France's first Five Nations' championship coming in 1954, to be followed by its first Grand Slam – that is to say victories in all four matches – in 1968. As Augustin and Garrigou put it: 'From the 1950s, France began to bring together very talented teams that imposed a style of play significantly known as *rugby-champagne*, a trademark showing that it is a part of the national heritage [*le patrimoine français*].'[12] To a France hungry for signs of a renewed unity and dynamism, success in international competition by the nation's athletes was to prove particularly appealing. The 32 medals won by the French at the London Olympics of 1948 would consequently be interpreted as evidence of the physical and moral regeneration of the recently defeated and occupied nation, while the achievements of the national football side (and especially the tournament's top scorer, Just Fontaine) in the 1956 football World Cup would be read a decade later as an indicator of France's continuing international importance against the background of the country's peculiarly, and perhaps even uniquely, traumatic retreat from overseas empire.

Thus, in the face of the two 'grand narratives' of post-war reconstruction – decolonization (with its attendant political and institutional fallout) on the one hand, and the radical economic and social modernization of *les trente glorieuses*, on the other[13] – sport seemed to offer a reassuringly simple vision of French achievement at home and abroad. More than any other sporting discipline, rugby union would constitute a privileged site for the 'playing-out' – understood here as the vicarious dramatization and cathartic resolution – of these and other post-war challenges to traditionally constructed models of national identity. The international brilliance of French rugby union in the post-war period had its roots in the organizational structures that survived intact from the Vichy period. For the union game had emerged from the war in a position of domestic strength that few could have predicted following a decade and a half of international isolation, compounded, inevitably, by the many and various traumas associated with the country's wartime defeat, occupation, and partition. Moreover, the maintenance of the administrative structures established by Vichy – if not actually the ideology that had inspired them – together with the great majority of the regime's sporting personnel, meant that French rugby's uniquely close relationship with the state was effectively preserved. The successes achieved on the pitch once international competition had been resumed were to provide a powerful incentive for the continuation and extension of this symbiotic relationship.

The post-war normalization of relations between the French and the other rugby-playing nations was to start somewhat slowly, with the Scottish Rugby Union in particular still very wary of entrenched French ways, including most obviously illicit professionalism and the violence, both on and off the pitch, with which it had become associated. Indeed, rumours were current at the time that Winston Churchill had intervened personally in order to persuade the Scots to travel to Colombes for the first post-war match between the two nations on New Year's Day 1947.[14] Whatever the truth or otherwise of this claim, the 8–3 victory recorded by France on that occasion was a hint of the great things to come on the international stage. France's first win on Welsh soil was achieved in 1948 (11–3 at the old St Helen's international ground), with an inspired performance by Robert Soro serving to make his reputation as 'le lion de Swansea'.[15] A rather different sign of the French game's new significance was provided by Vincent Auriol's attendance at the return fixture the following year, the first time that a President of the Republic had attended a rugby international: 'This proved that rugby had become a national phenomenon.'[16] Other significant French successes were to include first victories at Twickenham in 1951 and at Murrayfield in 1952, together with a first-ever victory over the touring New Zealand All Blacks – then as now the most powerful force in world rugby – by 3–0 at Colombes in February 1954. This provided the spingboard for France's first overall victory in that year's Five Nations competition, which effectively (if unofficially) designates the European rugby champions. Finishing as joint winners, a feat that they were to repeat the following season, *le XV de France* would go on to become outright champions for the first time in 1959, and for the next three seasons, 1960–1962, and then again in 1967. The culmination of this process of international improvement came with the achievement of France's first Grand Slam – that is to say, victory over all four of the other competing countries in the Five Nations tournament – in 1968.

However, impressive as this series of results undoubtedly was, the most significant French accomplishment in this period was to occur further afield, in that most impregnable of rugby fortresses, South Africa. Not only was the 1958 tour the very first by a French union side, but the Springboks' defeat at the hands of *les Tricolores* was the first ever recorded, by any touring side, in a test series in that country. As a historic sporting event, the South African exploit of the French XV compares favourably with the recent conspicuous success of the French football team in the 1998 World Cup and the 2000 European championship. It was commemorated in a variety of ways, including particularly in Denis Lalanne's epic narrative of the tour, *Le Grand Combat du quinze de France* (1959).[17] Much of the credit for the French success was attributed to the captain of the side, Lucien Mias from the Mazamet club. A medical student who would go on to specialize in geriatrics, Mias was both a theoretician and a practitioner of closely coordinated forward play – still something of a novelty in the French game – and was consequently nicknamed 'Dr Pack'.[18] His success in South Africa led to him being awarded the Grand Prix Deutsch de la Meurthe by the French Académie des Sports, following such great figures as the pioneering aviators Georges Guynemer and Jean Mermoz. Additionally, he was received by the new President of the Republic, General Charles de Gaulle, and by his sports minister, Maurice Herzog, the mountaineer who had conquered the first 8,000-metre Himalayan peak, Annapurna, in 1950. His image was also modelled in wax for the famous Musée Grévin, the French Madame Tussaud's.[19]

France's international success had its origins in the dominance of the national championship by a single, all-conquering, association: the Football Club Lourdais. Intriguingly, 1958, the year of General de Gaulle's return to power and of the birth of the new Republic, was also a key moment in the history of both of the institutions that have, in their very different ways, brought this otherwise insignificant Pyrenean town to the attention of a national and, indeed, an international audience. Shortly after Bernadette Soubirous reported her visions of the Virgin Mary in 1858, local demonstrations of religious devotion began, to be followed by the first national pilgrimage to Lourdes in 1873. The fourteen invalids who joined the second pilgrimage in 1874 were the first of the many hundreds of thousands, if not millions, who would subsequently be drawn to the town in the hope of miraculous cures. Figures for 1993 indicate that nearly 70,000 invalids were included in the over 5,500,000 pilgrims who visited the shrine in that year, in what has now become firmly established as the world's foremost Christian pilgrimage.[20] The centenary of Saint Bernadette's visions was the occasion for extensive celebrations, which included the construction of a major addition to the already extensive religious architecture that had grown up above and around the little cave in the side of the Massabielle rock. Indeed, the building erected to mark the centenary was as much a celebration of French engineering as it was a symbol of religious devotion. Some 200 metres long by 80 metres wide, and with a total surface area of over 12,000 square metres, the vast underground basilica consecrated on 25 March 1958 was only made possible by the innovative use of reinforced concrete,[21] as the technological dynamism of *les trente glorieuses* was harnessed in the service of traditional Catholic values. With a capacity of 20,000, the new basilica could easily hold the entire permanent population of Lourdes, a town that, at this time, was in the process of developing the modern tourist infrastructure needed to maximize profits from what we might regard as the 'Bernadette industry', with numbers of visitors steadily increasing as a result of post-war affluence and associated improvements in transport networks.

The post-war building boom that was to leave modern Lourdes looking something like a religious Blackpool was to be at the root of the town's other 'miracle': a period of sustained dominance by the local club of the French union game to rival anything achieved by the all-conquering Stade Bordelais and Stade Toulousain sides of earlier periods, and destined to assure France of a seat at the high table of world rugby after the sporting isolation of the 1930s. Although founded in 1911, the Football Club Lourdais was to rise to prominence only in the wake of the Second World War. Central to the club's development was the influx of young men from the countryside into the urban centres of the south-west in search of work. The FCL's president, Antoine Beguère, an entrepreneur responsible for large-scale public works projects ranging from dams for hydro-electric schemes in the nearby mountains, through to the Lourdes rugby stadium, and even the new basilica itself – and additionally the town mayor, and later a senator – was well placed to offer suitable incentives to those rugby players who sought employment or advancement once peace had been restored.[22] In this age of official amateurism, the generally used term for such indirect financial investment in players was 'social aid', positively described by Potter and Duthen in the following terms:

> A player getting married may be helped to find a flat. A loan may be granted on easy terms to a player establishing or developing a business. Aid may be given to a hard-up student to remain at a university; to a young doctor, dentist, or solicitor to start a practice. Jobs are sought for unemployed players, or better jobs for fellows worthy of them.
>
> Social aid . . . A leg-up for conscientious, hard-working, deserving players. No help for the unworthy.[23]

However, whether or not 'social aid' was used by the Lourdes club in quite the disinterested fashion suggested here – 'a shining example of social aid well accorded and well used'[24] – there can be little doubting the club's success in attracting talented players in the immediate post-war period. Robert Barran is, perhaps, rather more objective in drawing attention to the role of transfers by key players from the club's principal local rivals (most obviously Tarbes and Pau) to boost its recruitment. However, as he goes on to note: 'Things were like that then. This policy was a reaction to the circumstances of the times. What the Lourdes directors were doing, so were plenty of others. The difference was that they were not able to keep the effort up.'[25] For the FCL may have reached successive championship finals in 1945 and 1946 (where it was beaten by Agen and Pau respectively) on the basis of imported talent, but its real successes in the period 1948–58 would be the product of home-grown stars, with a leading role being played by the local hero Jean Prat in particular.

While there can be no doubt that the economically motivated influx of players to Lourdes was an important part of the FCL's success story, the role played by *Monsieur Rugby*, Jean Prat, in the rise both of the club and of French rugby as a whole was at least as significant.[26] Appropriately enough, the stadium where the sporting consecration of Lourdes was destined to be achieved was built on land acquired in 1927 from Monsieur Prat senior, a local farmer, and the family name would be to the fore throughout in this second transformation of the town into a household name. Jean Prat is undoubtedly one of the brightest stars in the French rugby firmament, an inspirational captain of Lourdes and the national XV who only missed a single Five Nations match in a period of eleven years, amassing fifty-one caps in the process. Ironically, the single match that he missed – against Ireland in 1951, as a result of a bout of influenza – was the first in which his brother Maurice was also selected. Jean Prat was, with his brother Maurice, at the heart of a Lourdes-based quantum leap in French rugby's fortunes. The impact of the Prat brothers and the other dozen or so FCL players who played for the national side in the period 1948–58 can be appreciated in a variety of ways. In that time only one French XV took the field in a major international fixture without a Lourdes player. At the height of the club's influence, in 1958, no less than seven FCL players were included in the same national side, while, over the ten-year period 1948–58, the Lourdes club won the national championship on six occasions: 1948, 1952 and 1953, and three years in succession between 1956 and 1958; they were also runners-up in 1955. The FCL played 178 official matches over this period, being defeated only fourteen times, and scoring 2,714 points 'for', with only 846 'against'. With further national championships added in 1960 and 1968, it is little wonder that Henri Garcia concludes that the Lourdes side of this period was nothing less than 'the greatest team ever produced by French rugby'.[27]

The FCL's dominance of the domestic game was the bedrock upon which the French international side would build itself into a major force. It was this success, followed by millions of new supporters of *le XV de France* in the press, on the radio, and, increasingly, on television, that would see the game develop a genuinely national audience as its traditional heartland in the south-west was united, at least periodically, with armchair *rugbymen* from Brittany to Alsace.[28] This media-led 'nationalization' of the game on the basis of the international success of *les Tricolores* would be the essential prerequisite for its successful adoption after 1958 by Gaullist politicians as a symbol of *la France qui gagne* [victorious France]. The game would thus perform an important symbolic function as General Charles de Gaulle sought to transform a nation still wedded to an outmoded colonial vision of international success into a modern industrial nation at the heart of the new European Economic Community. In the event, rugby was recuperated by successive French governments as the nation emerged from the trauma of two lengthy colonial wars – and the near civil war that resulted from the second of them – to become a symbol of a new national vigour and an associated determination to defend French interests in international competition in all spheres, from the economic to the strategic. Of course, without 'the second miracle of Lourdes', French rugby could not have become the convenient symbol of national dynamism that it undoubtedly did after the return to power of General de Gaulle. Central to this process of political appropriation would be a moral investment in rugby that saw politicians, together with influential journalists, draw broader lessons for French society from the successes of its sporting representatives. Henri Garcia's summing up of France's 16–6 demolition of Wales at Cardiff in 1958 gives an indication of the discourses of national unity, technical modernity, and abiding *grandeur* within which French rugby football would be inscribed in this period:

> It was the great rugby lesson of the Arms Park. Never, ever, has the French XV played a more collective or better organized game than in this combination of the ideas of Mias in the forwards and the Lourdes players in the backs. A stunned rugby world discovered a set of *Tricolores* who had become masters of collective play with that typically French touch of attacking sharpness and inventiveness.[29]

Just how this reassuringly essentialist vision of France and Frenchness was constructed for a new, national, audience of armchair rugby supporters will be considered in Chapter 7. Before we can do that, however, it is necessary to say something about the political stakes of international sport at this time.

More specifically, it is instructive to note that the rise of modern French rugby in the post-war period took place against the backdrop of a process of decolonization that included two major wars, in Indo-China (1946–54) and Algeria (1954–62), and which, in the case of the latter conflict, would involve an entire generation of young Frenchmen in an ultimately futile military campaign. So *rugbymen*, like the rest of this latest *génération du feu* [war generation], would be conscripted for military service in Algeria. These would include such famous names as Guy Boniface, whose glittering playing career is examined in more detail in the next chapter. Guy Etcheberry, son of the famous Basque star Jean Etcheberry, and himself an international player with the French army XV, saw service in Algeria, and describes coming across entire units made up of rugby players.[30] What is more, rugby would itself become associated with the subsequent commemoration of this period, most obviously in literature. This is somewhat paradoxical, in that the Algerian war historically provided one of the most striking examples of the political exploitation of sport's symbolic potential, but on the football pitch rather than the rugby field. What is referred to here is the widely reported and genuinely dramatic gesture made by the 10 Algerian professional footballers who, in April 1958, left France and the French football league for Tunis, where they joined the external leadership of the revolutionary Front de Libération Nationale (FLN), specifically in order to establish an Algerian national side. These included particularly Rachid Mekloufi of Saint-Etienne, who had already been selected for the 1958 French World Cup squad, and who was represented, in Pierre Lanfranchi's words, 'as the perfect example of a fraternal integration achieved within the context of a French Algeria whose complete legitimacy the political authorities were doing their utmost to prove'.[31] Announced by the FLN in a declaration published on the front page of *L'Equipe* on 15 April 1958 and in the national journal of record *Le Monde* two days later, the Algerian players' move may well have touched the metropolitan public more profoundly than many – if not all – of the grand declarations made by the nation's intellectuals in the course of the conflict. The FLN would shortly up the political stakes by ordering the withdrawal of ethnic clubs from colonial leagues, and by organizing the bombing of football stadiums in Algeria and the execution of leading political opponents at football matches in France. Where football had once been used for the purposes of colonial integration, and its associated propaganda, it was now used for revolutionary nationalist action and agitation. This, incidentally, is the background to the Algerian novelist Rachid Boudjedra's fictionalized account of the assassination by Mohammed Ben Sadok of the Bachaga Mohammed Ali Chekkal, former vice-president of the Algerian Assembly, at the Colombes stadium on 26 May 1957, during the French cup final.[32] The French were clearly not alone, then, in recognizing the political potential of popular cultural forms in this period, and especially that associated with the major participatory and spectator sports.

Rachid Boudjedra's use of football in his novel of the Algerian war may fruitfully be compared with two very different narratives by French authors in which rugby plays an important part: Gaston Bonheur's *La Croix de ma mère* (1976) and Guy Lagorce's *Le Train du soir* (1983).[33] Guy Lagorce's story of childhood love and courage takes place against the background of German reprisals in the southern zone of occupied France in the summer of 1944. At the heart of this tale is the love of two French schoolboys, Antoine and Julien, for their Jewish classmate, Monique; a love that will lead the boys to hide and protect Monique as the vengeful occupiers regroup and retreat before the Allies' advance. Adult life will eventually see the three grow apart, until Antoine's suicide forces Monique and Julien to reassess their complex set of relationships. Of central importance, we discover, is Antoine's military service in Algeria, during which he actively participated in the torture of 'native' suspects. However, also significant is the fact that Antoine and Julien played together as full internationals in the French rugby XV. For it is, we learn, in the contrast between the hard lessons of the rugby field and the much harsher ones of the Algerian war that we are ultimately able to find an explanation both for Antoine's radical transformation and for his despairing final gesture:

> At the start, and on the basis of what life had been like at the *lycée* Godefroy-de-Bouillon, the army seemed to them, all things considered, to be stupid rather than really nasty. The war, on the other hand, entered their lives, like a reunion with the horror that they thought they had forgotten since 1944 in Rochecourbe. But this time, it was up to them to play. And it was patently obvious that this particular match did not have much to do with fair play. Their childhood and top-class sport had got them used to a certain form of courage and had toughened them up at a very young age. The war taught them that they knew less than they thought about themselves or other people.[34]

In contrast to this tale of military *angst*, Gaston Bonheur's *La Croix de ma mère* is a novel in which rugby serves above all as the familiar marker of regional identity; that is to say, the game performs its traditional function as the 'national' game of a France to the south and west of the Loire. Nevertheless, it does so in a way that is both imaginative and instructive. A sweeping, and essentially baroque fiction, Bonheur's romance has as its larger-than-life hero the comically named Alban Hondedieu,[35] a Southern *châtelain* in the mould of Cyrano de Bergerac, who harks back to the *ancien régime* and before it to the Cathars. Set against the background of the counter-terrorism in Algeria and in metropolitan France of the Organisation de l'Armée Secrète (OAS), as de Gaulle eventually led his war-weary country towards a grudging acceptance of Algerian independence, Bonheur's tale centres on a quixotic attempt to establish an independent southern state called *Toulousie*, which will, among other things, be able to welcome into its midst the exiled European settler population of Algeria, the *pieds-noirs*. Alternately comic and tragic – a full-scale siege of the medieval fortress of Carcassonne is followed by a suicidal attack on a team of Gaullist undercover agents in Toulouse – the adventure combines history, fantasy, and reassuringly *folk-lorique* sporting references in equal measure. So not only is the now elderly

Alban a former rugby player of renown, but so are all of his fellow conspirators:

> Shortly, his close associates were gathered around Alban, who, because of his height, stood out like a beacon.
> First came the dearest of all, his brother-in-arms, the enormous Chabert. Together they had formed the most feared second-row in Occitan rugby between 1920 and 1924. [. . .] Alongside this reunited pairing of the most famous 'locks' of their day, Raymond-Roger Mourront, the solicitor, felt sheltered, as he had been on the pitch when they faced up to the hurricane from Béziers or the Catalan race. [. . .] Belted up tightly in a trench-coat, with a military-style stick in his hand, he still looked every inch a fly-half. The fourth member of the group, Joseph Bel, the dandy of the team, played full-back – when the fancy took him. He refused to train, but, on his good days, sometimes made dazzling solo runs . . . Those were the epic days of their youth.[36]

Small wonder, then, that while the wild plan of these four, far-right, musketeers for an independent southern state may look to the Algerian war for its immediate justification, its underlying rationale is rooted in the traditional *vertus rugbystiques* of the region:

> Would the autonomy of the South be feasible? From a military point of view, yes. [. . .] When you are warlike and rugby-playing, victory is in the bag. [. . .] Algeria was an Occitan colony, not a French one, and, once again, France had made a mess of everything. In any event, it was a good excuse for fighting the old fight once again. We had to take advantage of this national disgrace to impose our old slogan: *pretz et paratge*. Always difficult to translate: 'to be proud and to show it', 'to believe in yourself, and to not give a damn', 'pride and chivalry'. *Pretz*, is when you drive into the scrummage. *Paratge*, is when you attack with ball in hand rather than trying to kick.[37]

Although predictably doomed to failure, this southern myth – the dream of a *méridional* heartland that might as readily be called *Ovalie* as *Toulousie* – is at least as entertaining as the Gaullist myth of *la France qui gagne*. Indeed, de Gaulle's pragmatic recuperation of French rugby union's sparkling achievements in the 1950s and 1960s was arguably more cynically calculated than that attempted by the wartime Vichy regime. It is therefore the reinvention of this marker of popular south-western separateness in the image of a patrician northern centralist that must be considered next.

Notes

1. This term is also used by Sean Smith, *The Union Game: A Rugby History* (London, BBC, 1999), pp. 202–6, but was first suggested by Robert Barran, *Du rugby et des hommes* (Paris, Albin Michel, 1971), pp. 133–41, in his description of 'Lourdes, citadelle du rugby'. See also Jean Abadie, *Lourdes, une certaine idée du rugby* (Pau, Editions Marrimpouey Jeune, 1976).

2. See Jean-Pierre Augustin and Alain Garrigou, *Le Rugby démêlé: Essai sur les Associations Sportives, le Pouvoir et les Notables* (Bordeaux, Le Mascaret, 1985), pp. 315–17. There was a second 'rugby war' in the town in the early 1980s, as a result of a dispute regarding the movement of players between the union and league clubs.

3. Jean-Pierre Bodis, *Histoire mondiale du rugby* (Toulouse, Bibliothèque Historique Privat, 1987), p. 291.

4. Mike Rylance, *The Forbidden Game: The Untold Story of French Rugby League* (Brighouse, League Publications, 1999), p. 170.

5. Ibid. See also Louis Bonnery and Raymond Thomas, *Le Jeu à XIII* (Paris, PUF, 1986), pp. 3–4.

6. See Jill Forbes and Michael Kelly, *French Cultural Studies: An Introduction* (Oxford, Oxford University Press, 1995), p. 102.

7. Marianne Amar, *Nés pour courir: La Quatrième République face au sport* (Grenoble, P.U. de Grenoble, 1987), pp. 27–42. More generally, see Henry Rousso, *Le Syndrome de Vichy de 1944 à nos jours* (2nd edn, Paris, Seuil, 1990).

8. Jean Lacouture, *Le Rugby, c'est un monde* (Paris, Seuil, 1979), p. 22.

9. Rylance, *The Forbidden Game*, p. 171.

10. Ibid., p. 172.

11. Bodis, *Histoire mondiale du rugby*, pp. 293–4.

12. Augustin and Garrigou, *Le Rugby démêlé*, p. 337.

13. One of the few studies to interweave these two strands effectively is that of Kristin Ross, *Fast Cars, Clean Bodies: Decolonization and the Re-ordering of French Culture* (Cambridge, MA, MIT Press, 1995).

14. Henri Garcia, *La Fabuleuse histoire du rugby* (Paris, ODIL, 1973), pp. 305–6.

15. Henri Garcia, *Seigneurs et forçats du rugby: un siècle d'ovale en France* (Paris, Calmann-Lévy, 1994), p. 87.

16. Garcia, *La Fabuleuse histoire du rugby*, p. 321.

17. Denis Lalanne, *Le Grand Combat du quinze de France* (Paris, La Table Ronde, 1959).

18. Garcia *Seigneurs et forçats du rugby*, p. 98.

19. Denis Lalanne, *Les Conquérants du XV de France* (Paris, La Table Ronde, 1970), pp. 119–20.
20. Manufacture Française de Pneumatiques Michelin, *Guide de Tourisme Michelin: Pyrénées Aquitaine* (Clermond-Ferrand, Michelin, 1995), p. 166. See also Ruth Harris, *Lourdes: Body and Spirit in the Secular Age* (New York, Viking, 1999).
21. Michelin, *Pyrénées Aquitaine*, p. 166.
22. Barran, *Du Rugby et des hommes*, pp. 136–7.
23. Alex Potter and Georges Duthen, *The Rise of French Rugby* (London, Bailey & Swinfen, 1961), pp. 127–8.
24. Ibid., p. 128.
25. Barran, *Du Rugby et des hommes*, p. 137.
26. Jean Prat's nickname was given to him by British rugby commentators. See Garcia, *Seigneurs et forçats du rugby*, p. 85.
27. Garcia, *La Fabuleuse histoire du rugby*, p. 393.
28. Potter and Duthen, *The Rise of French Rugby*, p. 135.
29. Garcia, *La Fabuleuse histoire du rugby*, p. 390.
30. Interview with the author, July 1996.
31. Pierre Lanfranchi, 'Mekloufi, un footballeur français dans la guerre d'Algérie', *Actes de la Recherche en Sciences Sociales*, no. 103, June 1994, p. 70.
32. Rachid Boudjedra, *Le Vainqueur de coupe* (Paris, Denoël, 1981). See Philip Dine, 'Un héroïsme problématique – Le sport, la littérature et la guerre d'Algérie', *Europe*, nos. 806–7, June–July, 1996, pp. 177–85.
33. Gaston Bonheur, *La Croix de ma mère* (Paris, Julliard, 1976); Guy Lagorce, *Le Train du soir* (Paris, Grasset, 1983).
34. Lagorce, *Le Train du soir*, p. 193.
35. This is a play on the expression 'Nom de Dieu!': 'In the name of God!'.
36. Bonheur, *La Croix de ma mère*, p. 78.
37. Ibid., pp. 71–2.

– 7 –

'Mission Accomplished!' – 1968 and All That

This chapter will draw attention to rugby's changing cultural significance at a time of particularly profound social and political upheaval, beginning, in May–June 1958, with the institutional crisis prompted by the Algerian war, and reaching its climax with the carnivalesque *événements* [events] of May–June 1968. The period under consideration thus begins with de Gaulle's return to power, and coincides with the height of the economic boom of *les trente glorieuses*, before ending with the radical undermining of established social structures and accepted values in a riotous Parisian summer of protest. More specifically, we shall concentrate here on rugby football's pragmatic adoption by the governing politicians of the Fifth Republic. For the rise of French rugby in the 1950s and 1960s did not just coincide with the inauguration and consolidation of the new Gaullist regime. Rather, the nation's association of one with the other, and of both with itself, was systematically encouraged by General de Gaulle and his supporters. This policy of linking the national team's fortunes with those of the new (Fifth) Republic was part of a broader appeal to the discourse of sporting success in the construction of *la France qui gagne*, and one that was to receive a significant boost following the 1960 (Rome) Olympic games. Central to this process was the link between rugby football and rurality, a theme that, in other areas, such as political and cultural regionalism, had been thoroughly discredited by its association with the Vichy regime.[1] As a result of the post-Liberation failure to purge French sport of those individuals and associations tainted by wartime collaboration, rugby union, which had been ailing in 1939, found itself in a position to thrive. The fact that it was, from 1945 until the mid-1960s, also one of the few vectors for the expression of region-alist sentiment that remained open to respectable public opinion now significantly enhanced its appeal. Indeed, it was this that allowed rugby football to be seized upon by politicians and the media in this period of radical change as a means of linking tradition and modernity, and thereby of seeming to maintain what were held to be essential and even eternal French values.

Of course, for this particular cultural and ideological trick to be pulled off, French rugby had to be seen to be successful, and particularly in international competition. For in the brave new France of General de Gaulle, success was everything. Indeed, it might be argued that what was required of French sportsmen at this time was to act as symbols of the nation's economic dynamism and political confidence: a sporting representation of renewed French power suitable for consumption at home and abroad. Just such an opportunity for the political exploitation, or at least recuperation, of athletic achievement occurred in rugby football, with the beginning in the 1950s of its own golden age. The French *rugbymen* had won their first Five Nations championship, and additionally defeated New Zealand at Colombes, in 1954; a year that was itself a political watershed, which saw both France's catastrophic military defeat in Indo-China and the onset of the Algerian war. Led by Lucien Mias, *les Tricolores* went on to win their first overseas test series in South Africa in 1958; and they thus now embarked with justified confidence on what was French rugby's equivalent of the quest for the Holy Grail, namely the attempt to win France's first Five Nations 'Grand Slam', which was eventually achieved in 1968. It was this conspicuous success that allowed the governing politicians of the new, Gaullist, Fifth Republic to adopt rugby as the national sport. The boom years of post-war economic and social reconstruction thus became firmly associated with *le rugby-champagne*, or rather *le rugby-français*, as the union game, traditionally rooted in the south-west, for the first time came to be considered as part of the national heritage or *patrimoine*.

This 'nationalization' of French rugby football was encouraged by developments within the game itself, which were themselves amplified by well-placed journalistic commentators, including particularly (as is discussed below) Antoine Blondin at *L'Equipe*, the country's leading sporting newspaper. However, even more significant was the massive expansion of television sports coverage. It was the advent of television, and specifically the live outside broadcasting of sport from the mid-1950s onwards, that was to transform French rugby from a regional passion into a national preoccupation, at least for the duration of the annual Five Nations championship. The first televised game was the Grand Slam decider of 1955, which France lost at Colombes to the Welsh, with the first 'cross-Channel' games being shown by the state-run Organisation de la Radiodiffusion-Télévision Française (ORTF) the following season: 'Rugby thus became a national reality.'[2] In fact, the first televised matches would only be seen by a privileged few on the small screens of the day. However, with the development of more sophisticated technology and a steady rise in the access to television of an increasingly affluent urban population, rugby would rapidly become popular to the north and east of its traditional heartland. The mass mediatiz-ation of rugby may in consequence be accurately dated to the period 1960–65, with a key role being played in the popularization of the game by the shift early on in the style of commentary provided, away from that of the patrician Parisian Loys Van Lee, and towards the altogether more down-to-earth approach of a figure who was to become synonymous with French rugby, Roger Couderc.[3] As Pociello explains:

> . . . during the [1961 French tour of New Zealand], broadcast live by satellite, Roger Couderc invented a new style of commentary . . . which was to contribute significantly to the success of televised rugby. [. . .] It was a very immediate and affective style of commentary, with hardly any technical analysis, but vibrant with emotion. 'Come on lads! . . . [*Allez les petits!*] Get stuck into them!', and the like; all delivered, appropriately, in the sing-song accent of the south-west, and just the right thing to describe a valiant attack by our national XV.[4]

Such was Couderc's popularity in the 1960s that he became known as 'the French team's sixteenth player', with his devotees continuing to listen to his radio commentaries on Europe 1 whilst watching the television coverage – with the sound turned off – following his temporary replacement in 1968.[5] As Pociello's comments suggest, Couderc's lack of technical expertise was actually part of his attraction to a new national audience itself unfamiliar with an apparently simple but actually very complex game: 'The basis of Couderc's success did not reside in his understanding of the technical refine-ments of the game (such as the scrummage), in his mastery of its laws or his ability to explain why the whistle went; rather it was enough for him to possess the game's *habitus* and *ethos* in their most easily recognizable forms, that is to say to have the right accent, to be canny [*malin*], and above all to be chauvinistic.'[6] Technical competence was actually supplied by former international Pierre Albaladejo in later years, with the two men combining to form something of a comedy double-act that further added to rugby's appeal for a national audience.

The Couderc–Albaladejo partnership resembled another celebrated duo, itself an image of an essentialist French identity that also first came to public attention in the later 1950s and early 1960s, namely the wily Astérix the Gaul and his well-meaning if rather bumbling side-kick Obélix: 'In a continuing series of adventures, Astérix and his burly partner Obélix are depicted fighting with Romans around different areas of France, around neighbouring European countries, and in more distant lands, presenting national and regional stereotypes with gentle humour. The wisecracking warriors triumph through a mixture of luck, reckless courage, and a magic potion prepared by the druid.'[7] French rugby's celebration since its earliest days of counter-attacking valour and, especially, the virtues of *la ruse* [craftiness or guile] mapped easily on to these comic-book characters, as did the south-west's particular devotion to the ritualized consumption of totemic foods and drinks. Indeed, in *Astérix chez les Bretons* (1966), the two heroes even come across a game that bears a striking similarity to rugby (thereby incidentally – if spuriously – establishing its indigenous credentials): '[the game] is played with a gourd by thirty Bretons, divided into two teams of fifteen [with the matches] counting towards the Five Tribes tournament'.[8]

In their commentaries, Couderc's naïve, impulsive, and regularly outraged Obélix was balanced by Albaladejo's cool-headed, better informed, and generally more astute Astérix: 'Once these roles had been established, they mattered far more in their verbal adventures than the technical nature of their commentaries [which] at their most colourful relied (just like comic-books for both children and adults) on imagery drawn from a common store of fantasies expressed in fairy tales and ancient legends.'[9] As voiced by the Astérix stories, such archetypal folk-narratives could even be extended to take in de Gaulle's pursuit of a foreign policy that conceived of France as determinedly independent of both the American and the Soviet *blocs*. In a recent number of *Ethnologie française* devoted exclusively to the Astérix myth, Maurice Agulhon has underlined the crucial shift in French self-images that occurred in the 1950s. Whereas the nation's mythology had hitherto been rooted in an imperial conception of *grandeur*, under de Gaulle – and especially after the Algerian war – this was replaced by an anti-imperialist rhetoric 'of a France which disrupts, which refuses, which resists (not, properly speaking, occupation or aggression, but at least integration)': 'Astérix is thus rather like de Gaulle expelling NATO from its bases in France and standing up to the "Anglo-Saxons" in Montreal and Mexico.'[10] This had its sporting parallel in France's continued exclusion from rugby's ruling International Board, and the FFR's compensating investment in FIRA as an alternative world body. French national sides thus continued to play regularly against Italy and Romania, and even travelled to Prague in the spring of 1968 to play against Czechoslovakia, in what was an intriguing footnote to that country's all too brief experiment in 'socialism with a human face'.

The paradoxical nature of French neo-patriotism in this period becomes even more apparent when set against the country's long-term commitment to the project of Europeanization. For it was against the backdrop of the economic and political unification of Europe, together with the country's no less significant love–hate relationship with American popular culture, that the narrative of French 'anti-imperialism' was articulated. In this time of profound change, France looked in on itself in the search for abiding verities. Stéphane Baumont has identified some particularly significant continuities in Roger Couderc's quasi-mystical variety of popular nationalism: 'Who has not heard the legendary refrain of that bard of [French] rugby, Roger Couderc, a genuine Maurice Barrès of the microphone . . .; an authentic Paul Déroulède of the airwaves and rewarded as such with the *Légion d'Honneur*. "They're good, they're young, yes, yes, my children, come on lads [*allez les petits*], come on France".'[11] Like the sanctified Lorraine of Barrès, the rugby-playing south-west presented in the later 1950s and the 1960s by Couderc, Albaladejo, and others was essentially mythical: less *le Midi* than *l'Ovalie*, the land of the oval ball. A critical observer from one of the important and often overlooked rugby-playing enclaves in the south-east of the country has aptly characterized this standard French attitude to the sport: 'For them, rugby is something rather quaint which is inextricably mixed up with such familiar aspects of the region's local colour as its famous tourist sites and its gastronomic specialities; rugby is like the Lourdes basilica, the blue sky of Pau, *foie gras*, the volcanic mud of Dax, *cassoulet* [sausage and bean stew] from Toulouse, and raw ham from Bayonne, all rolled into one.'[12]

The linking of rugby to such well-known markers of regional specificity is closely related to its central myth as offered to, and enthusiastically consumed by, a new national television audience: that is to say the theme of rurality.[13] For rugby continued to be perceived above all as a sport of the countryside rather than of the towns; a sport of places where traditional patterns of festivity were still honoured; where the character of the inhabitants was essentially fixed and based upon clearly delineated ethnic affiliations – Basques, Gascons, Catalans, and the like; a last redoubt of *la France profonde*, in short, miraculously insulated against 'the headlong, dramatic, and breathless' processes of modernization, which together meant that 'French society was transformed after the war from a rural, empire-oriented, Catholic country into a fully industrialized, decolonized, and urban one'.[14] The fact that the south-west, like the rest of provincial France, was administratively reinvented in the post-war period was thus ignored in favour of an image of continuity. The rise of Toulouse as a regional capital, thanks both to government initiatives and private investment, especially in the aerospace industry, was thus less important than *le rugby-cassoulet* with which the city had long been associated. By the same token, the profound changes in the countryside that resulted from wide-ranging agricultural reforms – including particularly a flight from the land that is habitually described as a rural exodus, and is consequently associated with the 'desertification' of rural France – were less significant than the reassuring images of *le rugby des villages*.

In a television documentary shown in the early 1960s, Lucien Mias, captain of the side that achieved the historic series win in South Africa in 1958, is shown returning to his family home, 'a village lost in the mountains of the Aude . . . a village which is almost abandoned, but which does not want to die'.[15] Visiting the *école communale* where he was once a schoolmaster, Mias is pictured giving an impromptu lesson on the Gauls, a staple of the Republican education system given a new resonance by the popularity of the Astérix cartoons. As the voice-over commentary explains, 'the young schoolmaster from Laprade-Basse has kept his two promises: he became a doctor, and he has made *le XV de France* victorious'.[16] Although himself a living testimony both to the rural exodus and the triumph of technocracy over peasant value-systems, Mias is hailed as the incarnation of the region's and the nation's most abiding virtues. As a result, and despite the obvious visual signs of his native village's depopulation and decline, the authoritative voice-over can conclude reassuringly that 'nothing has changed'.[17] This is the most basic message, and the principal myth, underlying the political elite's symbolic appropriation of French rugby football at this time.

In the seemingly all-powerful figure of Mias and such sporting icons of the day we begin to glimpse the most basic rationale for the recuperation of this particular sport by the politicians of the new Fifth Republic, as by those of the Vichy regime before them. For it is precisely the appeal of a traditional, village-centred, and peasant-based construction of masculinity – and with it national identity – that was to be seized upon as an antidote to the radical newness of the urbanized and technologically driven France of *les trente glorieuses*. As Kristin Ross reminds us: 'The roughly ten-year period on either side of the end of the Algerian War in 1962 was perhaps the last time that French people were greeted by a resounding chorus proclaiming the "new": Françoise Giroud's coining of the term "New Wave" in 1958 to describe the emergent youth culture in the cities has become in subsequent years the commonplace marker for a historical moment when most people found themselves to be living two or more lives at once, and thus felt the invigoration and fatigue of confronting situations without having the appropriate habits or behaviours firmly in place.'[18] While cultural historians have conventionally focused on the well-known artistic locations of this 'newness' – the cinematic New Wave and the so-called New Novelists – 'an examination of the discursive production of the time shows that the noun most often modified by the adjective "new" was in fact that of "man": in the decade in question, the arrival of the "new man", of a new construction of (male) subjectivity was proclaimed from all sides, celebrated, analysed, and debated'.[19] If France's post-war industrial resurgence depended, at the level of rhetoric if nothing else, on a previously unknown socio-professional category, that of 'the new, forward-looking, corporate *jeune cadre* [young executive] . . . the transitory expression of a French society in transition',[20] French rugby's particular variation on the theme of *homo ludens*[21] was to provide an altogether more reassuring image of masculine mobility and dynamism. Indeed, rugby would prove to be a remarkable force for political (and specifically cross-party) consensus in these troubled and troubling times, thanks to its ability successfully to integrate a variety of 'still cherished pre-war outlooks'[22] within a qualitatively new form of technologically mediated sporting spectacle, thus elegantly and apparently effortlessly combining the most solid of traditions and the shock of the new.

General de Gaulle's outrage at the feeble performance by French athletes at the 1960 Olympic games in Rome underlined the importance that he attached to sport as an international marker of dynamism and competitiveness. The publication a few months later of a plan for national sporting *grandeur* (jointly written by senior Gaullist politician Louis Joxe and the celebrated mountaineer Maurice Herzog) was to lay the foundations for the Fifth Republic's sustained investment in sporting excellence.[23] In the absence of conspicuous successes in other sports – not only was French athletics in crisis, but the nation's football teams performed poorly after the heroics of the 1956 World Cup – de Gaulle and his supporters had to look elsewhere for a sporting incarnation of *la France qui gagne*, and they found it in rugby. The simultaneity of the establishment and consolidation of the Fifth Republic and rugby's rise to a position of totemic significance in the French national consciousness was by no means coincidental. On the contrary:

> The Gaullist administration contributed greatly to the new status of rugby. [. . .] In this Gaullist France, it became a part of national symbolism. As a positive representation of *la France qui gagne*, it was targeted for nationalistic investment by the government, which it was all the better suited to canalize as a regionally rooted sport [*sport de terroir*].[24]

Receptions at Matignon and the Elysée for successful French teams were one way in which this process of identification – and, crucially, mutual legitimation – was encouraged. De Gaulle's well-reported interest in the team's fortunes, including particularly his ban on Saturday afternoon meetings when Five Nations matches were being played, was another part of the new administration's very visible linking of itself to the national rugby team. The appointment of Jacques Chaban-Delmas to the post of Prime Minister by de Gaulle's successor as President of the Republic, Georges Pompidou, was arguably the culmination of this process.[25] As well as possessing unimpeachable Gaullist and Resistance credentials, Chaban-Delmas was also widely known as a sportsman, being a former international player of both tennis and rugby. It was this last qualification that made a particularly significant contribution to the former Bègles player's establishment of his municipal and regional power-base in Bordeaux, as he himself admitted in the early 1970s: 'I also owe my success to rugby [. . .] 100,000 people south of the Loire address me as "tu" and call me Jacques because of it.'[26]

In these and related ways, such as the sending of official messages of encouragement and congratulation, the performance of the national XV was to become an affair of state under de Gaulle and his successors. The captain of the victorious French side at Twickenham in 1967 could therefore, quite reasonably, send a telegram to the President of the Republic proclaiming 'Mission accomplished!'; while Georges Pompidou, for his part, would in 1969 feel entitled to inform the press of his nomination for the captaincy of *le XV de France*, with his choice, Walter Spanghero, duly being appointed by the FFR.[27] More recently, Daniel Herrero's public display of support for François Mitterrand in the 1974 presidential campaign and that of Jean-Pierre Rives for Valéry Giscard-d'Estaing in 1981 show a continued affinity between the political and rugby-playing elites, as do the regular interventions made in this area by that most determinedly opportunistic of French politicians, Jacques Chirac.[28] The telegram of commiseration sent by President of the Republic François Mitterrand to the French side defeated 29–9 by the All Blacks in Auckland in 1987 not only maintained this now traditional association, but also demonstrated the usefulness of rugby as a tool of international diplomacy: in this case as an important symbolic act in the re-establishment of normal relations with New Zealand in the wake of the sinking in the city's harbour of the Greenpeace environmentalist organization's vessel 'Rainbow Warrior' by French secret agents in 1985.[29]

As the foregoing reference to the first socialist president of the Fifth Republic will have made clear, rugby has been appealed to as a repository of essential French values across the political spectrum. This means that the former star of the 1950s and 1960s, the 'Duke' of Brive and the Corrèze, Amadée Domenech, may with justice proclaim that 'rugby votes on the Left'. However, the radical tradition of *le Midi rouge* does not mean that acceptance of the game's peculiar variety of nationalism – a brand of parochialism imbued with patriotic fervour – was any less common further to the Right, in this period or subsequently. So not only has rugby football been claimed as their own by the Gaullists, but also by prominent critics of de Gaulle and all his works, including especially that opponent of so much to be found in the France of *les trente glorieuses*, Antoine Blondin. Indeed, for Blondin, rugby is perhaps the last place that the most fundamental and time-honoured of French virtues may be discovered. Writing in *Paris-Match* in April 1962, he looks to rugby as the repository of an ethnic and mystical Frenchness that recalls that of Paul Voivenel in the Vichy period, and might even have been recognized by Barrès:

> Rugby is essentially traditional, chivalrous, and generous. It was only to be expected that it should have responded to the aspirations of communities whose folklore has remained particularly alive, where the local temperament readily lends itself to lyricism, and where exuberance often leads to extravagance.
>
> [. . .]
>
> This sport must certainly be possessed of secret virtues – and not just scenic ones – to be able to make men experience these unfamiliar sensations of solidarity with others, of forgetting oneself, of identification, of participation, in short, in the mystical sense of the word.
>
> Even more than the victories of the French team, this atmosphere of privileged ecstasy may be one of the keys to the national infatuation with rugby. If we wish to gather the last fruits of the sublime and the legendary, then we must seek them out in their last refuge: the stadium.[30]

Here the myth of the golden age joins those of the soil, the people, the nation, and, come to that, the myth of sport itself, in a powerfully affective amalgam. That such an emotional and moral investment was made in French rugby right across the political spectrum – and at precisely the moment when it did, indeed, enter its own golden age in terms of the sparkling *rugby-champagne* served up by the national side – is less a coincidence than a reflection of the political pragmatism of General de Gaulle and his political opponents alike. It is also a function of the particular attractiveness, not to say insidiousness, of sport-based constructions of masculine identity and factitious community.

Rugby's connection with *Paris-Match* is also of significance, in that this publication, established in 1949, and with sales in the millions by the early 1960s, was 'a dominant presence of the 1950s . . . with a particular preference for the life-style of French and international celebrities'.[31] International rugby players joined that select band, where they were courted by 'a more nebulous socialite Right' not unlike that which had centred on 'Le Boeuf sur le toit', the Right Bank night-club of the 1920s.[32] This set included such figures as the fashionable young novelist Françoise Sagan, whose *Bonjour Tristesse* had been the publishing event of 1954, and who danced the night away with members of *le XV de France* in post-match celebrations in London in 1961.[33] Central to the group was Antoine Blondin, who had come to sports journalism after a career as a committed right-wing activist and serious novelist. A member of the so-called *Hussards* literary movement – alongside Roger Nimier and Jacques Laurent, who shared both his iconoclasm and his nostalgia – Blondin looked to rugby, as well as cycling, from the 1950s on, as an antidote to the frenetically modernizing society that surrounded him: 'Sport, with its close sense of fraternity, which he experienced with his friends Nimier and Kléber Haedens, became the logical substitute for the camaraderie of political action and this reactionary anarchist became in the 1980s an affectionate Mitterrandiste.'[34] If sport was so important to Blondin, it was necessarily combined with the lifelong addiction of a writer who famously claimed to be 'not an author who drinks, but a drinker who writes'.[35] Rugby's micro-culture offered significant advantages from this point of view, and Blondin would establish particularly close relationships – which inevitably meant drinking partnerships – with a number of iconic rugby players, including especially Guy Boniface and (as we shall see in Chapter 8) Jean-Pierre Rives.

In the early hours of New Year's Day 1968, Guy Boniface was involved in a fatal car crash at the Hagetmau turn-off on RN133. He thus joined the pantheon of celebrity victims of the internal combustion engine, the international epitome of whom was at the time James Dean.[36] For French viewers of American films and, increasingly, of French films influenced by American representations of that country's 'road' culture, Dean's iconic status was established precisely by the fact and the manner of his death, as Kristin Ross has persuasively argued in her survey of the reordering of French culture in the post-war period, very significantly titled *Fast Cars, Clean Bodies*.[37] Thus, when the particular fast car containing Guy Boniface's clean body collided with a tree, the event was compared, not just within France but throughout the rugby-playing world, to the death of the Hollywood film star, with Boniface presented precisely as 'ce James Dean du rugby'.[38] Antoine Blondin described the loss at thirty years of age of a player whom many considered to be the finest centre three-quarter in the world in just these terms, likening it also to the deaths of his friend Nimier, of the journalist Robert Roy, and, a mere three days after Boniface's death, and only a few kilometres down the road, of Jean-Michel Capendeguy, the twenty-year-old winger for the national rugby side.[39] Such was the resonance of the event that the Olympic flame, *en route* for the 1968 winter games in Grenoble, came to a halt at the scene of Boniface's crash to honour the player.[40]

In the France of *les trente glorieuses*, the car – and particularly the fast car – became a potent symbol of the new social and geographical mobility necessitated by the root-and-branch modernization of the economy.[41] Moreover, the car crash became in its own right a bizarre, and often gruesome, marker of the modern, and with it of social distinction:

Françoise Sagan's 1954 car wreck in her Aston-Martin was a focus of print obsession for months, even years; Nimier's latest car accidents were featured in *Femina illustration*. Testimonies to a particular novelist's bold, risk-taking driving style in turn increased sales of both novels and magazines. [. . .] The violent automobile death of Nimier himself and novelist Sunsiaré de Larcone in 1962, along with those of Albert Camus and Michel Gallimard in 1960, Jean-René Huguenin in 1962, the two sons of André Malraux, the Ali Khan, and the near-fatal accident of Johny Hallyday in the surrounding months, each produced a torrent of horrified, lurid articles.[42]

Against this backdrop, Guy Boniface's death on the first day of 1968 may straightforwardly be read as conforming to a tradition of celebrity demise, in which death at the wheel continued to be associated with wealth, glamour, and stardom. However, it would be wrong either to inscribe his death within a Dean-inspired myth of youthful rebellion, or to see him as simply some variety of super-*cadre*, as mobile and *disponible* [available or flexible] off the pitch as he undoubtedly was on it. Nor, come to that, is it enough to focus merely on the *Hussard* connection, and to see in the sportsman who accompanied the alcoholic Blondin on his Parisian ramblings a relatively naïve figure flattered by the attentions of the highly cultured and deeply reactionary Right. Or at least, we have to go beyond these readings, each of which does, in fact, contain a grain of truth. For Guy Boniface in life and, *a fortiori*, in death, was able to reconcile in his person – or, more accurately, in the legend that became attached to it – directly competing images of French masculinity and nationhood. Once again, the manner of his death offers a clue to the player's ability to reconcile apparently contradictory notions: of mobility and rootedness; of modernity and tradition; of change and continuity; of the primacy of both the individual and the community; of the national and the local as determinants of identity. For while he may have died in a fast car on the *route nationale*, he was on his way to a New Year's Eve celebration with family and friends, and so finished his life where he had started it, amid the *bourgs* of his native *pays* in the Landes, in the heartland of French rugby football. If Guy Boniface was transfixed by death in a frozen image of high-speed and high-risk mobility, it was thus entirely in keeping with the dazzling, but inherently limited, movement of his performances on the pitches of the south-west, the Parc des Princes and Colombes, and the rest of the rugby-playing world. The player, like the game that he epitomized, was always moving quickly, but never actually going anywhere. This was the crux of his appeal to a France torn between the old and the new.

In fact, anyone who has ever heard of Guy Boniface will also have heard of his elder brother André, also a centre, and it is as *les frères Boni* that we now need to consider them. Products of the Mont-de-Marsan club, which they guided to the national championship in 1963, the pair had a long but chequered international career, with most commentators agreeing that inconsistent selection meant that they did not play together in the national colours as often as they should have done. Nevertheless, the brothers between them collected eighty-one international caps from 1954 to 1966, appearing together in the centre on eighteen occasions from 1960 on, when Guy was first picked for the national side; a French record which stood for twenty-six years. Two elements are central to an understanding of the significance of the Boniface brothers: firstly, the not-so-simple fact of their being brothers; and secondly, the contribution that they made to the establishment of a characteristically French style of play, in conjunction with a third, mutually adopted, brother-in-arms, Jean Gachassin. It is not uncommon for brothers to play an important role in the on-field culture and popular perception of a variety of sports, and this in many countries. The particular combinations of genetic inheritance and shared upbringing that lie behind the achievements of such famous siblings as, for instance, Bobby and Jackie Charlton in English football, or the Chappell brothers and the Waugh twins in Australian cricket – and, come to that, the unprecedented recent success of the American Williams sisters in tennis – although of undoubted interest, are not really what concerns us here. Rather it is the cultural significance attached to such family relationships that is of importance. For it would seem that sports writers and broadcasters, and their respective audiences, seem to take a particular interest in, and to derive a special form of pleasure from, the achievements of siblings. In the specific case of rugby, with its strong traditions of local rootedness and familial continuity, such an objectively disproportionate predilection for examining the activities of brothers seems self-evident, as does a fondness for rugby dynasties.

In France, at least as much as anywhere else – and for reasons that, as discussed in Chapter 3, would seem to be linked to long-term demographic trends – rugby union has historically had an important familial and dynastic dimension. In a book devoted precisely to this theme, Renaud de Laborderie details over 70 sets of rugby-playing brothers, all of which include at least one full international player.[43] Of these, some of the more famous include the following: the Moga brothers from the Bègles-Bordeaux club where Jacques Chaban-Delmas established his political power-base in the immediate post-war period; the FC Lourdes and France pairing of Jean and Maurice Prat, from the glory days of the late 1940s and 1950s; and, more recently, the Camberabero brothers from La Voulte, the Spanghero brothers from Narbonne, and, perhaps above all, *les frères* Boniface. The fact that the two were paired as centre three-quarters, both for the Stade Montois (Mont-de-Marsan) and for the national XV, is an important consideration here, and this for a variety of reasons. To begin with, this particular combination of players (numbers 12 and 13 in the modern team) is arguably the most visible in any rugby side. Where the Prat brothers had been split between the forwards and the three-quarters, and the Spanghero brothers – all four of them – would be confined to the relative anonymity of the pack, the *frères* Boniface were conspicuous as playmakers in the open spaces of the rugby pitch. Moreover, a particularly high level of understanding is required of an international pairing in this mid-field position (as it is, indeed, of the two half-backs, which may explain the success of the Camberabero brothers, both for La Voulte and France). In the case of *les Boni* this understanding attained a rare intensity of empathy, permitting the development of an expansive and adventurous style of attacking three-quarter play that built on the achievements of the great Lourdes side of the period, and which national and international audiences alike would now come to identify and celebrate as characteristically 'French'. In this effort they were significantly supported by the Lourdes club's most gifted player, the diminutive and mercurial fly-half, Jean Gachassin, who rapidly established himself as the pair's natural playing partner.

If the properly fraternal aspect of the brothers' playing career is thus one part of their enduring appeal, another is their undoubted excellence as runners with and passers of the ball. Although the ability to perform in this way might seem to an outsider to be a crucial prerequisite for any player of this handling variety of 'football', the fact of the matter is that very many individuals and teams, up to and including national sides, have been able to achieve remarkable success with only a minimal emphasis on running with and passing the ball, as opposed to kicking it, holding it, and otherwise moving it forward through an emphasis on strength and technique in the pack rather than speed and flair in the three-quarters. Among the other major rugby-playing nations, such tactics have for long been generally accepted as a perfectly valid part of the game, and may quite legitimately be applied by all teams at all levels. However, in France – as we shall see in more detail in Chapter 8 – the periodic dominance of such play, and the tactical thinking that underpins it, has given rise to considerable controversy. Indeed, both within the national club championship and, especially, in the approach to international competition of *le XV de France*, the conception of the game as a war of attrition to be conducted essentially by only nine or ten members of a fifteen-man team (the eight forwards, together with the scrum-half and, optionally, the fly-half) has, at various times, given rise to what amounts to a doctrinal struggle for the 'soul' of French rugby.

Following his retirement from the game in the wake of his younger brother's death, André Boniface would rapidly establish himself as the leading philosopher and prophet of *le beau jeu* [the beautiful game] or *le jeu ouvert* [the open game], a playing ethos that he also attempted to put into practice – with a degree of success – as a coach at the Mont-de-Marsan club. However, it was as players, and more specifically as the epitome of the French tradition of *rugby-champagne*, that André and Guy Boniface, willingly aided and abetted by Jean Gachassin, were to make their enduring mark on the game. Ironically, the finest illustration of their playing ethos came in defeat, and has been commemorated in fiction by Blondin's fellow *Hussard*, Kléber Haedens.

In his novel *Adios* (1974), Haedens opens the narrative with an accurate account of what was at the time an enormous French sporting disappointment. Victory in the 1966 Wales–France match at Cardiff Arms Park would have seen the *Tricolores* attain what had become their Holy Grail, namely France's first Grand Slam of victories over all four of the British and Irish 'home unions' in the annual Five Nations Championship, in which it had been competing since 1910. Some 65,000 spectators watched this match, including an unknown number of travelling French supporters. The growing significance of travelling support at this time was reflected in Robert Dhéry's film *Allez France!* (1964), a comedy centred on a group of south-western *rugbymen* visiting London for the England–France game.[44] For Haedens's narrator, a sports journalist sent to report on the game, the outcome of the match is evidence of an essential component of the French national character. Rather than seeking, as the great majority of sides would have done, simply to defend the two-point advantage over their adversaries that would surely have ensured victory – and against all expectations – the French players opted to attack. The principal actors in the resulting drama were the fly-half Jean Gachassin and the two Boniface brothers in the centre. Haedens's narrator takes up the tale:

> A movement by the three-quarter line, instantly illuminated by a deep incision by the fly-half, gave us a glimpse of a *dénouement* full of flags and fanfares. The drizzle stopped falling. The red umbrellas were put down, and eyes were narrowed beneath flat caps.
>
> The ball was launched into the grey sky in a very high pass, a floated pass, intended for the centre three-quarter who was running towards the Welsh goal-line flanked by our left winger. It was at that moment that a big fellow in a red jersey with three white feathers emblazoned on it leapt up to catch the flying ball and, clutching it to his chest with his right hand, set off over the springy turf on a zig-zagging eighty-yard dash against the wind.
>
> At the end of his sprint he had scored the try that sealed victory for the Welsh by a single point.[45]

That such an incident should form the point of departure for a major work by a serious novelist is not the primary issue here. Rather, what is of note is the way in which a number of parties responded to this snatching of defeat from the jaws of victory. For the French selectors, this incident – properly regarded as part and parcel of the game of rugby – amounted to the theft of their coveted first Grand Slam, and they reacted accordingly. Gachassin and the Boniface brothers were dropped from the team, together with the scrum-half Lilian Camberabero. The Boniface brothers were not even included in the squad that travelled to Naples two weeks later for what had become established as the national side's traditional end-of-season friendly against Italy. In spite of their record over the previous decade, the pair were summarily dismissed, without a word of explanation. Such was the popular appeal of *les Boni*, however, that the national sports newspaper, *L'Equipe*, organized a subscription on the part of its readers in order to invite the brothers to attend the France–Italy match as its guests of honour. Although individual donations by readers were limited to a single, symbolic, franc – as enshrined in French law, and particularly in the statutes relating to the awarding of damages – the many thousands of *L'Equipe* readers who contributed were together able to ensure that the end of a rugby era was appropriately marked.[46]

The extreme reaction by those at the top of the French rugby federation to the interception by Stuart Watkins of Gachassin's lobbed pass underlines the significant investment, both moral and material, made in the project of international competitive success by a politically influential group of sports administrators. While their commitment to triumph on the field may have been motivated less by the Gaullist vision of *la France qui gagne* than by older conceptions of regional and national pride, and not a little self-interest, it was no less real than that of de Gaulle himself. However, for *Maître* Jean Gachassin, the player whose misjudged pass almost certainly cost France a Grand Slam in 1966, 'not to have gone for the gap that opened up would have been to deny rugby itself, OUR attacking variety of rugby. The eternal French rugby, which belongs to the past, the present, and the future.'[47] In direct contrast to this position was that adopted by the then President of the FFR, Jean Delbert, for whom victory in the Five Nations championship had become both an affair of state and a personal matter.[48] The outrage expressed throughout the French press (and also in Britain) at his treatment of *les Boni* was also voiced by Roger Couderc on national television, and by a flood of letters of support to the players concerned, including notably one from Minister of the Interior Roger Frey, while thousands of well-wishers gathered to greet Gachassin himself on his return to his home in the small Pyrenean town of Bagnères-de-Bigorre. *En route*, a private dinner at the 'Pied de Cochon' in Les Halles, the old market district of Paris, at the invitation of Antoine Blondin, was, characteristically, also a part of this reception for the three players.[49]

It does not seem altogether inappropriate that Gachassin should choose to describe this popular fervour as 'an enormous sociological phenomenon'.[50] For what was at stake in Cardiff on 26 March 1966 was, of course, much more than simply the outcome of a rugby match or even the result of an international competition. What was being acted out on the stage of the Arms Park was a battle for the ideological core of French rugby, itself pre-dicated upon a conception of national identity that we may usefully term, borrowing from Gaullist terminology, *une certaine idée de la France*. For as the sociologist Pierre Sansot has argued, 'at times when our sense of social belonging [*notre insertion*] is in doubt, we need to reassure ourselves who we are. The [sports] team is able to respond to this desire in many different ways [and thus] combines a sporting role and a social role.'[51] In the France of the mid-1960s, the national rugby team undoubtedly fulfilled this dual function, as its self-belief on the field of play was used to bolster a nation radically altered by the economic and social transformations of the post-war period, and approaching the quasi-revolutionary political turmoil of May–June 1968. When the *Tricolores* finally completed their first Grand Slam on 25 March 1968 – appropriately enough beating Wales (14–9) at a rain-soaked Cardiff Arms Park – their achievement represented something more than a sporting victory. For French rugby, and the traditional model of masculinity upon which it was based, offered an image of strength, determ-ination, and, above all, continuity in the midst of crisis. Yet, paradoxically, French rugby was itself in the throes of a palace revolution at this time, which would result in nothing less than a struggle for the 'soul' of the newly national game.

Notes

1. See Robert Gildea, *France Since 1945* (Oxford, Oxford University Press, 1996), pp. 129–30.
2. Jean-Pierre Augustin and Jean-Pierre Bodis, *Rugby en Aquitaine: histoire d'une rencontre* (Bordeaux, Centre Régional des Lettres d'Aquitaine and Editions Aubéron, 1994), p. 163; Henri Garcia, *La Fabuleuse histoire du rugby* (Paris, ODIL, 1973), pp. 369 and 387.
3. See Christian Pociello, *Le Rugby ou la guerre des styles* (Paris, A. M. Métailié, 1983), pp. 272–5.
4. Ibid., p. 272.

5. Ibid.
6. Ibid., p. 273.
7. Jill Forbes and Michael Kelly, *French Cultural Studies: An Introduction* (Oxford, Oxford University Press, 1995), p. 134.
8. René Goscinny and Albert Uderzo, *Astérix chez les Bretons* (Paris, Dargaud, 1966); cited in Jean-Pierre Augustin and Alain Garrigou, *Le Rugby démêlé: Essai sur les Associations Sportives, le Pouvoir et les Notables* (Bordeaux, Le Mascaret, 1985), p. 338.
9. Pociello, *Le Rugby ou la guerre des styles*, pp. 274–5.
10. Maurice Agulhon, 'Le mythe gaulois' in 'Astérix: Un mythe et ses figures', special number of *Ethnologie française*, 1998/3, June–September, pp. 296–302; p. 300 for the quotation.
11. Stéphane Baumont, 'Le rugby et la politique . . .', *Midi*, no. 4, 1987, pp. 13–22, at p. 21.
12. René Barnoud, *Quel drôle de ballon!: Mêlées et démêlés* (Lyons, A. Rey, n.d. [1978?]), p. 166.
13. Pociello, *Le Rugby ou la guerre des styles*, pp. 275–6.
14. Kristin Ross, *Fast Cars, Clean Bodies: Decolonization and the Reordering of French Culture* (Cambridge, MA, MIT Press, 1995), p. 4.
15. Clip included in R. Driès, *100 ans de rugby en France: un film à la gloire du sport roi* (video; Paris, INA, 1988).
16. Ibid.
17. Ibid.
18. Ross, *Fast Cars, Clean Bodies*, p. 157.
19. Ibid., pp. 157–8.
20. Ibid., p. 166.
21. This term is suggested by Johan Huizinga's classic study of the play element in culture, *Homo Ludens* (London, Routledge & Kegan Paul, 1949).
22. Ibid., p. 4.
23. See Philip Dine, 'Sport and the State in contemporary France: from *la Charte des Sports* to decentralisation', *Modern & Contemporary France*, vol. 6, no. 3, 1998, pp. 301–11, at pp.306–7. It should be noted that the adjectives *gaulliste* (which refers specifically to the politics of de Gaulle and his supporters) and *gaullien* (which describes rather the general tone or style of de Gaulle's quasi-monarchical presidency) are both translated as 'Gaullist' in this discussion.
24. Augustin and Garrigou, *Le Rugby démêlé*, p. 338.
25. Ibid.
26. Cited by Pierre Duboscq (ed.), *Rugby, parabole du monde* (Paris, L'Harmattan, 1998), p. 109. On Bègles more generally see Jean-Pierre

Callède, 'La politique sportive de la municipalité de Bègles: Contribution à une approche généalogique de l'action sportive communale', *Spirales* (special number on 'Le sport et la ville: Les politiques municipales d'équipements sportifs, XIXe–XXe siècles'), no. 5, 1992.

27. Duboscq, *Rugby, parabole du monde*, p. 108; cf. Baumont, 'Le rugby et la politique', p. 14.

28. Baumont, 'Le rugby et la politique', pp. 17–19 and 22 n. 7. The rugby connection was particularly exploited by Chirac in his early career as a *député* for the Corrèze and then as agriculture minister.

29. Ibid., p. 21.

30. Cited in Paul Voivenel, *Mon beau rugby: L'Esprit du Sport* (Toulouse, Editions de l'Héraklès, 1942; Toulouse, Editions Midi Olympique, 1962), 1962, pp. 276–7.

31. Forbes and Kelly, *French Cultural Studies*, p. 147.

32. Ibid., p. 69. See also Nicholas Hewett, *Literature and the Right in Postwar France: The Story of the 'Hussards'* (Oxford and Washington, D.C., Berg, 1996), pp. 89–91.

33. Françoise Sagan, 'Cette enfance naturelle et drôle', in Roger Couderc and Pierre Albaladejo, *Le Livre d'or du rugby 1981* (Paris, Solar, 1981), pp.3–4.

34. Hewett, *Literature and the Right in Postwar France*, pp.140–1.

35. Ibid., p. 139.

36. Dean's demise may now have been eclipsed by the 'Princess Diana' phenomenon.

37. Ross, *Fast Cars, Clean Bodies*, p. 46.

38. Antoine Blondin, *Ma vie entre des lignes* (Paris, La Table Ronde, 1982), p. 223. Boniface was also the model for the central figure in Blondin's short story, 'Nous rentrerons à pied', according to Denis Tillinac, *Rugby blues* (Paris, La Table Ronde, 1993), p. 23. See also Denis Lalanne, *Les Conquérants du XV de France* (Paris, La Table Ronde, 1970), p. 290, regarding the 'mille javas sur la Rive Gauche' [thousand wild nights on the Left Bank] of Blondin and Boniface; cf. pp. 356–7. See also Yvan Audouard, *Monsieur Jadis est de retour: Antoine Blondin* (Paris, La Table Ronde, 1994), *passim*.

39. Blondin, *Ma vie entre des lignes*, p. 227.

40. Lalanne, *Les Conquérants du XV de France*, p. 360.

41. Ross, *Fast Cars, Clean Bodies*, p. 22.

42. Ibid., pp. 26–7.

43. Renaud de Laborderie, *Le Rugby dans le sang* (Paris, Calmann-Lévy, 1968).

44. *Allez France!* (Robert Dhéry, France, 1964). See also Augustin and Bodis, *Le Rugby en Aquitaine*, pp. 164–5. Cf. Alex Potter and Georges Duthen, *The Rise of French Rugby* (London, Bailey & Swinfen, 1961), pp.142–5, regarding the particular role of television in cafés in the popularization of the game. Also of interest in terms of rugby's increased public profile in the mid-1960s was the restoration and consecration of an abandoned chapel in the south-western village of Larrivière, near Grenade-sur-Adour, as 'Notre-Dame du Rugby'. See L'Abbé Michel Devert, *Les Grandes Heures de Notre-Dame du Rugby* (Mézos, the author, 1991). Two popular songs from this period might also be noted as adding to the prominence, in popular cultural terms, of the south-west: Charles Trenet, *Narbonne, mon amie* (1961) and Claude Nougaro, *Toulouse* (1966).

45. Kléber Haedens, *Adios* (Paris, Grasset, 1974), pp. 10–11.

46. Garcia, *La Fabuleuse histoire du rugby*, pp. 446–9.

47. Jean Gachassin (with Emmanuel Cazes), *Le Rugby est une fête* (Paris, Solar, 1969), p. 25. *Maître* is the term used in France to address lawyers, and thus Jean Gachassin's professional title.

48. Ibid., p. 39.

49. Ibid., pp. 40–5

50. Ibid., p. 40.

51. Pierre Sansot, *Les Formes sensibles de la vie sociale* (Paris, PUF, 1986), p. 77.

PART IV

Towards a Global Game, 1968–2000

– 8 –

The Struggle for the Soul of *le rugby français*

The *rugby-champagne* of the 1950s and 1960s had faithfully reflected the self-confidence of a nation successfully embracing technological and economic modernity, but still eager to preserve its rural heritage, albeit in a mythified form. This heady sporting brew had seen 'the adopted game'[1] taken in new and distinctively Gallic directions, permitting the combination of artistry and imagination to gloriously intoxicating effect. In the following two decades this comfortable image of France and Frenchness would come under increasing strain, both on and off the field. For just as the country's post-war economic miracle ground to a halt, and as its associated political consensus began to fragment, so the newly national game lost its sense of direction in the 1970s and 1980s. What resulted was, on the one hand, a heated dispute between competing visions of how the game should be played, and, on the other, an unprecedented struggle for control of the national rugby federation. The confirmation in the post-war period of rugby's privileged status as part of the national cultural heritage or *patrimoine* was to prove central to the debates surrounding its development in the 1970s and 1980s. Three teams would be at the heart of these frequently heated exchanges of views: the AS Béziers and Stade Toulousain clubs, and the French national side. Meanwhile, three individuals would emerge as both actors and icons within the fiercely contested French game: FFR president Albert Ferrasse; captain and later trainer of the national side Jacques Fouroux; and French rugby's most famous player and first real celebrity, Jean-Pierre Rives. It is in terms of the network of power relations existing between these key teams and leading figures that the story of French rugby in the 1970s and 1980s will be considered here. More specifically, that historical narrative will be shown to centre on a behind-the-scenes battle for control of the national rugby federation, and on an inextricably linked public struggle for the 'soul' of *le rugby français*. In order to understand the technical arguments underpinning this debate, it is necessary to consider on-field developments in some detail, as well as the new ways in which the union game was depicted at this time. This will lead us to a consideration of the media's representation of Jean-Pierre Rives, French rugby's most glamorous figure, whose development of an international persona may itself be productively set against the backdrop of significant developments elsewhere in the rugby world, and particularly in South Africa.

In its way, 1968 was as much a watershed for French rugby as it was for the French polity. The apparently eternal verities that had informed the French game since 1945 were subjected for the first time to a sustained challenge, just as were the most basic assumptions and organizational structures of French society as a whole. Yet in the midst of the educational, industrial, and political turmoil of May–June 1968, rugby appeared initially to be a bastion of solidity, continuity, and traditional values rooted in *la France profonde*. Indeed, recent events seemed to underline the durability of this element at least of the Gaullist vision of *la France qui gagne*. However, the accidental death of Guy Boniface just a few months earlier may, with hindsight, be regarded as symbolic of the passing at this time of one conception of French rugby and its replacement by an alternative model. Critics of this new, hard-nosed, approach to playing the game would attack its perceived lack of movement, intelligence, and artistry, going so far as to suggest that the sacrifice of style to results was actually incompatible with Frenchness. For the impassioned defenders of *le rugby-champagne* against the depredations of what we might term *le rugby-rendement*,[2] what was at stake in the 1970s and 1980s was nothing less than the distinctive character of the French game.

It is perhaps not entirely coincidental that this sporting version of the conflict between the ancients and the moderns, between artistry and industry, and between idealism and pragmatism occurred just as France as a whole began to realize that the golden age of *les trente glorieuses* had given way to a new era of economic and social crisis, under the combined shocks of the 1968 *événements* and the oil crises of 1973 and 1979. Denis Tillinac, a leading practitioner of French rugby's literature of nostalgia, has gone so far as to draw a parallel between the presidency of the first non-Gaullist President of the Fifth Republic, Valéry Giscard-d'Estaing (1974–1981) and the effective reign of the AS Béziers rugby club: 'Historians will note that the Giscard years coincided with Béziers's dominance. Techno years, morose years, as the France of middle-managers took over from that of de Gaulle's one-nation [*le peuple gaullien*]. We all wanted to be rational, and so we abandoned poetry . . . Gone were the glory days of the Boniface brothers. . . .'[3] The desire to return to French rugby's golden age in the 1950s and 1960s may thus not have been the product of sporting nostalgia alone. This is a pattern that was to be repeated and intensified in the 1980s and 1990s. What was conveniently forgotten by many of those who looked back with pride to the glories of *les Boni* and their adopted brother, the mercurial Jean Gachassin, was that it was not their combined fireworks in the three-quarters that had finally brought France its long-awaited first Grand Slam, but rather a competent performance by a pack in which the captain Christian Carrère was ably supported by such work-horses as Walter Spanghero, Benoît Dauga and Elie Cester, with the team's scoring opportunities coming predominantly through the kicking of the Camberabero brothers at half-back. It was no coincidence that Carrère himself was from the Toulon club, while the Camberaberos, although originally from Tyrosse, had made their home in La Voulte, in the Rhône valley: south-eastern pragmatism had triumphed where south-western adventurism had not, in short. Indeed, it was precisely the defeat of the national side (11–9) by a south-eastern selection led by the Camberaberos, in a practice match held just before the championship, that had led to the complete overhaul of the *XV de France* and thus to the successful Grand Slam.

The 1967–68 season may also be considered a turning-point in the development of the French game in that this was the last time that the great Lourdes club would be crowned champions of France (for a record-equalling eighth time).[4] The Bègles club from the suburbs of Bordeaux took the championship in 1969, and the Camberabero brothers' La Voulte side won it in 1970, but the tournament would henceforth be virtually monopolized by the AS Béziers club. Although Béziers had been involved in four out of five championship finals in the early 1960s, winning the title for the first time in 1961, it was over the period 1971 to 1984 that the club's hegemony was firmly established, with no less than ten championships in fourteen seasons. If the fact of the pre-eminence of the Association Sportive Bitteroise (ASB) in this period could not be doubted, the manner of the club's establishment of its position of dominance gave rise to considerable debate. While those within the club such as its coach Raoul Barrière and its captain Richard Astre justified their success in terms of professional levels of commitment and a scientific approach to preparing for and playing the game, others were to take Béziers to task for the forward-dominated game used to crush all opposition for a decade.[5] To the fore in the denunciation of a club that was widely feared but rarely admired was Jean Lacouture, biographer of de Gaulle and fervent defender of *le rugby-champagne* in the pages of the national journal of record, *Le Monde*.[6] For Lacouture, the advocate of running rugby *à la française*, it is the Béziers club's almost exclusive reliance on forward-power and territorial domination that must inevitably lead to its condemnation by all true lovers of the French game. This is what underpins his attack on 'the monotony of its system of play . . . [and] its absence of imagination'.[7] Typically, this technical critique is set against a cultural backdrop based on an essentialist history of the south-west:

> In Béziers, ever since the Cathars were burnt at the stake, people have learned to harden themselves against the Tramontane wind and the flames that it can whip up. They know how to insulate themselves against misfortune [*donner moindre prise au mal*] and to hunch their shoulders. They know how to make themselves smaller than normal and thus how to win a victory whilst falling back, a victory which springs solely from the failure of the other side. The citadel remains intact, but the flag which flies above it does not flap very loudly.[8]

However, in spite of Lacouture's best efforts, not only would the predominance of *le style biterrois* be successfully maintained, but it would also be extended to the national side.

In order to understand this even more controversial retreat from the attacking tradition of French rugby, it is necessary to appreciate that France's long-awaited first Grand Slam was followed by one of the leanest periods in post-war French rugby history. A disastrous tour of New Zealand and Australia, which included four straight test defeats, was thus the prelude to losses in both matches against the touring South Africans, against lowly Romania in Bucharest, and then in the first three matches of the 1969 Five Nations competition. This series of reverses only came to an end with a draw against Wales (8–8) at Colombes in March 1969. France, winners of the Grand Slam just twelve months earlier, finished last in the 1969 Five Nations championship, with just a single point from its four matches. Clearly, a new approach was needed, and the selectors would before long look to the methods employed so successfully by the rising stars of the Béziers club. Thus began a period in which Béziers would not only supply many key personnel to a resurgent French side, but also its technical expertise and even its philosophical inspiration. In particular, it was through the establishment as fixtures in the team of a succession of redoubtable ASB forwards, especially in the 'tight' front five positions, that the club really exerted its stranglehold on the national side and its playing ethos. Alain Estève in particular would become established as a hate-figure for the supporters of other clubs and other countries, with the press on both sides of the Channel only too happy to participate in the process of demonization to which this massive, bearded, and rather shambling second-row forward – nicknamed 'the beast' or 'the assassin' – was subjected.[9] This systematic reinforcement of the French forwards undoubtedly had an effect in terms of results, with France performing consistently well throughout the early 1970s, without for all that achieving the longed-for second Grand Slam. That was to come in 1977, with a significant impact from two ASB forwards, Alain Paco, the multi-talented hooker who had famously started his playing career as a fly-half, and Michel Palmié, a fearsome second-row in the Estève mould.

The performance of the *XV de France* that won the 1977 Grand Slam was unique in several respects, the first of which was that it really was only fifteen players who were involved in the campaign. Whereas Christian Carrère's side that had won France's first Grand Slam in 1968 had actually involved twenty-seven players over the four matches, Jacques Fouroux's team was the same one in each case, with no changes made by the selectors and substitutions during matches not permitted in this period. What is also remarkable is that the defensive strength of this side was such that it won the four games without a single try being scored against it, another unique achievement. However, in spite of its own attacking effectiveness, Fouroux's side was not generally appreciated by French rugby-followers. This was the result of its determination to play an essentially static and forward-based game of territorial domination, exploiting to the full the tactical kicking skills of fly-half Michel Romeu, rather than the open and attacking game of movement in the three-quarters so beloved of French rugby's tradition-alists. The critics who had previously attacked Béziers were once again to the fore in the face of this even more glaring denial of what they perceived to be the nation's sporting heritage. The uniquely successful if undoubtedly unspectacular campaign by *la bande à Fouroux* [Fouroux's gang] was lamented by Jean Lacouture, in particular. Having opened his account of the team's campaign with a caustic analysis of its method of 'Winning with eight and a half players' – a reference to the pack of forwards, together with the diminutive Fouroux – he concluded it by asking bitterly 'Are the strongest always the best?'[10] Likening the French team to an 'inexorable steamroller driven by little Fouroux' and 'a muscular hurricane', and their game to a 'commando operation . . . [a] paratrooper's way of playing rugby', Lacouture argued that there was 'something excessive, almost inhuman' and above all un-French about the national side's way of competing and winning.[11] Adopting the nostalgic tone that would become increasingly typical of an influential school of French rugby writers, Lacouture underlined his principal grievance against Fouroux's side and all it represented:

> In the days of Jean Prat and the Boniface brothers, French rugby had its own style. Then came a period of decadence. In order to regenerate itself, at the end of the 1960s, French rugby could have opted for a New Zealand transplant or some Welsh therapy. Instead, it was deemed preferable to inject it with hormones brought from Pretoria. And now look at it: laden with muscles and proud of its ponderous weight, setting off to accomplish the labours of Hercules – a hero who never claimed to be able to solve the riddles of the Sphinx.[12]

This characteristic appeal to an authentically French and, moreover, aesthetically and intellectually acceptable version of rugby – qualities invoked through the regular use of terms such as *l'art*, *l'intelligence*, *la virtuosité*, *la grâce*, *la beauté* – is most sharply focused in its condemnation of Fouroux, the side's captain and inspiration, and its principal on-field 'enforcer', the ex-boxer Gérard Cholley from the Castres club. So Lacouture ironically observes that Fouroux was 'naturally better in London when he didn't get any ball [to play with] than in Paris where good possession was available in abundance', while Cholley is castigated as 'the author [in the Scotland–France game] of an indescribable act that television stations showed in twenty countries, in close-up, and in all its crudity'.[13] Cholley's felling of an opponent with a punch was just one among many instances of a renewed French predilection for *le jeu dur* that earned Fouroux's 'gang' a thoroughly unsavoury reputation on the other side of the English Channel. This reached its climax with the 'Sanson Affair', which resulted from the FFR's objection to a Scottish referee known for his hard line on foul play. If moves to replace him as the match official for what was the crucial game against England at Twickenham had been made as was usual in British rugby circles – i.e. behind closed doors and on the basis of individual contacts – then all might well have passed off without incident. However, the French authorities, in just one of many such failures to appreciate and respect the unspoken conventions of anglophone rugby culture, made their opposition to Sanson public. The British media were unanimous in denouncing the French as cheats who were afraid of being found out, and the reception given to the French side when it did travel to Twickenham was unprecedentedly hostile. Moroever the FFR's stance was roundly condemned by seasoned commentators such as Georges Duthen on the French side.[14]

Such expressions of outrage fell on deaf ears, however, and the French rugby authorities continued to back Fouroux and his team. As ever, the real power in the French game remained where it had been throughout the post-war period: with the FFR and especially the office of federal president. Under the dictatorial reign of Albert Ferrasse, this control had been significantly consolidated and reinforced. Ferrasse had been a player with the SU Agen club, and then a top-class referee, before becoming its president. It was thus as the spokesman of the reigning champions of France that he had orchestrated the 1966 revolt against the then FFR president Jean Delbert. The most vocal of a small group of ambitious administrators who became known as the 'Young Turks', Ferrasse had warned Delbert that 'We are going to kick you out on your arse' [*Nous allons vous foutre dehors*],[15] in an early illustration of the blunt and bullying manner that would characterize his domination of French rugby for the next quarter of a century.

Born near Agen, and brought up on the family farm of his maternal grand-parents, Ferrasse was the son of a railway worker with no rugby connections, and thus as much of a self-made man in the rugby world as he was in his plumbing materials business. With only elementary schooling, and, in particular, no knowledge of the English language – and, what is more, not the slightest desire to learn it[16] – Ferrasse and his ethos could hardly have been further removed from the privileged backgrounds, and, crucially, the 'old-school-tie' mentality typical of rugby's administrators in the British Isles. The power behind the throne of Delbert's very temporary replacement, Marcel Batigne, Ferrasse became president himself in a palace revolution formally endorsed by the FFR's annual congress in Paris on 22 June 1968. The tumultuous backdrop of the 1968 *événements* was well chosen. Henceforth, relations between Ferrasse and the British 'home unions' would always be prickly at best, while in France he ruled the game in an author-itarian fashion that was wholly his own.

From his Agen power-base, Ferrasse – also known as 'Bébert' [Bertie], 'le roi Albert' [King Albert], and 'Tonton' [Uncle] among other, rather less affectionate, nicknames[17] – the FFR's new strong man, would bestride the French game like a colossus throughout the 1970s and 1980s. Indeed, just as the later 1950s and 1960s had been French society's *années gaulliennes*, this period in French rugby's history might well be thought of as *les années ferrassiennes*. One of Ferrasse's many critics, the novelist and chronicler Denis Tillinac, has accurately summed up his impact on the French game as follows:

> Before Ferrasse, French rugby belonged to the players. Under his reign they had to keep quiet; King Albert only had time for sycophants . . . From then on, an abusive Jacobinism sought to suppress the revolts that came from a south-west [*Occitanie*] that had only devoted itself to rugby in the first place in order to cultivate its differences. [. . .]
>
> [. . .] All we ever saw henceforth was the blue of Agen: Bertie was better known than the internationals, while in contrast even the most fanatical British rugby fan – quite rightly – couldn't even tell you the names of the game's admin-istrators.[18]

Ferrasse was thus able to exert the same sort of stranglehold on the French game off the field that the AS Béziers club did on it, and, by 1977, it could safely be said that Ferrasse's word was law, both on and off the pitch. His decision to throw the weight of his autocratic regime behind 'the Little Corporal', as Fouroux was appropriately nicknamed, was to stand him in good stead for over a decade. However, it would ultimately prove his undoing, as *le Petit Caporal* himself discovered the field-marshal's baton that according to his celebrated namesake, Napoléon Bonaparte, every foot-soldier carries in his kitbag. For the time being, however, the power struggle between the two men was still a long way off, and, as Ferrasse's protégé, Fouroux looked to an apparently bright future in the Byzantine corridors of power of 'la fédération ferrassienne de rugby'.[19] Indeed, in 1980, just three years after the Grand Slam success of his uniquely self-reliant *bande*, Fouroux was named as coach of the national side.

As trainer of *les Tricolores*, Fouroux would come in for even more criticism. His rapid promotion was itself a source of hostility, and only exacerbated by his own tendency to make it ever more obvious that he considered himself to be the heir apparent to the omnipotent Ferrasse. However, external criticism seemed, if anything, only to reinforce the internal cohesion of Fouroux's group of players, much as it had in 1977.[20] What is more, and as Napoleon himself would have appreciated, luck was also on *le Petit Caporal*'s side. Within a few months of his taking charge, the unfancied *XV de France* had battled its way to a third Grand Slam: 'without doubt the most un-expected in its history'.[21] Fouroux's side was to take its definitive shape over the 1980s, with its nucleus formed of players drawn from the SU Agen club, FFR president Ferrasse's own power-base. This arrangement was obviously of mutual benefit, although it resulted in some predictable criticism of what was widely perceived to be an overly cosy relationship. The side was to find its fullest expression in its 1987 incarnation, which achieved France's fourth Grand Slam, with five SUA players in the line-up. Although significantly more rounded than the 1977 team, with such enterprising players as Pierre Berbizier and Philippe Sella in the side, as well as the attacking flair of the incomparable Serge Blanco at full-back, the 1987 Grand Slam side was still subject to severe criticism. This time, the attacks came not so much from idealistic conservatives within the media, as from strategically placed coaches who were looking to modernize the French game through a version of total rugby *à la française*. Fogel and Jaurena take up the story, emphasizing the role of the one club that had at last emerged to challenge the stranglehold of Béziers and its narrow philosophy on the French game, the reborn 'red virgin' of the great Stade Toulousain:

> What a difference between the perpetual motion produced by the players in red and black [of Toulouse] and the systematic reliance on the setting up of rucks with the ball placed on the ground – and thus halted – by the powerful blue forwards [of France]! French rugby at this time went through a real war of styles against the backdrop of a latent war for control of the FFR itself. Albert Ferrasse treated with disdain the 'PE teachers', dismissing them as 'moaning minnies' [*zozos brailleurs*]. The targets of his comments were the Toulouse trainers [Pierre]

Villepreux and [Jean-Luc] Skrela as well as Daniel Herrero from Toulon, who took his side to the national championship in 1987. Fouroux, as a faithful guard-dog, bit everyone that his president pointed out to him.[22]

Ferrasse and Fouroux had certainly identified their principal detractors with their reference to these three coaches. All three did, indeed, have a background in physical education, as, ironically, did Béziers's Raoul Barrière.[23] Together they would offer a technically modern and tactically pragmatic approach to playing rugby that would in time see their model adopted throughout the French game, and would lead to Skrela and Villepreux being appointed as coaches of the national side in the 1990s (with Jo Maso, the former Perpignan and France star of the 1970s, who is also for ever associated with the French tradition of running rugby). Stade Toulousain, for their part, would go on to become champions of France seven times between 1985 and 1997, making a record fourteen championships in total, with the last four in successive years, as well as becoming the inaugural European club champions in 1996, when they defeated Cardiff in the final (21–18) at the Welsh side's own Arms Park stadium. The undisputed champions of a reinvented version of *le beau jeu*, the club remain the standard by which all other French clubs must be judged.

Daniel Herrero has undoubtedly gone furthest in his impassioned denunciation of both Ferrasse – who had effectively usurped authority over the heart and soul of French rugby, displacing its natural centre from Toulouse to his personal *fief* in Agen[24] – and his protégé Jacques Fouroux, as the man directly responsible for a style of play that Herrero considers to be an affront to the heritage of French rugby and thus to France itself. So in spite of the creditable results achieved by Fouroux's side in the inaugural rugby World Cup in 1987 (where *les Tricolores* finished runners-up to the All Blacks), Herrero remains deeply critical of the trainer's power-based methods, as opposed to what he considers to be the 'Latin' way of playing traditionally associated with the French game, with its emphasis on dazzling attacking skills. At the deepest level, his hostility to Fouroux and Ferrasse is based on his conviction of 'real' French rugby's unique contribution to the national culture:

> Classically based on the cultural and philosophical values of the South, the manner of playing of our national team was disrupted by the frantic thirst for power and combat. [. . .] The soul of our peoples expresses itself in the whirlwind motion of the ball. France in its geographic, ethnic and cultural diversity has generated an imaginary [*imaginaire*] of liberty, creativity and independence. [. . .]
>
> [. . .]

If the French XV systematically plays close to the pack rather than spreading the ball wide, I'll go along with that! If our backs play like donkeys, that's fine by me! But if they become donkeys . . . No! That's a betrayal.

If we use the rolling maul a bit more often than attacking with the ball in hand: no big deal! But if we stop passing the ball altogether, then we betray Vercingétorix, François Villon, Chateaubriand, Henri IV, Dame Carcas, Thierry-la-Fronde, de Gaulle and Jean Moulin, the Cathars, the troubadours and Brassens, the bulls of the Camargue and the last bears in the Ariège. Yes! We betray my grandad and your own, even if you do come from Agen.[25]

Neither Herrero's playful mixing of registers, from the colloquial through the technical to the social scientific, nor his ironic listing of national heroes and heroines of all varieties, up to and including France's distinctive fauna, should be allowed to detract from the seriousness of the point that he is making here. His conviction that France has its own unique tradition on the rugby pitch – and thus a sporting variety of the *mission civilisatrice* [civilizing mission] historically enshrined in both the Roman Catholic and French Revolutionary traditions – is expressed here with complete sincerity, as it has been by many other French commentators on the fortunes of the national rugby team.

Yet *le XV de France* had done enough to enable Ferrasse to maintain Fouroux in his position as national coach, at least for the time being. However, the inability of *le Petit Caporal* to adapt his playing philosophy meant that France's World Cup defeat by the All Blacks had merely confirmed Fouroux in his belief in the virtues of force over artistry.[26] He thus embarked on an intensification of the national side's determinedly muscular and confront-ational style of play, which has been aptly characterized as *le rugby-Rambo*.[27] The results of this pale imitation of the All Blacks' rugged style were predictable, with a string of mediocre performances recorded over the next few years, which resulted in Fouroux's resignation in 1990. This tactical withdrawal meant that he could devote himself henceforth to intrigues and manoeuvres within the national rugby federation designed to bring about the palace revolution that he hoped would enable him both to depose and to succeed his long-time protector, Albert Ferrasse. This is a sordid tale to which we shall return in Chapter 9.

Even in French rugby's darkest days in the 1970s and 1980s, and in the midst of the fiercest criticism from press and supporters alike of the methods adopted by the national side, one player rose above the controversy and was received with unanimous praise, in France and abroad: Jean-Pierre Rives. Such was the popular enthusiasm generated by this relatively small but immensely powerful and talented player, capped 59 times as a wing-forward between 1975 and 1984, that he can safely be regarded as the French game's greatest star, and the only one successfully to have transcended the limitations of his chosen sport by becoming a national icon in his own right.[28] In fact, Rives was just one half of a back-row pairing that was to illuminate both the domestic and international scenes over a decade, the other member being his fellow wing-forward in the Stade Toulousain and French sides: Jean-Luc Skrela. Complementing each other physically – Rives, stocky and blond, Skrela, tall and dark – just as they did in their approaches to both attack and defence, the pair had few rivals either on the pitch or in the imagination of the French sporting public. The international esteem in which the two players were held is most clearly borne out by the fact that they were picked to play together for the prestigious Barbarians against the touring New Zealanders in 1978, the first Frenchmen to be recognized in this way by what is one of the principal bastions of the British rugby establishment. The pair were also central to the revival of Stade Toulousain at this time, which provided the basis for the club's own hegemony after the eventual eclipse of Béziers in the mid-1980s; a process overseen by Skrela and Pierre Villepreux, in a coaching partnership transferred to the national side in the 1990s.

However indebted to his playing partner Rives may have been on the field, it was he rather than Skrela who was durably to capture the French public imagination. The player's long blond hair, a double rarity in the French game, was undoubtedly an important part of his appeal. Nicknamed *Casque d'Or* [Golden Helmet] by the leading television commentator Roger Couderc, Rives thus acquired a sobriquet that had previously been applied to the great Jacques Bouquet in the 1950s and 1960s.[29] However, at least as much as his distinctive appearance, it was Rives's playing style that marked him out, even when French sides were primarily remarkable for their unattractive approach to the game. Jean Lacouture, so critical of this general dearth of inspiration, could thus write of the winning try in a dour French victory over Scotland (10–9) in 1975:

> . . . who else would have prepared it [. . .] but Jean-Pierre Rives, who made his blond mane dance above this sombre match, like a burning flame in the deserts of Arabia? This boy's dramatic appearance on the international scene . . . is at one and the same time miraculous and altogether reasonable.
>
> It's a miracle to see this *duc de Reichstadt*, pink and blond, rolling in the mud under the studs of the Scottish bisons and then bursting into flame again in the vanguard of the next attack. Here is a young man who plays rugby for fun, because as a first-year medical student there's still a little free time remaining for something other than anatomy and pathology. We don't know what Dr Rives will turn out like, but we are already very fond of Rives the student.[30]

In fact, Rives would not actually complete his medical studies, becoming instead – and rather less glamorously – a court bailiff, among other things, before being recruited to a public relations post with Pernod-Ricard, France's leading manufacturer of the *pastis* [aniseed spirit] so beloved of the *Midi*. Since his retirement from rugby in 1984, Rives has devoted himself essentially to sculpture, living a semi-reclusive existence that has in turn added to the player's mystique. Yet the principal elements of Rives's *légende* are already present in this snapshot from his first season as an international player: his striking physical appearance; his attacking play; his willingness to 'lay his body on the line', as the current journalistic cliché has it; his obvious enjoyment of a game that, like himself, he does not take too seriously; and the sympathetic emotional response that he generates. While a certain tension would subsequently make itself felt between the traditionally elitist ethic of amateurism celebrated here and Rives's high-profile position with Pernod-Ricard (which effectively made him French rugby's first full-time professional in all but name, as the post self-evidently depended upon his performances on the field rather than off it), these basic elements would remain in place throughout his career. This said, the ratio in which they appeared would vary significantly over time, in response to the circumstances in which Rives found himself.

In the early stages of his career, when he and Skrela were two of the much-criticized *bande à Fouroux* that won the 1977 Grand Slam, Rives was immune to criticism because of his self-evident attacking flair. 'Who could reproach "Golden Helmet" with anything at all . . .?', ask Fogel and Jauréna: 'The public adulates this [attacking] Rives because he represents the imagination and the charm [*la fantaisie et la séduction*] which is so lacking from these victory-obsessed mercenaries.'[31] Later in his career, the player would establish a reputation instead as a fearless defender who would spare no effort and suffer any and every assault in the French cause. It was this aspect of his game that was, in fact, to become the most enduring image of his unstinting service in the blue jersey of *le XV de France*. More specifically, it would be Rives's intensely mediated shedding of his blood in the defence of the sporting nation that would bring him to a wider public.[32] The regularity and visibility of Rives's self-sacrifice was such that it was affectionately lampooned by the satirical magazine *Les Quatre-Saisons*, produced quarterly by a group centred on the ageing champion of the literary far-right, and columnist for *L'Equipe*, Antoine Blondin, formerly a close associate of Guy Boniface and now a friend of Rives. Like Guy Boniface, Rives represented for Blondin the maintenance of ancient and noble virtues, with chivalry to the fore, and thus the preservation of an ethnic and mystical Frenchness, in an age of cosmopolitan rootlessness. More prosaically, and as Boniface too had done before him, he also used to supply Blondin with his old rugby jerseys, which the writer took enormous pride in wearing.[33] Blondin himself ascribed considerable significance to the fact that Rives, whom he met for the first time in 1981, was born on 31 December (1952), the same day that his great friend Guy Boniface had died (in 1968). Blondin saw this as a sign of the passing on to Rives of responsibility for the soul of French rugby. His affectionate nickname for Rives – *mon petit blondinet* – could itself be read as meaning both 'my little blond one' and 'my little Blondin', indicating the extent to which Rives became an integral part of the writer's personal universe.[34] Blondin's satirical review showed a characteristic photograph of the bloodied Rives (for added effect in the white change strip used by *les Tricolores* to avoid colour clashes), together with a do-it-yourself pattern for a similar jersey.[35] The development of this strange phenomenon of public martyrdom was most marked during the thirty-four games that Rives played as captain of the national side from 1978 to 1984. At times the disregard for his personal safety of French rugby's very own 'Captain Courageous'[36] was to be pushed to extremes that verged on the genuinely reckless, and, indeed, on the absurd. Most strikingly, Rives's determination to lead his side in the second test against Australia in Sydney in July 1981 with a shoulder he had dislocated four times just a fortnight earlier must be reckoned a form of valour which few would understand, let alone wish to emulate: 'Australia's Mark Loane, a doctor, said of his decision to play, "It was bravery to the point of insanity."'[37]

Whatever the wisdom, or come to that the practical usefulness, of such self-sacrifice, there could be no doubt that Rives brought a breath of fresh air to a French game that had become bogged down in the dour forward battles of Raoul Barrière's Béziers and Jacques Fouroux's France. For Rives's intense personal commitment and adventurous spirit met with a fair measure of success on the pitch, and, crucially, consistent public support off it. So not only was the achievement of the 1981 Grand Slam (France's third) hailed by French rugby supporters, but also the manner in which national teams led by Rives competed generally in this period.[38] Rives's period of captaincy thus confirmed Pierre Villepreux's often stated belief that 'In France, to win is not enough; it is important for the public that French teams play and win in the right manner.'[39] By combining his own conception of the traditional *beau jeu* with a selfless devotion to the national cause, Rives endeared himself for ever to French rugby supporters. Moreover, through his regular appearances in the rapidly developing world of show business, Rives made himself familiar to a much wider audience.[40] Above all, Rives brought glamour to the French game, and thus incarnated what had become 'the emergent meaning of sport . . . once post-war reconstruction was done'.[41] Through his unprecedented transformation into a genuine celebrity, *Casque d'Or* showed the way forward for the union game and for French sport as whole.

The basis of the flamboyant rugby-player's cultural metamorphosis was his well-publicized friendship with such high-profile figures as the actor Jean-Paul Belmondo and Princess Stéphanie of Monaco.[42] This process of identification with the toast of Parisian society was clearly facilitated by Rives's move to the capital as a result of his recruitment by Pernod-Ricard, with the company itself standing to gain from any and every boost thus given to their employee's public profile. Other members of Rives's new circle of show-business friends and acquaintances included the Formula 1 star Alain Prost, the tennis-player Yannick Noah, the rock musician Jacques Higelin, the sculptor Albert Feraud, and, especially, the successful comedian Patrick Sébastien.[43] Himself a former player with the CA Brive club, Patrick Boutaud – 'Sébastien' is a stage name – would go on to become its president and thus a key figure in the sparkling European success of the *Brivistes* in the 1990s. In May 1984, for his *Carnaval* television show, the entertainer came up with the idea of having the blond Rives come on painted black, while his fellow international the black Serge Blanco appeared painted white. This stunt was allegedly conceived as a blow for racial tolerance in a period when racism – as exemplified by the far-right Front National – was coming increasingly to the fore in French political life.[44] However such a gag may strike us now, there can be no doubt that Rives's regular appearance on French television screens and in the French press contributed significantly to the development of his public persona. He was additionally an accomplished skier, golfer, and tennis-player, and so often depicted engaging in these and other socially prestigious sporting activities. Rives's employment by Pernod-Ricard also meant that he transferred from Stade Toulousain to the *doyen* of French rugby clubs, and still its most socially exclusive, the Racing Club de France. The club's particularly solid network of contacts with Parisian high society was thus made available to Rives, to the mutual benefit of club and player.[45] Moreover, the RCF's elitist tradition of *le rugby-chic*, as opposed specifically to *le rugby-choc* of Béziers and Fouroux's France, bolstered the image of Rives as French rugby's perfect gentleman. In addition, Rives's rapidly developing association with *le show-biz* would set a precedent for important business developments in the French game in the 1990s, while his encouragement of a miniature 'rural exodus' to the RCF from the south-west would see the club crowned champions of France in 1990, for the first time since 1959. As for Rives's friendship with the sculptor Albert Feraud, and his own subsequent development as an artist – together with his reported love of classical music and talent as a pianist[46]

– this could only add to the player's distinctly Parisian mystique. In the person of Jean-Pierre Rives, in short, *le rugby-Rambo* had been attractively combined with *le rugby-Rimbaud*.

While Rives may have been the acceptable public face of French rugby in the 1970s and 1980s, its real guiding spirit was, as we have seen, the omnipotent Albert Ferrasse. The link between the two men was closer and more prosaic than either might have wished publicly to acknowledge, in that the 'Corinthian' Rives actually began his career in public relations thanks to the personal contact established between Ferrasse and the managing director of a south-western firm producing and marketing *foie gras*, one of the region's most celebrated *produits du terroir*.[47] More importantly, Rives shared the federal president's views on what had become the most burning issue in French sport. Specifically, and in marked contrast to his public display of 'colour blindness' on Patrick Sébastien's comedy show, Rives was much closer to Ferrasse in his stance on sporting relations with the South Africa of the apartheid period than would now appear to be compatible with a genuine rejection of racist politics. So, as opposed to players such as the Welsh star John Taylor, the All Black captain Graham Mourie, and even Rives's fellow television performer, Serge Blanco, who all elected to withdraw as individuals from their respective national tours to South Africa, even before the full sporting boycott of that country between 1985 and 1992, Rives continued to cling to the fig-leaf of sport's long proclaimed independence of politics: 'The only part of life in South Africa where people are the same, where they wear the same jersey and come under the same rules, is on a rugby field.'[48] As a consequence of this view, Rives continued to visit the Republic even after the FFR had cancelled its planned tours there in response to increasing pressure from the French government (which banned both the 1979 Springbok and 1983 French tours). Although avowedly hostile to apartheid itself, Rives believed that such was the white South Africans' love of sport that more could be done to encourage change through continuing sporting relations with them than by ostracizing their country.[49]

This was very much the position of Albert Ferrasse, who, in his memoirs, proudly proclaims: 'Yes, I always relied on rugby . . . to defeat apartheid!'[50] At least as important in Ferrasse's calculations, however, was the firm friendship that he had established with the South African representative on the International Board, Dr Danie Craven. Although highly educated and a very different personality in many other respects, Craven, from his own power-base in the Afrikaaner 'Oxbridge' at Stellenbosch, could share many of the anti-British sentiments habitually felt by Ferrasse, and the pair would continue to agitate for South Africa's international sporting rehabilitation throughout the period of its isolation. France's last pre-boycott tour was in

1980, when the Springboks overwhelmed the French, despite what Ferrasse himself describes as 'the superhuman courage of the French captain, Jean-Pierre Rives'.[51] With the new Socialist government's hostility underlined in 1982, Ferrasse did not attempt to organize another tour until 1989. It was that year's centenary of the founding of the South African Rugby Board that persuaded him to attempt to circumvent the world-wide boycott and thus to offer some precious support to his beleaguered friend Danie Craven. Following discussions between Ferrasse and the Secretary of State for Youth and Sport, the (black) former Olympic athlete Roger Bambuck, with national coach Jacques Fouroux also in attendance, a team of French international players visited South Africa, officially on an individual basis. The fierce political debate that consequently erupted was perhaps most remarkable for Ferrasse's agreement to participate in a debate, broadcast on the France-Inter radio station, with Harlem Désir, the chairman of the SOS-Racisme protest organization. The resulting total lack of comprehension between the two speakers was, perhaps, predictable enough.[52]

Subsequent developments in South Africa would prove Ferrasse and Rives to have been partially correct, at least, in their belief in the potential of rugby in that country to act as a force for social change. Indeed, Ferrasse, a frequent visitor to South Africa, where he met not only Danie Craven, but also both P. W. Botha and his successor as president F. W. de Klerk, may even have contributed directly to the final overthrow of apartheid. This, at least, is the view expressed by Craven, as cited – with a wholly characteristic lack of anything resembling false modesty – by Ferrasse himself: 'Rugby fundamentally made the situation move forward. Albert's action played a decisive role.'[53] This is undoubtedly a large claim, and one that would be incomprehensible were it not for the role as a catalyst for much more profound political change played by the South African Rugby Board's series of secret meetings with the African National Congress late in 1988. These culminated in the 15 October meeting in Harare, the capital of neighbouring Zimbabwe, at which a joint project for a single multiracial rugby federation was published. This was a genuinely seismic event, as Craven had now taken a stance openly against apartheid, and the outraged reaction of both the ruling National Party and conservatives even further to the right indicated the significance of this step.[54] Craven's death in 1993 would prevent his seeing South African rugby's full rehabilitation, but he did at least witness the first stages of the momentous process that would include the release from prison of Nelson Mandela and his subsequent election as the country's first multi-racial president. The 1995 rugby World Cup, held in South Africa and crowned by the victory of the Springbok side, was hailed by Mandela himself as the symbol of the spirit of reconciliation that informed the new 'rainbow nation', and would thus constitute the dramatic finale of this revolutionary social transformation. The impact in France of the multiple forces of globalization released by that genuinely historic sporting event, and particularly the no longer avoidable professionalization of the avowedly amateur rugby union game, will form the focus of our final chapter.

Notes

1. This expression is suggested by Sean Smith, *The Union Game: A Rugby History* (London, BBC, 1999), pp. 186–231.
2. The term *rendement* is understood here in its combined technological and economic sense as 'output'.
3. Denis Tillinac, *Rugby blues* (Paris, La Table Ronde, 1993), p. 73.
4. It should be noted that Stade Français's eight wins came at a time when only a handful of clubs were involved in the championship. This historic club's wholesale reinvention of itself in the 1990s, including its altogether remarkable ninth and tenth championship successes in 1998 and 2000, is discussed in Chapter 9.
5. For a more balanced analysis of the Béziers phenomenon, see Jean-François Fogel and Christian Jaurena, *Le Rugby* (Paris, Jean-Claude Lattès, 1994), pp. 75–91. See also Georges Pastre, *Rugby, capitale Béziers* (Paris, Solar, 1972); cf. Didier Beaune, *Les Invincibles: l'épopée des rugbymen de Béziers* (Paris, Calmann-Lévy, 1972).
6. For a helpful introduction to the rhetoric of French rugby journalism, including particularly the work of Roger Couderc and Jean Lacouture, and even the 'poetics of rugby' as practised by Haedens and other writers, see Christian Pociello, *Le Rugby ou la guerre des styles* (Paris, A. M. Métailié, 1983), pp. 270–320. It is worthy of note that an interest in rugby was also reflected in other media at this time. These included S.-R. Lavigne's *L'Auvergnat marque un essai* (Paris, Editions Guy Authier, 1978), a rugby-themed detective novel in a popular series of stories; also a television series, which subsequently gave rise to a novel by the scriptwriters, Denis Lalanne and Jean Chouquet, *Allez la Rafale!* (Paris, Antenne 2 and Editions Mengès, 1977).
7. Jean Lacouture, *Le Rugby, c'est un monde* (Paris, Seuil, 1979), p. 102.
8. Ibid., p. 81.
9. See, for instance, the article by Jean Hatzfeld, 'Alain Estève: Le rugbyman assassin', *Libération*, 22–23 May 1981; cited by Pociello, *Le Rugby ou la guerre des styles*, p. 108.
10. Lacouture, *Le Rugby, c'est un monde*, pp. 184–8.

11. Ibid., pp. 173–6. The use of the term 'paras', virtually a dirty word for *Le Monde*'s liberal readership in the wake of the Algerian war, is particularly striking here.
12. Ibid., p. 174.
13. Ibid., pp. 180, 183.
14. Cited in Jean Cormier, *Grand Chelem* (Paris, Denoël, 1977), pp. 126–32. See also Fogel and Jaurena, *Le Rugby*, p. 121, regarding Ferrasse's post-match criticism of Cholley, who was then defended by Fouroux, intriguingly.
15. Richard Escot and Jacques Rivière, *Un siècle de rugby* (Paris, Calmann-Lévy, 1997), p. 161. It is worthy of note that another prominent member of this group was André Moga, one of the famous brothers who dominated the Bègles-Bordeaux club, where they were close associates of Jacques Chaban-Delmas, who was to become Prime Minister under President Georges Pompidou in 1969. See Claude Askolovitch and Sylvain Attal, 'La Mafia de l'ovale', in eidem, *La France du piston* (Paris, Robert Laffont, 1992), pp. 99–123, at pp. 110–11.
16. Albert Ferrasse, *Mêlées ouvertes* (Paris, Albin Michel, 1993), p. 13.
17. The nickname 'Tonton' was, of course, also applied to François Mitterrand.
18. Denis Tillinac, *Rugby blues* (Paris, La Table Ronde, 1993), pp. 48–9.
19. Fogel and Jaurena, *Le Rugby*, p. 125.
20. Ibid., pp. 179–80.
21. Escot and Rivière, *Un siècle de rugby*, p. 101.
22. Fogel and Jaurena, *Le Rugby*, pp. 180–1. As its title suggests, Christian Pociello's sociological study, *Le Rugby ou la guerre des styles*, underlines this doctrinal conflict as being of central importance to any reading of the French game.
23. See Raoul Barrière, *Le Rugby et sa valeur educative* (Paris, J. Vrin, 1980).
24. Daniel Herrero, *Passion ovale* (Monaco and Paris, Editions du Rocher, 1990), p. 138.
25. Ibid., pp. 113–14.
26. Fouroux was subsequently to adopt a similar strategy as coach of Grenoble, where his heavyweight team became known as 'the mammoths'.
27. Escot and Rivière, *Un siècle de rugby*, pp. 193–4.
28. Henri Garcia, *Seigneurs et forçats du rugby: un siècle d'ovale en France* (Paris, Calmann-Lévy, 1994), p. 136.
29. Rives thus inherited from the CS Vienne and France three-quarter a nickname that had its origins in Jacques Becker's classic 1952 *film noir*, with the celebrated Simone Signoret in the title role.

30. Lacouture, *Le Rugby, c'est un monde*, pp. 137–8.
31. Fogel and Jaurena, *Le Rugby*, p. 126.
32. Pascal Duret and Marion Wolff, 'The semiotics of sport heroism', *International Review for the Sociology of Sport*, no. 29, 1994, p. 144.
33. Yvan Audouard, *Monsieur Jadis est de retour: Antoine Blondin* (Paris, La Table Ronde, 1994), p. 34.
34. Jean Cormier, *Il était une fois Jean-Pierre Rives* (Paris, Robert Laffont, 1985) p. 177.
35. Peter Bills, *Jean-Pierre Rives: A Modern Corinthian* (London, Allen & Unwin, 1986), in illustrations between pp. 110 and 111.
36. Ibid., Ch. 1., pp. 1–20.
37. Ibid., p. 9.
38. Ibid., p. 97.
39. Ibid., p. 83. See also A. Greaves, 'Sport in France' in Malcolm Cook (ed.), *French Culture since 1945* (London, Longman, 1993), pp. 125–48.
40. This process probably started with Roger Couderc's involvement in the 1960s with variety shows, on which rugby players often featured as guests. See Roger Couderc, *Le Rugby, la télé et moi* (Paris, Solar, 1966), and the same author's *Adieu, les petits!* (Paris, Solar, 1983), *passim*.
41. Fred Inglis, *Popular Culture and Political Power* (London, Harvester Wheatsheaf, 1988), p. 138.
42. Cormier, *Jean-Pierre Rives*, p. 181.
43. Ibid., pp. 181–6. See also Bills, *Jean-Pierre Rives*, pp. 118–35.
44. Cormier, *Jean-Pierre Rives*, p. 188.
45. See Askolovitch and Attal, 'La Mafia de l'ovale', pp. 99–102 et seq.
46. Bills, *Jean-Pierre Rives*, pp. 154–5.
47. Julien Giarrizzi, 'Le rugby n'aime pas qu'on lui parle d'argent et pourtant . . .', in the same author's *Le Sport et l'argent* (Paris, A. Lefeuvre, 1981), pp.117–21, at pp.120–1. Interestingly, Rives's fellow international, the great Walter Spanghero, has himself become the head of a major firm working in this field, which still bears the family name. Other business links with French rugby are investigated in Chapter 9.
48. Bills, *Jean-Pierre Rives*, p. 137.
49. Ibid., p. 138.
50. Ferrasse, *Mêlées ouvertes*, p. 161.
51. Ibid., p. 157.
52. Ibid., pp. 66–8.
53. Ibid., p. 176.
54. Escot and Rivière, *Un siècle de rugby*, p. 239.

– 9 –

Out of Africa: Professionalism's Winds of Change

The evolution of French rugby football in the 1990s followed the pattern established over the previous two decades, in that the most significant developments were to take place off the pitch rather than on it. The focus of this final chapter will consequently be on the range of pressures exerted on managers of the French game at this time, both by internal and external forces. Central to this process were the contrasting responses of players and administrators to the issue of professionalism, which came to a head with the 1995 World Cup competition. From a position of relative weakness in the early 1990s – reflected in a string of disappointing results against neigh-bouring England – French rugby would effectively reinvent itself and restore its prestige over the course of the decade. However, for this to happen, the administrative paralysis long associated with the federal president Albert Ferrasse's seemingly endless reign now had to be brought to an end. Opposition to Ferrasse resulted in a war of succession between personalities and policies competing for dominance of the increasingly 'globalized' French game, with such familiar names as Jacques Fouroux being challenged by a variety of new actors. However, it was in the end a new entrepreneurial spirit imported from the increasingly dominant southern hemisphere that would have the biggest impact on this restructuring of the French game. With professionalism the key, it is inevitably the responses of French rugby's elite players to the qualitatively new circumstances of the post-1995 rugby world that will form the core of the discussion here.

Perhaps the hardest series of results for supporters of French rugby to digest in the early 1990s were the eight successive defeats by England, home and away, between 1989 and 1995 inclusive. The England XV, hitherto dominated by France in the post-war period, went on to win unprecedented back-to-back Grand Slams in 1991 and 1992, adding another in 1995, to rub salt into French wounds and to establish itself henceforth as France's only serious rival for supremacy in the northern hemisphere of the rugby world. The encounters between the two sides at this time were seldom particularly attractive spectacles, with England every bit as devoted to the ethos of overwhelming forward strength as the French had been in the Fouroux era and continued to be under his successor Daniel Dubroca. Although even here there were some notable exceptions, with the sweeping attack that culminated in a score by the French captain Philippe Saint-André at Twickenham in 1991 widely acclaimed as 'the try of the century'. However, the two teams' hard-fought confrontations more often resembled siege warfare, with little movement and a reliance on the maintenance of possession and tactical kicking, rather than on running with the ball. Nevertheless, they regularly generated an intensity that captured the imagination of the public and the press alike on both sides of the English Channel, thanks in part to a new generation of French 'hard men', such as the massive Olivier Merle – from the AS Montferrand club, and nicknamed 'le Puy de Dôme', after the local mountain – who took on the mantle of Alain Estève as the latest, frequently demonized, incarnation of *le jeu dur* in the British press.[1] Similar developments were reflected in the French domestic championship with the re-emergence of the Bègles-Bordeaux club, which won the national championship in 1991. The winning side's reliance on a slowly advancing rolling maul by their shaven-headed forwards – a technique known as *la tortue* [the tortoise] – aptly sums up their approach to the game; as does the court case brought against one of their players, Serge Simon, for the serious injuries allegedly inflicted on an opponent.

Unsurprisingly, these France–England games often degenerated into violence on the pitch and polemic off it, most spectacularly during the second rugby World Cup in 1991, hosted jointly by Britain and France, where the two sides met in the quarter-final at the Parc des Princes in Paris. The tone was set early on, when the English set out, cynically, but very effectively, to unsettle the French side's captain and undoubted star, Serge Blanco, with a succession of high kicks and very hard – if not actually illegally late – follow-up tackles. So upset was Blanco, a player admired around the world for his elegant running, particularly in daring counter-attacks, that he was drawn, quite out of character, into the fist-fight that resulted. Although the French side attempted to settle down after this and to establish their own rhythm, the ill-tempered game was dominated by the tactical kicking of the English half-backs, with England finishing the comfortable winners (19–10). At least as dramatic as the events on the field were those that occurred off it. Daniel Dubroca, the former national captain and stalwart of Ferrasse's SU Agen club, who had been appointed just a year earlier as Fouroux's successor as coach of the *XV de France*, was incensed by the result of this crucial game. In an incident reminiscent of the notorious Baxter and Sanson 'affairs' (of 1913 and 1977 respectively), Dubroca violently confronted the match referee, the New Zealander David Bishop, after the final whistle. This incident would result in his resignation a few days later, under the combined pressure of the World Cup organizing committee and the FFR president Albert Ferrasse.[2]

By the early 1990s, Albert Ferrasse had been in undisputed control of the French rugby federation for nearly a quarter of a century. Having been elected to the presidency of the FFR against the backdrop of the quasi-revolutionary carnival of May–June 1968, the new incumbent would become as much an icon of stability, and, indeed, of immobility, as the then President of the Republic, General Charles de Gaulle. With due allowance for the obvious differences of scale, it is possible to argue that Ferrasse's fall, when it came, would be comparable to that of the country's pre-eminent post-war politician. For if a vein of social conservatism had always underpinned the statesman's radical conception of France's place in the world, Ferrasse's patriarchal reign, although innovative externally, would throughout be marked by the parochialism that the economic and social restructuring of *les trente glorieuses* had so effectively swept away in other spheres. Like de Gaulle, Ferrasse had risen to power on the promise of change, and like the country's political giant, the president of the FFR would be found out by an inability to manage change so sweeping that it denied his personal vision of national *grandeur*. However, in marked contrast to de Gaulle, who resigned as soon as it became clear that he no longer had a clear personal mandate from the French people, the dictatorial Ferrasse was determined to cling on to power regardless of the mood of the players, administrators, supporters, and journalists who together made up his national constituency.

As president of the FFR – an organization that, like all other national sporting bodies in France, has the responsibility for running its particular sport merely delegated to it by the state, rather than permanently ceded – Ferrasse served not only under de Gaulle, but also under Presidents Pompidou, Giscard-d'Estaing, and Mitterrand, and thus dealt directly with a succession of sports ministers. He was also on particularly good terms with de Gaulle's Minister of the Interior, Roger Frey. A former rugby player himself, and a keen huntsman, Frey invited Ferrasse to the shooting parties he often hosted for very select guests. Ferrasse was also regularly invited to presidential events of this kind by the socialist François Mitterrand – in spite of the President's personal lack of interest in hunting – on state-owned properties at Rambouillet and elsewhere.[3] For his part, Ferrasse would make invitations to his own hunting parties a tool for rewarding and controlling his placemen within the FFR hierarchy. This kind of activity was also part of a taste for the good things in life that was most typically demonstrated by his love of fine food and wine. Under his leadership, the business of the FFR was routinely conducted in the best restaurants of Paris and the south-west, with lavish entertainment again used as a means of manipulation and control. In his memoirs, Ferrasse himself is keen to point out that 'contrary to an idea which is all too widely held, I have never been a big eater . . ., but I do like good plain cooking, which is also called traditional in that it is based on the dishes that our forebears used to make'.[4] This rhetorical emphasis on the reassuring simplicity of the past is itself a key to under-standing the FFR under Ferrasse. For in French rugby's governing body, as Pierre Duboscq has argued, 'le pouvoir est au bout du terroir'.[5] By this, he means that legitimacy within the federation has always been based on a perceived fidelity to the traditional values of the south-west: to a conception of authenticity rooted in *le rugby des villages*, in short. Eating and drinking, like hunting, shooting, and fishing, together with his love of the traditional *belote* card-game, and even his pronounced south-western accent, were thus all markers of Ferrasse's authentic *culture rugbystique*. However, for Ferrasse's increasingly vocal critics, the propensity of French rugby's highest-ranking officials to deal with the game's affairs first and foremost 'with the prongs of their forks'[6] was merely the most visible sign of a corrupt system of administration that was patently unfit to manage the sport's rapid evolution in the 1990s. It was widely hoped that an opportunity for the necessary changes – particularly as regards the management of professionalism, revenues from television rights, and new forms of European competition – would occur when the ageing Ferrasse eventually retired, as he had promised to do in April 1990.

Having first been elected in 1968 at the age of 51, Ferrasse was thus well into his seventies when he announced in October 1990 that he had changed his mind, and would, after all, be standing again for the FFR presidency when elections were next due in 1992. In the face of Albert Ferrasse's deter-mination to carry on at all costs, three main poles of opposition emerged, all based on former captains of the national side. The first was that of Jacques Fouroux, who, as Ferrasse's protégé and heir apparent, had been waiting in the wings for over a decade, and had only recently been appointed to the FFR's central committee, following his resignation as coach of the national side. With support drawn essentially from the regional committees of the north and east, which had long been excluded from power by the effective cartel of the south-west, Fouroux offered a new, if inherently impractical, vision of developing rugby across the whole of the national territory, rather than just in its traditional heartlands. The second group was headed by Robert Paparemborde, the former prop forward from Pau, who had been a central figure in Fouroux's 1977 Grand Slam side, and who had now established himself in Paris as a highly influential administrator with the reinvigorated Racing Club de France. 'Patou', as this terror of opposition front rows was fondly known, was supported, revealingly, by another ten or so former members of the 1977 *bande à Fouroux*, as well as by the Perpignan-based epitome of *le beau jeu*, Jo Maso. Like Fouroux, Paparemborde offered new men and a new, more business-oriented, vision of French rugby's future, but did not seek to change the federal structures that had enabled Ferrasse to exert his dictatorial control for so long. Jean Fabre, from an earlier generation, and yet paradoxically with an altogether more radical view of the changes needed within the French game, was the third figure to challenge Ferrasse. With a doctorate in pure mathematics, and a career spent as an *Inspecteur Général de l'Education Nationale*, Fabre was, perhaps, predisposed to consider the problems faced by French rugby at least as much in terms of systems as of personalities. Moreover, as the president since 1981 of Stade Toulousain, the club that had taken over from AS Béziers as the undisputed standard by which other French clubs were to be judged, he spoke from a position of considerable strength. As Richard Escot, *L'Equipe*'s senior rugby correspondent, has put it: 'Toulouse was built around a new idea of how rugby could be played. The idea that a prop could act like a centre was introduced by Toulouse in 1985. They were ahead of everyone. They worked together like a family [under] Villepreux and Skrela. . . .'[7] Like his club's 'total' approach to the game on the pitch, Fabre's project for the administrative reorganization of French rugby was a revolutionary one, in that he wanted to take power away from the regional committees – the primary bastions of traditionalism and the means by which Ferrasse had exerted almost dictatorial control for over two decades – and to give it to the clubs, increasingly revealed as the real focus of the modern game.[8]

An important factor in Ferrasse's belated appreciation of the seriousness of the crisis that now existed was the stand taken by Roger Bambuck, the Minister for Youth and Sport in the socialist Mitterrand administration. Writing to Ferrasse on 9 January 1991, Bambuck informed the FFR's head that, in response to requests from a number of leading clubs – led by Fabre at Stade Toulousain, although neither was named – 'it would be opportune to put the question [of the reform of federal structures] on the agenda of the forthcoming general assembly and thus to allow this body to decide on the various proposals'.[9] The regional delegates duly came together to discuss the future of the French game on 16 February 1991. In the event, Fabre would not be able to mobilize sufficient support among the clubs to permit the proposed overhaul of the committee-based federal structure. However, such was the seriousness of his challenge that Ferrasse was forced to come to a compromise. In a move that itself epitomizes the Byzantine intrigues of the FFR, against which Fabre himself had railed so recently and so vocally, the Toulouse president came to a private understanding with Ferrasse, whereby Ferrasse would continue in his position until after the 1991 World Cup, with Fabre serving as his vice-president. It was then generally assumed that Fabre would take over as president in his own right and embark on the root-and-branch overhaul of the French game for which he had argued so vigorously. For Ferrasse, this compromise had the advantage of ruling the now detested Fouroux out of the equation. Fouroux, sensing that the game was up, shifted his own allegiances to Paparemborde and withdrew from the contest. However, his fall from federal grace was to include an element of ritual humiliation appropriate to a would-be parricide and regicide. His fate was sealed in the course of one of Ferrasse's lavish shooting parties at a country retreat in the Landes. The classical unities of place (the house in the forest), time (a single day), and action (the 'trial' of Fouroux, culminating in his 'death-sentence') were thus all respected as the feudal sovereign and his barons plotted the upstart's demise. Indeed, a regional newspaper that reported on this day of the long knives drew directly on the title, plot, and menacing chiaroscuro of *Partie de chasse* [The Hunting Party], the best-selling *bande dessinée* [comic-book] adventure by Bilal and Christin, in its coverage of the relevant events.[10]

However, if Ferrasse had decided belatedly to bow out with a semblance of good grace, he had not yet fired his final shot in the French federation's wars of succession. Party political comparisons are valuable in attempting to make sense of the internecine rivalries of the FFR at this time. For in much the same way as the internal politics of the Parti Communiste Français (PCF) were dominated in this same period by the desire of a group of 'renovators' to break with the monolithic structures and outdated dogmas of the past, at least as much as with the leadership of the veteran Georges Marchais, so Fabre and his supporters were threatening more than just Ferrasse and his clan. What they now had in their sights was the Ferrassian equivalent of the Stalinist 'system of democratic centralism, which had nothing democratic about it, no dissent to the line laid down by the political bureau and central committee [being] tolerated'.[11] When he challenged Ferrasse, Fabre was also threatening a deeply rooted, although now outmoded, conception of French rugby, for federal management styles and power structures were inextricably linked to the game's traditionalist ethos. The 'political management' of rugby union in France was thus inevitably tied up with 'its cultural management in the deepest sense of the term', as Ferrasse maintained his implacable hostility 'to the rugby modernists, to the technicians, and perhaps also to a certain type of financier and wheeler-dealer'.[12]

For if Ferrasse had no real objection to money changing hands in the French game, his preference was for a variety of low-key, discreetly financed, and locally managed semi-professionalism – what we might conveniently term *le professionnalisme de papa* [old-time professionalism] – rather than the potentially far more damaging switch to full-blown professionalism, as in association football, cycling, and every other major competitive sport. In this stance, Ferrasse was broadly in line with the majority of administrators in the other rugby-playing nations of the northern hemisphere, but wholly out of step with developments in rugby's ever more dominant southern hemisphere, where overt professionalism was becoming the norm. However, the preservation of the increasingly shaky myth of French rugby's amateurism was central to his battle to preserve both *la culture du rugby* and his own position. Hence the complete secrecy that was maintained in 1991, when, in the build-up to their World Cup quarter-final match against Australia, the French national squad refused to play unless they were paid. The threatened strike led the two leading candidates for the presidency of the FFR, Jean Fabre and Bernard Lapasset, the only other serious pretender to Ferrasse's crown to have emerged, to make concessions quickly in order to avert disaster ahead of the big game. They offered all the members of the French World Cup squad an 'official' (although wholly clandestine) fee of seven thousand francs (£700) each: a very modest sum by today's standards, but one that was nevertheless of enormous symbolic significance. Never before had leading players challenged the FFR's hierarchy in this way; and what is more, the authorities had caved in immediately in the face of their threatened action.[13]

Lapasset's emergence as Fabre's main rival for the federal succession was the result of his own expertise in manipulating the FFR's power structures, together with the decisive intervention of Ferrasse, cunning to the last. An archetypal federal *cadre*, Lapasset was consequently deeply conservative and thus doubly attractive to Ferrasse and the rest of the old guard. With typical wiliness, the outgoing president had sworn support to Fabre while working all the time to undermine him in favour of his new protégé, Lapasset.[14] He was helped in this by the fact that 'Fabre's plan . . . to bring the Federation into line with the new era . . . could not fail to frighten the *apparatchiks*': 'Behind the scenes, a *rapprochement* between Lapasset and Paparemborde cut out Jean Fabre, who was judged to be too radical, a belief which was only reinforced by his announcement of Pierre Villepreux's appointment as head of the FFR's playing operations.'[15] Betrayed by the *Ferrassiens* and the new generation alike, Fabre was doomed even before the management committee met for its secret vote on 14 December 1991. After two years of in-fighting that had left the FFR seriously weakened, and just weeks after the close of a World Cup competition that underlined both the southern hemisphere's continuing dominance and the onward march of professionalism, a successor to Ferrasse was finally elected. By an absolute majority on the first round of voting, Lapasset had triumphed, and with him the old men and their old ways, once again. Personalities and policies had conspired to deny Fabre and his vision of renewal, and it would be left to a Ferrasse 'clone' to attempt to deal with the radical challenges that confronted French rugby, as indeed they did the union game around the world.

A brief examination of Fabre's home club at this time will readily suggest just how much French rugby lost by this conservative choice. The commitment to the new world order of Fabre and Stade Toulousain went far beyond the usual club interest in the outcome of the national championship on the one hand, and in supplying players for the national side on the other. In fact, the club's loss of confidence in both of these spheres, historically administered by the traditionalists of the FFR, lies behind its commitment to a new era of international competition at club level. Indeed, it is precisely in the glaring mismatch between Stade Toulousain's dominance of the French domestic game throughout the 1980s and 1990s and its inability to impose itself – before the advent of Skrela and Villepreux – on the national selectors that the appeal of alternative varieties of international competition can be found.[16] Moreover, such are the spiteful internal politics of the FFR, that the very fact that the club conclusively demonstrated its ability to take on – and beat – all comers at its own international 'Masters' tournaments in 1986 and 1990 is likely to have figured significantly in the vengeful calculations of international selectors drawn from other, and lesser, clubs. These first world club championships had been organized with the financial backing of prestigious industrial partners, who had to come to symbolize Toulouse's transformation in the post-war period from a modest provincial centre into a major pole of the French economic and technological miracle. Aerospace and aviation companies were particularly visible in this regard, with Matra Espace, Aérospatiale, and the UTA airline all supporting Stade Toulousain's initiative, and with the crucial media backing provided by the newly launched and privately funded La Cinq television network. However, in spite of the commercial and sporting success of the Toulouse innovation, the reluctance of Ferrasse's FFR to support regular international competition between clubs meant that attempts to encourage a European club tournament – along the lines of association football's highly profitable UEFA cup competitions – remained fruitless.[17] It was only in 1996, with Ferrasse safely out of the way, and in the era of full professionalism, that rugby's European Cup competition belatedly came into being. In one of the more agreeable ironies of French rugby history, Stade Toulousain, which had done so much to encourage the new competition, became the first-ever champions of Europe, defeating the Welsh champions Cardiff at their own Arms Park stadium (21–18). With Brive winning the following season, it was not until Bath's victory in 1998 that a non-French team became European champions, and it was not until 2000, when Northampton defeated Munster, that a French side did not figure in the final. Brive's 1997 European campaign, in particular, combined the best and worst of French rugby's traditions, with a dazzling display in the final that completely overwhelmed the English champions Leicester, but also some very unsavoury incidents both during and after their earlier matches against the (far from blameless) Welsh champions Pontypridd.[18]

In the southern hemisphere, events were moving much more quickly. The 1987 and 1991 editions of the rugby World Cup had convinced many of the money to be made from a game whose amateur status and traditionalist ethos had prevented it from competing effectively with other sports for mass-market attention. The build-up to the 1995 World Cup served to crystallize the issues and interests involved, with the real drive for change coming essentially from two very powerful Australian-based media groups, headed by Rupert Murdoch and Kerry Packer. Murdoch's News Corporation had already had a significant impact on both rugby union and rugby league in Great Britain and his native Australia. Having secured control of the thirteen-a-side code in both Australasia and the north of England, its two main centres, Murdoch turned his attention to France, where the *treizistes* had been in apparently terminal decline since the glory days of the early post-war period. On 7 November 1994, in a luxurious hotel near the Trocadéro in Paris, and in a *coup de théâtre* typical of the man, it was Jacques Fouroux, of all people, who announced the planned creation of 'France Rugby League'. This was to be a championship based on sixteen professional clubs, which would in turn constitute a route into Murdoch's new Super League, in which the top clubs from England, Australia, and New Zealand would compete to decide the game's world champions. While Fouroux's dramatic switch of allegiance was perceived as a betrayal in French rugby union circles, his ambitious project's lack of a sound financial basis soon became clear. The sixteen planned professional sides were rapidly reduced to eight, which played out a rather desultory competition, with little media or public interest, during the summer months. France Rugby League was then abandoned, and replaced by PSG Rugby, a rugby league section of the successful Paris Saint-Germain football club, which had to be bought in from scratch, so that the French could have a representative in Murdoch's Super League, to be televised exclusively by his Sky satellite channel.[19] The poor results of the side in its first season, when it was composed essentially of established *treizistes* reinforced by a small number of players recently recruited from French rugby union, led to the wholesale replacement of the squad by some twenty Australians the following season. With little popular support for rugby league even within the south-west, and with scarcely any at all in the national capital, the venture was doomed from the outset.[20] While this double failure marked the end of the road for Jacques Fouroux's ambitions, it was no more than a little local difficulty for Murdoch. Although his worldwide influence has not, to date, been felt as directly in France as it has elsewhere in the rugby-playing world, Murdoch's thinking and that of his like-minded Australian competitors has nevertheless had a significant impact on the recent evolution of the game in France. One such development was the creation in March 1995 of a 'presidents' club', to defend the interests of the country's ten leading rugby clubs. The establishment of this organization was a belated recognition of Jean Fabre's foresight, and was intended to protect French rugby's elite in the face of the FFR's determination to dilute their strength in a forty-club first division of the national championship. The club presidents who came together in this way were able to share valuable insights, particularly in so far as thorny issues such as the payment of ever larger 'expenses' to players, the transfer market, and the division of revenue from television contracts were concerned.[21]

The 1995 World Cup would be an event of monumental importance for the newly democratic South Africa that hosted it, and also for the rugby-playing world as a whole. On the eve of the final between the host nation and New Zealand, the presidents of the South African, New Zealand, and Australian rugby unions announced that they had just signed with Rupert Murdoch the biggest commercial contract in rugby history: equivalent to £275 million, for the exclusive television rights to international rugby union in the southern hemisphere for ten years, including particularly two new tournaments created for him and due to run from 1996, a 'Tri–Nations' series of home and away matches between the three countries, and a 'Super Twelve' competition between their leading provincial sides.[22] By this simple expedient, the media magnate had effectively guaranteed the full-blown professionalization of world rugby. The defenders of amateurism, in France, as elsewhere, now came under intense pressure to admit defeat and go along with the media moguls and the southern hemisphere giants. The pressure for change was intensified by demands from the country's top players, who were everywhere forming associations or unions to defend their own interests, and by attempts to launch a variety of alternative international circuits to rival that announced by Rupert Murdoch. In France, the players had, as we have seen, begun to flex their collective muscles some four years earlier, with their 1991 World Cup strike threat, and were now in no mood any longer to forgo what they considered to be their rightful share of the substantial profits increasingly generated by the world game. In this mood, and with the FFR continuing to resist out-and-out professionalism, they were also easy targets for Murdoch's Australian rivals. On 26 June 1995, just three days after Murdoch's southern hemisphere *coup* and two days after the World Cup final, a secret meeting was held at the Maxim's restaurant at Orly airport between the representatives of the Australian multi-millionaire Kerry Packer, and his partner on this occasion Ross Turnbull, and representatives of the French international XV. The Packer–Turnbull project involved a world rugby circus, based on a dozen national sides, as a direct rival to Rupert Murdoch's own organization.[23] In return for signing professional contracts, individual French international players were offered a million francs (£100,000) per year. Lesser amounts were on offer to club players recruited by the internationals. Not surprisingly, within three weeks, Packer and Turnbull had signed up no less than 127 French players. In the event, the project would be abandoned, as Packer made his peace with Murdoch in return for a deal concerning television rights to horse-racing in Asia.[24] However, by voting overwhelmingly for professionalism, France's elite rugby players had cut the remaining ground from under the feet of the traditionalists within the FFR.

In another delicious irony, it fell to Ferrasse's conservatively inclined successor, Bernard Lapasset, to preside over the historic meeting of the International Board that finally dropped rugby union's official insistence on the amateur credentials of its players, whether past or present. Meeting in the style to which the FFR had grown accustomed, at the Hotel Ambassador, not far from the Opera in Paris, the Board agreed to put an end to the hypocrisy that had characterized high-level rugby's finances for at least the previous fifteen years. In spite of a determined rearguard action fought especially by smaller nations like Scotland and Ireland, who were justifiably afraid of what the future might hold, it thus fell to Lapasset to announce, on 26 August 1995, the end of amateurism and the advent of the 'open', that is to say, overtly professional, era. However, the actual management of this dramatic change was to be left to individual rugby unions, with the Board requiring only that the books should be balanced in each country. Almost immediately, established French players became subject to lucrative offers from other countries. Thierry Lacroix and Olivier Roumat, both from the Dax club, were thus recruited by the South African province of Natal, where they helped the side to success in that season's Currie Cup. In the final match, they defeated a Western Province side itself reinforced by their international team-mate, the flanker Laurent Cabannes. This was merely the beginning of a new age of player mobility that would see French stars move to leading sides around the world. The FFR, fearing the possible negative impact of just such a flight of talent on the quality of the French national championship, and thus on both the likely revenue from television rights and, ultimately, the standard of the national side, announced that the three players, who had gone to play in South Africa without official approval, would no longer be selected for *le XV de France*.

Once again, however, it was the players themselves who held all the trump cards. On 9 November, on the eve of the first test against the visiting All Blacks, the French international players refused to attend an official reception and thus effectively went on strike. At issue were the size of match bonuses, the (lucrative) allocation of international match tickets to each player, and the continued refusal of the federation to allow players to sell their public image, as well as the ban recently imposed on the South African 'exiles'. In the face of the players' action, Lapasset was, as before, forced to climb down, thus further underlining that power in the French game had shifted decisively from the federal administrators to the playing elite. By beating the mighty All Blacks (22–15) in the match proper, the French international players further underlined their strength and their determination, both on the field and off it; as well, of course, as enhancing their value as commercial commodities.[25] In the weeks after the New Zealand game, a group of leading international players, including the captain of *les Tricolores*, Philippe Saint-André – who had scored the winning try in the big match, in spite of the determined defence of the phenomenal Jonah Lomu – began to organize a formally constituted trade union. With the help of the Panini firm, they organized a mail-shot for the 2,000 players active in the French first division, and were also offered the use of the established infrastructures of the French professional footballers' association. On 15 December, the statutes of the Association des Joueurs de Rugby (AJR) were formally lodged in Paris. Henceforth, the players would be able to enter into negotiations with the FFR and individual clubs alike on altogether more favourable terms.[26]

Lapasset, who had announced just three months earlier that 'French rugby has chosen not to become professional',[27] had been overtaken by events, and the federal authorities would shortly be obliged to accept complete professionalization. However, the FFR was quite right to fear the shake-up that would result from the overt payment of players, and especially from the fierce international competition that was certain to develop for the French game's outstanding performers. As *Le Monde*'s correspondent put it: 'The clubs, even the richest ones, do not have the resources to keep a "pro" team going, that is to say to guarantee salaries which are sufficiently high to persuade players to commit themselves completely to a career which is both short and uncertain.'[28] The changes went even deeper, in fact, and it was the new spirit of entrepreneurialism that professionalization brought in its wake that constituted the principal challenge to the established *culture du rugby*. For the new class of business-oriented managers that now emerged to challenge the existing *dirigeants* [administrators] would call into question not only the appropriateness in the modern age of the French game's organizational structures, but also the fundamental legitimacy of its prevailing ethos.[29] It is for this reason that Richard Escot has commented that 'the end of amateurism is, relatively speaking, a bit like the equivalent of the fall of the Berlin Wall'.[30] In French rugby's south-western heartland, there had long been a widespread acceptance of both the necessity and the justice of rewarding those who played the game for the entertainment and, crucially, the municipal pride of their local communities. Yet this traditional model of remuneration – normally a combination of material and social benefits – was radically challenged by the eruption into French rugby in August 1995 of the unbridled market economics of a worldwide sporting industry financed by global media corporations. Money was not the only issue, in consequence, nor even the primary one. What was at stake, once again, was the much-debated 'soul' of the French game.

Under Albert Ferrasse, from the mid-1960s to the early 1990s, French rugby as a whole had developed a 'management style' that closely reflected that of its federal president. For if Ferrasse had genuinely distinguished himself on the international stage, his real interests never strayed very far from his native Agen. So while his record abroad may be creditable – including particularly his previously discussed role in the evolution of South African rugby, his successful campaign to gain French admission to the International Board in 1978, and his encouragement of a rugby World Cup (which he himself was the first to present to the victorious New Zealanders in 1987) – it is much closer to home that the abiding legacy of Ferrasse's long reign may be found. For Jean Fabre, one of his most cogent critics, Ferrasse's *culture d'entreprise* had taken hold in French rugby as a whole by the 1990s:

> A personalized mode of functioning, with little regard for rules and regulations, was very often found in the [regional] committees and even in certain clubs. In this way, a parallel network [of control] had been created in which the oral tradition played a major role, and where the relationships and behaviour were reminiscent of certain secret societies.[31]

Central to this mode of operation was the Ferrasian 'clan', with the close personal relationships of Ferrasse and his loyal lieutenants, the so-called 'barons', regularly reasserted through communal eating and drinking, as well as through Ferrasse's hunting and fishing parties, and, more modestly, his weekly *belote* card-schools with his closest associates. The stranglehold exerted by this group at the national level was replicated in similarly organized groups of *notables* at the local level, in which a dynastic element was very often visible: from former prime minister Jacques Chaban-Delmas and the nationally influential Moga brothers in Bordeaux, to the more modest, and often related or otherwise associated, local worthies who typically run smaller French clubs. At all levels of the French game, this traditional mode of management has both encouraged and depended upon an administrative culture of personal loyalties, dealings behind closed doors, and a strict code of silence. French rugby's much vaunted existence as an extended family – *la grande famille du rugby* – thus has a distinctly darker side; with its concentration of absolute power in the hands of clan chieftains, its periodic family feuds, and its equivalent of the law of *omertà* together making the FFR's key personnel seem more like old-time *mafiosi* than modern sports administrators.

Where Will Carling, the then captain of the England XV, had, at the height of the 1995 professionalization crisis, famously dismissed the RFU's administrators as out-of-touch 'old farts', Jean Fabre, a former captain of *le XV de France*, was more inclined to see the FFR's *dirigeants* as political animals whose power remained only too real. Indeed, it was precisely their stranglehold that was blocking the necessary evolution of the French game.[32] However, new forces were beginning to make themselves felt, with player power and, especially, a new breed of sporting entrepreneur to the fore. The mediatization of sport in general and French rugby in particular was to become ever more marked in the 1990s. One of its most obvious impacts in the French context has been to give a renewed importance to Parisian clubs, and particularly the two longest-established clubs in the country, Racing Club de France and Stade Français. The overlap between sport and show business is something that has been particularly marked at these clubs, albeit in very different ways: the re-emergence of the RCF has been based on a mixture of its traditionally glamorous brand of social exclusivity and a new variety of rugby-focused entrepreneurialism; while that of Stade Français has consisted in a wholesale reinvention of the ailing club, made possible by new corporate sponsors and a new age of player mobility at the highest level. Two players from these different clubs sum up the sorts of changes that have been taking place in rugby in the capital: Franck Mesnel of the Racing Club and Serge Simon of Stade Français.

Franck Mesnel's transformation, as a recent admiring article in the British business press has put it, 'from rugby god to fashion entrepreneur',[33] has as much to do with the French game's traditional celebration of festivity as it does with the new opportunities for personal profit that opened up for the top players after the 1995 World Cup. Indeed, it is necessary to go back to 1987, the year of the inaugural edition of that competition, to find the roots of Mesnel's subsequent commercial success. In that year, in the French national championship – arguably the most hard-fought domestic rugby competition in the world – Mesnel's RCF travelled to Bayonne for an important fixture against the local side, the famous Aviron Bayonnais, who first established their reputation for sparkling rugby with a celebrated win in the 1913 championship final. For all the seriousness of the occasion, Mesnel and four of his fellow three-quarters felt that a touch of theatre was called for, and they consequently trotted out on to the pitch wearing the *bérets basques* that the Bayonne club's players had worn in its heyday. The home crowd, justifiably proud of the club's heritage, might have reacted badly, but instead responded well to the visitors.[34] With seasoned internationals like Mesnel and Jean-Baptiste Lafond in their side, and with the iconic Robert Paparemborde now in charge of the club, Racing went all the way to that year's championship final. However, their campaign was marked at least as much by their humorous approach to matches as by their considerable success on the pitch. So as the final rounds of this notoriously unforgiving competition brought them up against the toughest teams in the land, they appeared in turn in blazers against Brive, in long shorts and golden boots against Toulouse in the semi-final, and, most famously, in pink bow-ties against the forward might of Toulon in the final. Although narrowly defeated by Toulon (15–12), the private 'Show-Bizz' [*sic*] club that Mesnel and Lafond had founded, together with Eric Blanc, Yvon Rousset, and Philippe Guillard, during a stay at an Alpine ski resort on New Year's Day 1987, was guaranteed a public prominence that went well beyond the conventional rugby press.[35]

Three years later the club went one better. Reinforced by impressive new tight forwards such as Laurent Bénézech and Michel Tachdjian, and with the remarkable international flanker Laurent Cabannes in the back row, Mesnel and his fellow 'Show-Bizz' backs were provided with the perfect platform on which to build a win against the altogether more traditional SU Agen. Appearing in their trademark pink bow-ties – one of which they offered to the President of the Republic, François Mitterrand, as the two teams were presented to him before the match – Mesnel, Blanc, Guillard, and Lafond had champagne brought out to them at half-time by the injured Yvon Rousset, dressed for the occasion as a waiter. Although held 9–9 at full time, the Racing Club went on to win 22–12 after extra time.[36] However, this combination of festivity and playing success was only the beginning of the story for Mesnel and his associates. Together they formed the Eden Park menswear company: the name was inspired by the celebrated stadium in Auckland, New Zealand, while the new firm shrewdly adopted as its logo the pink bow-tie that had brought the 'Show-Bizz' players their national celebrity. By 1999 the firm had expanded its operations to include 22 shops across France and a new flagship store in London. While all of the group have maintained their interest in the company, it is Mesnel as its chief executive who has dominated its dealings. The son of a company director and a native of the very select Parisian suburb of Neuilly-sur-Seine, Mesnel studied architecture at the Ecole des Beaux Arts before turning his attention full-time to rugby and then his business.[37] He thus represents a doubly unusual – because *bourgeois* and Parisian – image of the modern French game, but one that may have important lessons for its future development in the professionalized era. Indeed, it may even be that a century of south-western hegemony is at last coming to an end, as French rugby's centre of gravity moves back to the national capital, where its story first began.

However, if Franck Mesnel and the Racing Club represent an obvious continuity as regards the commercial and social activities of the Parisian elite, the reinvention of Stade Français must be regarded as French rugby's equivalent of an epistemological break. Revealingly, alternative constructions of masculinity are also to the fore as the union game enters the new millennium. Mesnel himself has commented as follows on the symbolism of the Racing Club's now famous pink bow-tie: 'In rugby, because we are Parisians . . . we are all homosexuals! [. . .] As students we have many cultural and artistic interests so we decide to play with this joke. If we are called the homosexuals of French rugby we will be happy! We will laugh! We will wear our pink bow-ties!'[38] This ironic playing with the game's conventional representations of masculinity might, perhaps, be regarded as characteristically post-modern. However, a more authentic challenge to rugby's patriarchal assumptions is almost certainly posed by the involvement of Max Guazzini, the flamboyant owner of the NRJ commercial radio station, with the historic Stade Français club. From this point of view, the venerable sports association's adoption as its signature tune of Gloria Gaynor's 'I Will Survive', a hit from the 1970s that became a gay anthem in the 1990s, is of obvious significance.

Guazzini might usefully be compared with entrepreneurs across the Channel such as Sir John Hall at Newcastle and Nigel Wray at Saracens, whose financial backing has allowed ailing clubs to become powerful forces again, albeit in a reinvented form. It was just such investment that would take Philippe Sella, the most capped international player of all time, from Agen to Saracens, Thierry Lacroix from Dax to Harlequins, and Philippe Saint-André, as player-coach, from Montferrand to Gloucester. By the same token, Guazzini's money has helped Stade Français to rise from long-term obscurity to something both like and unlike the club's former greatness. Starting virtually from scratch in 1993, the club rose from the lower divisions of the French championship to become national title-holders in 1998, for the first time since 1908, thanks wholly to talent imported from elsewhere in France and from overseas. A key moment in this development was the arrival in May 1995 of Bernard Laporte, who had guided Bègles-Bordeaux to the national championship in 1991, and who was subsequently to replace Jean-Luc Skrela as the coach of the French national side in November 1999. In July 2000, when Stade Français took the title again, for the tenth time in the club's history, the squad included some fifteen overseas players, now under the guidance of John Connolly, ex-coach of the Queensland Reds. The club's purchases of established stars included, amongst others, the whole front row of the Bègles-Bordeaux 1991 championship-winning side, made up of Serge Simon, Vincent Moscato, and Philippe Gimbert. Renowned for their extremely physical style of play, this combination would ensure that the club's expensively imported creative talents had the required possession to weave their spells in the backs. Serge Simon, in particular, is a player whose personal itinerary is just as fascinating as that of Franck Mesnel. On the face of it, his career epitomizes the traditional *jeu dur* of the south-west, in much the same way as the playfulness of Mesnel and his friends is a throwback to the aristocratic elitism of the early days of the Racing Club and Stade Français. He first came to public prominence at Bègles-Bordeaux, where his robust approach to the game resulted in a court case for the serious injuries that he allegedly inflicted on an opponent in the course of a game. However, he was also captain of the French Universities XV, which he led to a student world championship in 1991, before qualifying as a medical practitioner. More recently, this most down-to-earth of players has also revealed himself to be a shrewd analyst of French rugby football as it adapts to the new cultural landscape of the professional era. He has thus proved himself to be every bit as open to personal reinvention as Franck Mesnel, and has additionally examined *la culture du rugby* from within to good effect. Thus, we learn that this modern *rugbyman* is fully conscious of his role in the construction of both memories and identities:

> . . . for a player is well aware that the stadium is a bearer of collective memories. We find ourselves in the midst of the irrational, but we remain there. When we speak of former players turning in their graves, that seems to get very close to the truth. [. . .] A question that I have not yet raised is that of mediatization and the role that we play locally as a result of the televising of matches. For our image is thus injected right into our own homes and more widely into our 'territorial

bases' [*foyers territoriaux*], if I may put it that way. The dimensions of the real community are constantly tending to expand. The concept of [the French rugby] community is thus one that is liable to modification.[39]

In the post-Murdoch era, and perhaps even in the putatively 'post-modern' one, the allegedly rational logic of global commerce is combining with the traditional logic of locally rooted associationism to produce unprecedented cultural syntheses in the sporting sphere. The 'diminishing contrasts and increasing varieties'[40] constitutive of the post-modern condition apply as much to rugby football as they do to any other cultural domain. Nevertheless, French rugby's distinctive character, while it may evolve, seems destined to survive for the foreseeable future. After all, 'Where else . . . but in French club rugby?'[41] could a pink bow-tie make a player's fortune, and a gay anthem help to turn an *assassin* into a cultural critic?

Notes

1. See, for instance, Robert Armstrong, 'Merle may pay dear for "cheap shots", *The Guardian*, 24 January 1995, p. 17; Steve Bale, 'French drop Merle and attack Cooke', *The Independent*, 26 January 1995, p. 40. See also Jean-Jacques Bozonnet, 'Malentendu franco-britannique', *Le Monde*, 18 February 1995, p. 14.
2. Richard Escot and Jacques Rivière, *Un siècle de rugby* (Paris, Calmann-Lévy, 1997), p. 260.
3. Albert Ferrasse, *Mêlées ouvertes* (Paris, Albin Michel, 1993), pp. 131–2.
4. Ibid., p. 141.
5. Pierre Duboscq (ed.), *Rugby, parabole du monde* (Paris, L'Harmattan, 1998), pp. 76–8.
6. Jean Fabre and Pierre Capdeville, *Rugby: La quatrième mi-temps* (Toulouse, Cépaduès-Editions, 1999), p. 43.
7. Cited in Donald McRae, *Winter Colours: Changing Seasons in World Rugby* (Edinburgh, Mainstream, 1998), p. 207. See also Jean-François Fogel and Christian Jaurena, 'Le désordre règne: Stade toulousain (1985–1989)', in the same authors' *Le Rugby* (Paris, Jean-Claude Lattès, 1994), pp. 159–76. Also of interest is Pierre Capdeville and Roger Surjus, *De la vierge rouge aux anges blonds* (Toulouse, Cépaduès-Editions, 1984).
8. Fabre and Capdeville, *Rugby*, pp. 23–8.
9. Ibid., p. 65. This ministerial intervention had an obvious precedent in the action taken by the government in 1980 to calm the strained relations between rugby union and rugby league in France at that time. See Jean-

Pierre Augustin and Alain Garrigou, *Le Rugby démêlé: Essai sur les Assoc-iations Sportives, le Pouvoir et les Notables* (Bordeaux, Le Mascaret, 1985), pp. 316–17.

10. Duboscq, *Rugby, parabole du monde*, pp. 77–8.

11. Robert Gildea, *France Since 1945* (Oxford, Oxford University Press, 1996), p. 185.

12. Michel Bergès in Duboscq *Rugby, parabole du monde*, p. 282. Bergès looks even further back into the partisan divisions of the French Left for a model, suggesting that the FFR of the early 1990s resembled nothing so much as the Section Française de l'Internationale Ouvrière (SFIO, the French socialist party) of 1920: *la vieille maison* [the old house] that Léon Blum had vainly tried to keep together in the face of the challenge mounted on its Left by the new forces of Bolshevism.

13. Escot and Rivière, *Un siècle de rugby*, p. 25.

14. He was supported in this endeavour by no less a figure than Jean-Pierre Rives. See Escot and Rivière, *Un siècle de rugby*, p. 261.

15. Ibid.

16. Fabre and Capdeville, *Rugby*, p. 32.

17. Ibid., pp. 36–8. See also Richard Escot, *Rugby Pro: Histoires Secrètes* (Paris, Solar, 1996), pp. 69–87.

18. Mick Cleary, 'French artists on a new high', *The Observer*, 26 January 1997, 'Sport', p. 9. Cleary's sub-title – 'Brive breeze past English rivals with muscle and guile to become European rulers' – is a fair reflection of their complete domination of Leicester (28–9) in the final. The back-to-back Grand Slams achieved by *le XV de France* in 1997 and 1998 provided further evidence of the renewal of the game in France in the wake of professionalization. This achievement too was duly celebrated by Mick Cleary, 'This French team have greatness in their grasp', *The Daily Telegraph*, 6 April 1998, p. S6. On the Brive-Pontypridd violence in 1997, see McRae, *Winter Colours*, pp. 203–5. On the earlier history of the Brive club (a classic *bourg*-based association, with an enormous reputation), see Thierry Degoulange, *Brive, un grand parmi les grands du rugby* (Brive, Chastrusse, 1976).

19. A similar initiative has also been taken in basketball.

20. Escot and Rivière, *Un siècle de rugby*, p. 273.

21. Ibid., p. 277.

22. Ibid., p. 283.

23. The project was sold to French players by the former player Eric Blondeau and a Paris-based lawyer, *Maître* Robert Simpson. See Escot, *Rugby Pro*, pp. 89–108 et seq. Of particular interest is the role played by French rugby's most celebrated player, Jean-Pierre Rives, who

offered himself as an intermediary to the Australians, but was overtaken by the pace of events, and was never really able to compete with the commercial determination of the other parties. Escot is particularly revealing on the background negotiations to the whole process of professionalization in France. Extracts from this book were also published as 'Sous la mêlée, l'argent caché', *L'Equipe Magazine*, no. 722, 20 January 1996, pp. 40–5. Also of interest is Julien Giarrizzi, 'Le rugby n'aime pas qu'on lui parle d'argent et pourtant . . .', in idem, *Le Sport et l'argent* (Paris, A. Lefeuvre, 1981), pp. 117–21; also Claude Askolovitch and Sylvain Attal, 'La Mafia de l'ovale', in eidem, *La France du piston* (Paris, Robert Laffont, 1992), pp. 99–123. On the role of the Australian entrepreneurs see, among others, Sean Smith, *The Union Game: A Rugby History* (London, BBC, 1999), 'Australia and the death of the amateur game', pp. 232–81.

24. Escot and Rivière, *Un siècle de rugby*, pp. 283–4.
25. The French success in Paris against the All Blacks followed an unprecedented series win in New Zealand on their 1994 tour. This included a last-minute and match-winning try in the Second Test in Christchurch by Jean-Luc Sadourny that would subsequently become known as *l'essai du bout du monde* [the try from the end of the world].
26. Escot and Rivière, *Un siècle de rugby*, pp. 284–7.
27. Jean-Jacques Bozonnet, 'Le rugby français remet sa professionnalisation à plus tard', *Le Monde*, 15 September 1995, p. 21.
28. Ibid.; see also Jacques Maigne and Marie-Ange Rodeaud, 'Lapasset veut en finir avec l'amateurisme marron', *Libération*, 19 September 1994, p. 29.
29. On this subject see especially Olivier Nier, 'Professionnalisation du rugby et stratégies de clubs de l'élite européenne' (unpublished doctoral thesis), Université Claude Bernard – Lyon 1, Lyons, 1998. See also Jean-Pierre Augustin, 'From one stage to another: French rugby caught between local and global cultures', *Journal of European Area Studies*, vol. 7, no. 2, November 1999, pp. 197–210.
30. Escot, *Rugby Pro*, p. 5.
31. Fabre and Capdeville, *Rugby*, p. 27.
32. Ibid., pp. 38–9.
33. Sandra Harris, 'Allez la France', [British Airways] *Business Life*, February 1999, pp. 20–5; the quotation appears on the front cover.
34. Ibid., p. 22; see also McRae, *Winter Colours*, pp. 194–200. Interestingly, Pierre Sansot sees the 'Show-Bizz' club's antics as a departure from French rugby's traditional ethos. I would be more inclined to see such behaviour as part of the game's established patterns of festivity rather

than simply a modern obsession with 'fun', as he suggests. See Pierre Sansot, *Le Rugby est une fête* (Paris, Plon, 1990), p. 33. Denis Charvet, the Stade Toulousain and international centre, had previously established a notable connection with the world of show business when he appeared in Louis Guillermou's film *La Messe en si mineur* (1990), alongside Margaux Hemingway. See Escot and Rivière, *Un siècle de rugby*, p. 246.

35. Escot and Rivière, *Un siècle de rugby*, p. 231.
36. Ibid., p. 249.
37. Former Biarritz and France full-back Serge Blanco has also launched his own chain of menswear shops, using his name and his number 15 shirt as a logo. Now a senior administrator, Blanco has been a leading campaigner for reform of rugby's competitive structures, both within France and at a European level.
38. Cited by McRae, *Winter Colours*, p. 197. There would not seem to be any direct French equivalent at the present time of the gay King's Cross Steelers RFC in London.
39. Cited in Duboscq, *Rugby, parabole du monde*, pp. 247 and 255.
40. Joseph Maguire, 'Globalisation, sport and national identities: "The Empire strikes back"?', *Loisir et société*, vol. 16, no. 2, 1993, pp. 293–322; p. 310 for the quotation.
41. McRae, *Winter Colours*, p. 197.

Conclusion: *A la recherche du rugby perdu*

In what remains one of the most incisive studies of rugby football – of either code, and in any language – Geoffrey Moorhouse has pointed out that 'it is at least a matter for argument that man at play down the ages has been as significant as man at war and man at work.' The American historian Barbara Tuchman is one who has argued this, and gone so far as to suggest that, "In human activity, the invention of the ball may be said to rank with the invention of the wheel."'[1] Various theories may be adduced in support of this claim, including Alain Ehrenberg's hypothesis that sport serves to effect a symbolic resolution of the fundamental paradox that lies at the heart of democracy, and thus of Western social experience as a whole, as first identified by Tocqueville: that is to say, the self-evident disparity between the principle of equality and the reality of inequality. For Ehrenberg, 'sporting competition is a way of reconciling this contradiction through spectacle [and] may be to the democratic imagination what the Oedipus myth was to [the Ancient] Greek [world-view]'.[2] The philosopher Raymond Abellio has gone even further in his analysis of rugby's specificity. Adopting a view of the game as characterized at least as much by immobility (associated with the mutual defence of territory) as by movement, quite unlike other team games, he has suggested that the sport constitutes a privileged vector for understanding, and even conquering, time itself.[3] This theme has been fruitfully developed by Pierre Sansot:

> Rugby, in some respects, resembles other sports. But it stands out as a result of the emotions that it provokes, and of the discourse that it generates. It continues to present itself as a singular game. It contains a certain form of resistance to time, a certain anachronism that does not displease those who love it: take, for example, its amateurism at a time when sports are becoming professional.[4]

There is obviously considerable irony here, in view of the fact that rugby union itself, 'the last great bastion [of] amateurism . . ., has also begun to crumble dramatically'.[5] Indeed, it is precisely the mismatch between a fondly remembered past and the altogether more troublesome present that French rugby's foremost literary chroniclers have chosen to examine in recent years, in a nostalgic quest for the lost rugby of their preferred golden ages.

Central to this particular attempt to recapture the past through art is the theme of childhood, which, as Sansot notes, has throughout been associated with rugby: 'Rugby reawakens our childhood in many ways, and primarily because it always leads to confrontations, like those of our earliest years.'[6] As described by Daniel Herrero in his *Passion ovale* (1990), not only is rugby's formative influence felt throughout childhood, but it may even change the nature of the adulthood that follows: 'I left home as a pubescent teenager, dreaming of becoming an adult. I returned a joyful child, and proud of being so; a child that I was determined to remain for the rest of my life.'[7] Having opened his autobiography with an account of his 'Terrains d'enfance' [childhood pitches], Herrero then takes his readers on a 'Voyage initiatique en Ovalie' [an introductory tour of rugby-playing France]. This is a pattern that recurs in Denis Tillinac's *Rugby blues* (1993) and Jean-Paul Rey's *Qu'ont-ils fait de notre rugby?* [What have they done with our rugby?] (1997).[8] As both titles suggest, these works are dominated not only by nostalgia, but also by an atmosphere of gloom as regards the direction taken by the modern French game. As Tillinac puts it:

> . . . the village cockerel has been turned into a bloated factory-farmed broiler. Will it crow once again? Nothing is less certain.
> [. . .] The history of rugby cultures is coming to an end, and the undeniable achievements of current champions cannot console me for the loss. The future promises us a wholly different sport.[9]

For Rey, as for Tillinac, what is at stake in the continuing transformation of the French game, hitherto synonymous with *le rugby des villages*, is fidelity to a communitarian tradition of sociability at least as much as to a national style of play. He explains why, after a lifetime spent covering French rugby for its leading journal, *Midi-Olympique*, he is now embarking on a final tour of rugby-playing France:

> To cheer myself up, I suddenly decided to go. To see once again the little oval world that is an entire universe. To rediscover the *pays* of my friends, and the memories. [. . .] More particularly to reassure myself that I hadn't been mistaken all along . . . about a certain type of rugby . . . A light and airy rugby, like Gachassin floating on the curls of smoke from the *Voltigeur* cigar that my grandfather used to look forward to lighting up, before he put on his beret, stretched his braces, and set off for the ground. A rugby of holding hands with my parents, on the way to the Jules-Soulé stadium in Tarbes. A rugby of bell-towers and *cassoulets*, of picnics in the spring and of coloured ribbons on the way to the final rounds of the championship.

Conclusion: A la recherche du rugby perdu

Not the rugby 'made in Australia', by Murdoch, Packer, [and company,] stealing our childhoods just to make . . . a quick buck out of our beloved game.[10]

Of course, nostalgia has always been part of French rugby, just as it has at all times been central to the discourse of modern athletic sports in general: each sporting generation typically compares its iconic players and key performances with those that have gone before. Moreover, it is at least as clear in this field as in any other that nostalgia is liable to serve as 'a cultural "security-blanket"'.[11] The lure of nostalgia is most obvious to those directly challenged by societal change, for whom the appeal to a glorified past may serve to protect entrenched systems of knowledge and power. However, as with so much else in rugby football, nostalgia too is 'a contested cultural terrain':

Nostalgia can be used by dominant power groups to legitimate their position by promoting a sense of cultural security through cultural practices common to many members of society. People also use nostalgia to resist rapid changes in society and to challenge new ways of thinking promoted by political and cultural elites.[12]

Viewed in this light, sporting nostalgia may not always be the politically reactionary force that it often appears, and may actually represent an important site of struggle against the homogenizing forces of globalization. French rugby's literature of nostalgia may thus be seen not simply as the ramblings of a variety of ageing, and still objectively privileged, men.[13] Rather, it may be considered as part of a broader cultural investment in the politics of memory that is typical of modern Western societies, including especially France: 'Rather than increasing unity and integration on a global scale, it is quite possible that the rational reaction to modern internationalism and the demise of the nation-state, in its original form, will be that local, regional and national communities will hold on even tighter to those symbols and traditions, including sporting traditions, which once gave various nations and peoples a sense of identity.'[14] In France, with its particularly rich museographic tradition, it was only to be expected that rugby too would have a museum dedicated to it sooner or later. 'L'Ovalie', a permanent multi-media celebration of the game conceived by Jean Lacouture, and housed in a purpose-built edifice that combines the distinctive shapes of a scrummage and a line-out, was duly opened in 1987. Appropriately, the exhibition is located not in a conventional setting in the national capital, but rather at the Port-Lauragais services on the A61 motorway, just outside Toulouse. A joint venture by the motorway operating company, Les Autoroutes du Sud, the Ministry of Youth and Culture, the Midi-Pyrénées region, the

Haute-Garonne *département*, and, of course, the FFR, the museum had already attracted two and a half million paying visitors by 1996.[15] It may therefore be regarded in its own right as a sociological phenomenon of some significance.

However, if French rugby is to survive it must, inevitably, evolve. The basic structures of the game in the northern hemisphere have recently changed with the admission of Italy to the annual European nations' championship, henceforth the 'Six Nations', as of the 1999–2000 season. France's continued and commendable investment in the future of the game outside the former British imperial *bloc* has thus finally been rewarded. Although the Italians, in spite of a shock win against Scotland in their opening match, are unlikely to trouble European rugby's established hierarchy in the near future, it should be remembered that French rugby too was dismissed as an irrelevance in its early days. However, as Donald McRae has argued, the decision finally to include 'little' Italy did not thereby remove the vulnerability of 'a tournament which had traded in nostalgia for so long', and that appears increasingly out of step with international competitions dominated by the World Cup and the southern hemisphere's Tri-Nations tournament.[16] If the three southern-hemisphere giants ever decided to admit a fourth nation to their annual superpower struggle, there is ample evidence to suggest that their preference would be for France, the only European side consistently to trouble them both home and away.[17] However, the continued French ability to combine, to startling effect, teams made up – in Pierre Danos's memorable phrase, of both 'piano-shifters' and 'piano-players'[18] – should not blind us to the French game's failures to adapt to a changing cultural landscape.

Most obviously, a game that prides itself on its ability historically to integrate immigrants of crisis (whether fleeing Franco's Spain, like the parents of the Herrero brothers; or Mussolini's Italy, like those of the Spanghero family), has proved singularly unattractive to the community of North African ethnic origin that today makes up France's largest and most frequently discussed 'immigrant' population. The case of Abdelatif Benazzi is an exceptional one in this regard. A product of the Union Sportive d'Oujda in his native Morocco, Benazzi was recruited by Albert Ferrasse's SU Agen, and was naturalized after only two years in France – just in time for the 1991 World Cup – thanks to Ferrasse's personal intervention with the President of the Republic François Mitterrand.[19] An outstanding forward who can play in any position in the second or back rows, Benazzi was *Midi-Olympique*'s player of the year in 1995, and would go on to captain France to its fifth Grand Slam in 1997. As such he has regularly been identified as an image of successful racial integration, both at national and local level.[20]

However, Benazzi's undeniable North African presence in French rugby has been very much the exception in what remains an overwhelmingly white game (although black players such as Roger Bougarel, Serge Blanco, and Emile Ntamack have been slightly more frequently visible). Rugby union's image of Frenchness is thus very different from the 'multicultural' one communicated by the nation's hugely successful football team. It may be that it is in this aspect of its adaptation to the brave new world of professionalism more than any other that French rugby needs to make the most significant advances. 'France, spins yet another truism, traditionally play rugby like Brazil play football.'[21] If the national side could only look rather more like Brazilians too, then the future of the modern rugby game in France might well be assured. Then, for the first time, ideology, sociability, and festivity might truly be reconciled, and the game that the French have undoubtedly made their own might offer its unique attractions to the nation, or at least to its younger masculine component, as a whole:

> One of rugby's most eminent virtues is its ability to counter solitude and sullenness. When the Republic swaps her [Revolutionary] Phrygian bonnet for a nightcap, there's nothing to be lost by dressing her up in a scrum-cap. From the Pyrenees to the Alps, it sometimes seems to me that the underlying solidarity of the French people is only kept together by a chain forged by this fascinating oval ball, and that the finest resources of our energy derive from the springing forth of an advancing [three-quarter] line, launching an attack with the ball in hand.[22]

Notes

1. Geoffrey Moorhouse, *At the George, and Other Essays on Rugby League* (London, Hodder & Stoughton, 1989; paperback edition London, Sceptre, 1990), pp. 2–3.
2. Alain Ehrenberg, 'Spectacle sportif et imaginaire individualiste: Essai de problématisation' in Pierre Arnaud and Jean Camy (eds), *La Naissance du mouvement sportif associatif en France: sociabilités et formes de pratiques sportives* (Lyons, P.U. de Lyon, 1986), pp.147–60, at p. 153.
3. Raymond Abellio, 'Le rugby et la maîtrise du temps', *Cahiers Raymond Abellio*, no. 1, November 1983, pp. 75–6. See also Jean Barry, 'Le rugby ou le temps maîtrisé, *Midi*, no. 4, 1987, pp. 23–5.
4. Pierre Sansot, *Le Rugby est une fête* (Paris, Plon, 1990), pp. 10–11.
5. Lincoln Allison, *The Changing Politics of Sport* (Manchester, Manchester University Press, 1993), p. 8.
6. Sansot, *Le Rugby est une fête*, p. 13.

7. Daniel Herrero, *Passion ovale* (Monaco and Paris, Editions du Rocher, 1990), p. 79. It should be noted that Herrero also talks of the formative influence of other events in his life at this time, including particularly an extended trip to South America, intended specifically to fill the gaps left by an over-concentration on sport.

8. Denis Tillinac, *Rugby blues* (Paris, La Table Ronde, 1993); Jean-Paul Rey, *Qu'ont-ils fait de notre rugby?* (Paris, Solar, 1997).

9. Tillinac, *Rugby blues*, pp. xiii–xiv. The familiar symbolism of *le coq gaulois* has a particular resonance in French rugby, where it not only appears as the national emblem on the jerseys worn by *les Tricolores*, but also extends to the smuggling of live cockerels into international matches, where they are released on to the pitch.

10. Rey, *Qu'ont-ils fait de notre rugby*, p. 14.

11. John Nauright and Timothy J. L. Chandler (eds), *Making Men: Rugby and Masculine Identity* (London, Frank Cass, 1996), p. 3.

12. Timothy J. L. Chandler and John Nauright (eds), *Making the Rugby World: Race, Gender, Commerce* (London, Frank Cass, 1999), p. 228.

13. Other works of particular interest from this point of view include Georges Pastre, *Les Ovaliques* (Paris, Editions Dehedin, 1990) and Jean Colombier, *Béloni* (Paris, Calmann-Lévy, 1992).

14. Grant Jarvie, 'Sport, nationalism and cultural identity' in Lincoln Allison (ed.), *The Changing Politics of Sport* (Manchester, Manchester University Press, 1993), pp. 58–83; p. 76 for the quotation.

15. This information is derived from the museum's own promotional material.

16. Donald McRae, *Winter Colours: Changing Seasons in World Rugby* (Edinburgh, Mainstream, 1998), p. 212.

17. Ibid., p. 339.

18. Ibid., p. 10.

19. Michel Gardère, *Abdelatif Benazzi: L'homme aux trois patries: la France, le Maroc, le Rugby* (Paris, La Table Ronde, 1995), p. 105.

20. Ibid., pp. 155–6. McRae, *Winter Colours*, pp. 346–8, in his interview with Benazzi, reveals that the player had to endure racist abuse from both opponents and team-mates in his early days at Agen.

21. McRae, *Winter Colours*, p. 195.

22. Antoine Blondin, preface to Henri Garcia, *La Fabuleuse histoire du rugby* (Paris, ODIL, 1973), p. 7.

Bibliography

Abadie, Jean, *Lourdes, une certaine idée du rugby* (Pau, Editions Marrimpouey Jeune, 1976).

Abellio, Raymond, 'Le rugby et la maîtrise du temps', *Cahiers Raymond Abellio*, no. 1, November 1983, pp. 75–6.

Agulhon, Maurice, 'La fabrication de la France, problèmes et controverses' in Martine Segalen (ed.), *L'Autre et le semblable: Regards sur l'ethnologie des sociétés contemporaines* (Paris, Presses du CNRS, 1989), pp. 109–20.

—— *La République, 1880 à nos jours* (Paris, Hachette, 1990).

—— 'Le mythe gaulois' in 'Astérix: Un mythe et ses figures', special number of *Ethnologie française*, no. 3, 1998/3, June–September, pp. 296–302.

Allison, Lincoln (ed.), *The Changing Politics of Sport* (Manchester, Manchester University Press, 1993).

—— 'Sport and civil society', *Political Studies*, XLVI, 1998, pp. 709–26

Amar, Marianne, *Nés pour courir: La Quatrième République face au sport* (Grenoble, P.U. de Grenoble, 1987).

Amouroux, Henri, *La Vie des Français sous l'Occupation* (Paris, Fayard, 1961 and 1990).

Amson, Daniel, *Borotra: De Wimbledon à Vichy* (Paris, Tallandier, 1999).

Anderson, Benedict, *Imagined Communities: Reflections on the Origin and Spread of Nationalism* (London, Verso, 1983 and 1991).

Armstrong, Robert, 'Merle may pay dear for "cheap shots"', *The Guardian*, 24 January 1995, p. 17.

Arnaud, Pierre (ed.), *Les Athlètes de la République: gymnastique, sport et idéologie républicaine 1870–1914* (Toulouse, Privat, 1987).

—— (ed.), *Le Militaire, l'écolier, le gymnaste: Naissance de l'éducation physique en France (1869–1889)* (Lyons, P.U. de Lyon, 1991).

—— and Jean Camy, *La Naissance du mouvement sportif associatif en France: sociabilités et formes de pratiques sportives* (Lyons, P.U. de Lyon, 1986).

Askolovitch, Claude and Sylvain Attal, 'La Mafia de l'ovale', in the same authors' *La France du piston* (Paris, Robert Laffont, 1992), pp. 99–123.

Audouard, Yvan, *Monsieur Jadis est de retour: Antoine Blondin* (Paris, La Table Ronde, 1994).

Augustin, Jean-Pierre, 'Formes de ballons et formes de croyances', *Les Cahiers de l'animation*, 2/40, 1983.

—— 'Les patronages du Sud-Ouest: la socialisation politique et le mouvement sportif, 1870–1914' in Pierre Arnaud and Jean Camy (eds), *La Naissance du mouvement sportif associatif en France: sociabilités et formes de pratiques sportives* (Lyons, P.U. de Lyon, 1986).

—— 'L'étonnante implantation du rugby dans le Midi', *Midi*, no. 4, 1987, pp. 3–12.

—— 'From one stage to another: French rugby caught between local and global cultures', *Journal of European Area Studies*, vol. 7, no. 2, November 1999, pp. 197–210.

—— and Jean-Pierre Bodis, *Rugby en Aquitaine: histoire d'une rencontre* (Bordeaux, Centre Régional des Lettres d'Aquitaine and Eds. Aubéron, 1994).

—— and Alain Garrigou, *Le Rugby démêlé: Essai sur les Associations Sportives, le Pouvoir et les Notables* (Bordeaux, Le Mascaret, 1985).

Bakhtin, Mikhail, *Rabelais and His World*, trans. Hélène Iswolsky (Cambridge, MA and London, MIT Press, 1968).

Bale, Steve, 'French drop Merle and attack Cooke', *The Independent*, 26 January 1995, p. 40.

Barber, Malcolm, *The Cathars in Languedoc* (London, Longman, 2000).

Barnoud, René, *Quel drôle de ballon!: Mêlées et démêlés* (Lyons, A. Rey, n.d. [1978?]).

Barran, Robert, *Du rugby et des hommes* (Paris, Albin Michel, 1971).

—— *Le Rugby des villages* (Paris, Les Editeurs Français Réunis, 1974).

Barrière, Raoul, *Le Rugby et sa valeur éducative* (Paris, J. Vrin, 1980).

Barry, Jean, 'Le rugby ou le temps maîtrisé', *Midi*, no. 4, 1987, pp. 23–5.

Baschet, Eric (ed.), *L'Illustration: Histoire d'un siècle, 1843–1944, VII. années 1892–1898* (Paris, Le Livre de Paris, 1988).

Baumont, Stéphane, 'Le rugby et la politique . . .', *Midi*, no. 4, 1987, pp. 13–22.

Beaune, Didier, *Les Invincibles: l'épopée des rugbymen de Béziers* (Paris, Calmann-Lévy, 1972).

Bills, Peter, *Jean-Pierre Rives: A Modern Corinthian* (London, Allen & Unwin, 1986).

Blondin, Antoine, *Ma vie entre des lignes* (Paris, La Table Ronde, 1982).

—— *L'Ironie du sport: Chronique de L'Equipe, 1954–1982* (Paris, Editions François Bourin, 1988).

Bodis, Jean-Pierre, 'Rugby, politique et société dans le monde des origines du jeu à nos jours (1972): Etude comparée' (unpublished thesis for the Doctorat d'Etat, Université de Toulouse-Le Mirail, 1986).

—— *Histoire mondiale du rugby* (Toulouse, Bibliothèque Historique Privat, 1987).

—— 'Le rugby en France jusqu'à la seconde guerre mondiale: aspects politiques et sociaux', *Revue de Pau et du Béarn*, no. 17, 1990, pp. 217–44.

—— *Le Rugby* (Toulouse, Editions Privat, 1999).

Bonheur, Gaston, *La Croix de ma mère* (Paris, Julliard, 1976).

Bonnéry, Louis and Raymond Thomas, *Le Jeu à XIII* (Paris, PUF, 1986).

Booth, Douglas, 'Recapturing the moment? Global rugby, economics and the politics of nation in post-apartheid South Africa' in Timothy J. L. Chandler and John Nauright (eds), *Making the Rugby World: Race, Gender, Commerce* (London, Frank Cass, 1999), pp. 181–207.

Boudjedra, Rachid, *Le Vainqueur de coupe* (Paris, Denoël, 1981).

Bourdieu, Pierre, *La Distinction: critique sociale du jugement* (Paris, Minuit, 1979).

—— 'Comment peut-on être sportif?' in the same author's *Questions de Sociologie* (Paris, Minuit, 1981).

Bourgeois, René, *Géo-Charles: Un poète de la vie moderne* (Echirolles, Editions Galerie-Musée Géo-Charles, 1985).

Bozonnet, Jean-Jacques, 'Malentendu franco-britannique', *Le Monde*, 18 February 1995, p. 14.

—— 'Le rugby français remet sa professionnalisation à plus tard', *Le Monde*, 15 September 1995, p. 21.

Braesch, François and Hervé Bride, *Vous ne plaquerez pas l'Alsace et la Lorraine* (Colmar, Editions d'Alsace, 1980).

Braudel, Fernand, *The Identity of France: I. History and Environment* (trans. Siân Reynolds; London, Collins, 1988); *II. People and Production* (trans. Siân Reynolds; London, Collins, 1990).

Brohm, Jean-Marie, *Critiques du Sport* (Paris, Bourgeois, 1976).

Busson, Bernard, *Héros du sport, Héros de France* (Paris, Editions d'Art Athos, 1947).

Callède, Jean-Paul, *L'Esprit sportif: Essai sur le développement associatif de la culture sportive* (Bordeaux, P.U. de Bordeaux, 1987).

—— 'La politique sportive de la municipalité de Bègles: Contribution à une approche généalogique de l'action sportive communale', *Spirales* (special number on 'Le sport et la ville: Les politiques municipales d'équipements sportifs, XIXe–XXe siècles', no. 5, 1992).

—— *Histoire du sport en France: du Stade Bordelais au SBUC, 1889–1939* (Bordeaux, Editions de la Maison des Sciences de l'Homme d'Aquitaine, 1993).

—— and M. Dané, *Sociologie des politiques sportives locales: Trente ans d'action sportive à Bègles (Gironde)* (Talence, Eds. de la Maison des Sciences de l'Homme d'Aquitaine, 1991).

Canyameres, Ferran, *L'Homme de la Belle Epoque* (Paris, Les Editions Universelles, 1946).

Capdeville, Pierre and Roger Surjus, *De la vierge rouge aux anges blonds* (Toulouse, Cépaduès-Editions, 1984).

Carle, Alison and John Nauright, 'Crossing the line: women playing rugby union' in Timothy J. L. Chandler and John Nauright (eds), *Making the Rugby World: Race, Gender, Commerce* (London, Frank Cass, 1999), pp.128–48.

Chandler, Timothy J. L. and John Nauright (eds), *Making the Rugby World: Race, Gender, Commerce* (London, Frank Cass, 1999).

Charney, Leo and Vanessa R. Schwartz (eds), *Cinema and the Invention of Modern Life* (Berkeley, CA, University of California Press, 1995).

Charreton, Pierre, *Les Fêtes du corps: Histoire et tendances de la littérature à thème sportif en France, 1870–1970* (Saint-Etienne, CIEREC de l'Université de Saint-Etienne, 1985).

—— 'Le mythe littéraire du rapprochement social par le sport' in Pierre Arnaud and Jean Camy (eds), *La Naissance du mouvement sportif associatif en France: sociabilités et formes de pratiques sportives* (Lyons, P.U. de Lyon, 1986), pp. 391–402.

Bibliography

—— 'Sport et sociabilité mondaine dans la littérature française, 1880–1930', *Sport-Histoire*, no. 1, 1988, pp. 101–12.

—— *Le Sport, l'ascèse, le plaisir: éthique et poétique du sport dans la littérature française moderne* (Saint-Etienne, CIEREC, 1990).

Chevallier, Gabriel, *Clochemerle* (Paris, Presses Universitaires de France, 1934).

Cleary, Mick, 'French artists on a new high', *The Observer*, 26 January 1997, 'Sport', p. 9.

—— 'This French team have greatness in their grasp', *The Daily Telegraph*, 6 April 1998, p. S6.

—— 'Only fabulous French can do this', *The Daily Telegraph*, 1 November 1999, p. S1.

Collective, *L'Univers du rugby: Actes du Colloque de Larrazet* (Montauban, Edicopie, 1988).

Collier, E., 'Willy Holt, du Racing Club de France à Auschwitz, en passant par la Résistance', *Le Monde*, 11 December 1998, p. 25.

Colombier, Jean, *Béloni* (Paris, Calmann-Lévy, 1992).

Commissariat Général à l'Education Générale et aux Sports, *Toulouse, capitale du rugby . . .*, *Les Cahiers de la France Sportive*, no. 3, March 1941, unpaginated.

Cormier, Jean, *Grand Chelem* (Paris, Denoël, 1977).

—— *Il était une fois Jean-Pierre Rives* (Paris, Robert Laffont, 1985).

Coubertin, Pierre de, *Essais de psychologie sportive* (Grenoble, Jérôme Millon, 1992).

Couderc, Roger, *Le Rugby, la télé et moi* (Paris, Solar, 1966).

—— *Adieu, les petits!* (Paris, Solar, 1983).

Cronin, Mike and David Mayall (eds), *Sporting Nationalisms: Identity, Ethnicity, Immigration and Assimilation* (London, Frank Cass, 1998).

Darbon, Sébastien, *Rugby, mode de vie: Ethnographie d'un club, Saint-Vincent-de-Tyrosse* (Paris, Editions Jean-Michel Place, 1995).

—— *Rugby d'ici: Une manière d'être au monde* (Paris, Editions Autrement, 1999).

Degoulange, Thierry, *Brive, un grand parmi les grands du rugby* (Brive, Chastrusse, 1976).

Devert, L'Abbé Michel, *Les Grandes Heures de Notre-Dame du Rugby* (Mézos, the author, 1991).

Dhéry, Robert, *Allez France!* (film; France, 1964).

Dine, Philip, 'The tradition of violence in French sport' in Renate Günther and Jan Windebank, *Violence and Conflict in Modern France* (Sheffield, Sheffield Academic Press, 1995), pp. 245–60.

—— 'Money, identity and conflict: rugby league in France', *The Sports Historian*, no. 16, May 1996, pp. 99–116.

—— 'Un héroïsme problématique – Le sport, la littérature et la guerre d'Algérie', *Europe*, nos. 806–7, June–July 1996, pp. 177–85.

—— 'The historical development of rugby in south-east France: *En marge de l'Ovalie?*' in Maurice Roche (ed.), *Sport, Popular Culture and Identity* (Aachen, Meyer & Meyer Verlag, 1998), pp. 211–24.

—— 'Sport and the State in contemporary France: from *la Charte des Sports* to decentralisation', *Modern & Contemporary France*, vol. 6, no. 3, 1998, pp. 301–11.

—— 'Sporting assimilation and cultural confusion in Brittany' in Grant Jarvie (ed.), *Sport in the Making of Celtic Cultures* (London and Leicester, Cassell and Leicester University Press, 1999), pp. 112–30.

Dreyfus, H. L., *Michel Foucault* (Brighton, Harvester Press, 1982).

Driès, R., *100 ans de rugby en France: un film à la gloire du sport roi* (video; Paris, INA, 1988).

Duboscq, Pierre (ed.), *Terrains et terres du rugby*, Université de Toulouse and Editions du CNRS, 1983).

—— 'Représentation de la nation' in Collective, *L'Univers du rugby: Actes du Colloque de Larrazet* (Montauban, Edicopie, 1988), pp. 93–106.

—— 'Sur les terrains du sport et du pouvoir: rugby', *Pouvoirs*, no. 61, 1992, pp. 107–15.

—— (ed.), *Rugby, parabole du monde* (Paris, L'Harmattan, 1998).

Dubreuil, B., 'La naissance du sport catholique' in Alain Ehrenberg, 'Aimez-vous les stades?: Les origines historiques des politiques sportives en France (1870–1930)', special number of *Recherches*, no. 43, April 1980, pp. 221–51.

Du Gay, Paul (ed.), *Production of Cultures / Cultures of Production* (London, Sage and Open University, 1997).

Duhau, Claude, *Histoire de l'Aviron Bayonnais, I: L'époque héroïque, 1904–1914* (Bayonne, Editions Christian Mendibourne, 1968 and 1983.)

Dunning, Eric and Kenneth Sheard, *Barbarians, Gentlemen and Players: A Sociological Study of the Development of Rugby Football* (Oxford, Martin Robertson, 1979).

Duret, Pascal and Marion Wolff, 'The semiotics of sport heroism', *International Review for the Sociology of Sport*, no. 29, 1994.

Ehrenberg, Alain (ed.), 'Aimez-vous les stades?: Les origines historiques des politiques sportives en France (1870–1930)', special number of *Recherches*, no. 43, April 1980.

—— 'Spectacle sportif et imaginaire individualiste: Essai de problématisation' in Pierre Arnaud and Jean Camy (eds), *La Naissance du mouvement sportif associatif en France: sociabilités et formes de pratiques sportives* (Lyons, P.U. de Lyon, 1986), pp.147–60.

—— *Le Culte de la performance* (Paris, Calmann-Lévy, 1991).

Escot, Richard, *Rugby Pro: Histoires Secrètes* (Paris, Solar, 1996).

—— 'Sous la mêlée, l'argent caché', *L'Equipe Magazine*, no. 722, 20 January 1996, pp. 40–5.

—— and Jacques Rivière, *Un siècle de rugby* (Paris, Calmann-Lévy, 1997).

Fabre, Daniel, 'Les dessous de la mêlée: urnes et mascottes', *Autrement*, special number on Occitanie, no. 25, June 1980, pp. 121–6.

Fabre, Jean and Pierre Capdeville, *Rugby: La quatrième mi-temps* (Toulouse, Cépaduès-Editions, 1999).

Ferrasse, Albert, *Mêlées ouvertes* (Paris, Albin Michel, 1993).

Fleuriel, S., 'Forms of resistance to the economic hold on sport: a national spirit versus the world market – the case of French rugby', *Culture, Sport, Society*, 1(3), 2000.

Fogel, Jean-François and Christian Jaurena, *Le Rugby* (Paris, Jean-Claude Lattès, 1994).

Fontès, Martin, *Un siècle et plus de rugby en Albi: XV–XIII* (Aiguelèze, Association Connaissances et Traditions de France, 1997).

Fontorbes, Jean-Pascal and A. M. Granié, *Le Rugby dans le cuir*, (video; Paris, Mission du Patrimoine Ethnologique, 1985).

Forbes, Jill and Michael Kelly, *French Cultural Studies: An Introduction* (Oxford, Oxford University Press, 1995).

Fukuyama, Francis, *The End of History and The Last Man* (London, Hamish Hamilton, 1992).

Gachassin, Jean (with E. Cazes), *Le Rugby est une fête* (Paris, Solar, 1969).

Garcia, Henri, *Rugby-Champagne* (Paris, La Table Ronde, 1960).

—— *Les Contes du rugby* (Paris, La Table Ronde, 1961).

—— *La Fabuleuse histoire du rugby* (Paris, ODIL, 1973). [Republished as follows: Paris, ODIL, 1985; Paris: Nathan, 1991; Paris, La Martinière, 1993.]

—— *Seigneurs et forçats du rugby: un siècle d'ovale en France* (Paris, Calmann-Lévy, 1994).

Gardère, Michel, *Abdelatif Benazzi: L'homme aux trois patries: la France, le Maroc, le Rugby* (Paris, La Table Ronde, 1995).

Gardian, Daniel-Guy, *100 ans au FCL: 1893–1993* (Caluire, FC Lyon, 1993).

Garrigou, Alain, 'Le travail, la fête et l'athlétisme: les enjeux des styles de jeu' in Société Française de Sociologie du Sport, *Sport et changement social* (Talence, Maison des Sciences de l'Homme d'Aquitaine, 1987), pp. 147–55.

Gay-Lescot, Jean-Louis, *Sport et éducation sous Vichy, 1940–1944* (Lyons, P.U. de Lyon, 1991).

Geertz, Clifford, 'Deep play: notes on the Balinese cockfight', in idem, *The Interpretation of Cultures* (New York, Basic Books, 1973; London, Hutchinson, 1975).

Giarrizzi, Julien, 'Le rugby n'aime pas qu'on lui parle d'argent et pourtant . . .', in the same author's *Le Sport et l'argent* (Paris, A. Lefeuvre, 1981), pp. 117–21.

Gildea, Robert, *France Since 1945* (Oxford, Oxford University Press, 1996).

Girardet, Raoul, *Mythes et mythologies politiques* (Paris, Seuil, 1986).

Giraudoux, Jean, *Le Sport* (Paris, Grasset, 1928).

Girette, Hervé, 'De Jean Galia à Vichy: Les origines du XIII en France', *L'Indépendant* [Perpignan], 26 July 1995, unpaginated.

Goffman, Erving, *The Presentation of Self in Everyday Life* (Harmondsworth, Penguin, 1969).

Goscinny, René and Albert Uderzo, *Astérix chez les Bretons* (Paris, Dargaud, 1966).

Greaves, A., 'Sport in France' in Malcolm Cook (ed.), *French Culture since 1945* (London, Longman, 1993), pp. 125–48.

Haedens, Kléber, *Adios* (Paris, Grasset, 1974).

Halls, W. D., *The Youth of Vichy France* (Oxford, Clarendon Press, 1981).

Harris, Ruth, *Murderers and Madness: Medicine, Law and Society in the Fin de Siècle* (Cambridge, MA, Harvard University Press, 1989).

—— *Lourdes: Body and Spirit in the Secular Age* (New York, Viking, 1999).

Harris, Sandra, 'Allez la France', [British Airways] *Business Life*, February 1999, pp. 20–5.

Bibliography

Hatzfeld, Jean, 'Alain Estève: Le rugbyman assassin', *Libération*, 22–23 May 1981.

Herrero, Daniel, *Passion ovale* (Monaco and Paris, Editions du Rocher, 1990).

Hewett, Nicholas, *Literature and the Right in Postwar France: The Story of the 'Hussards'* (Oxford and Washington, DC, Berg, 1996).

Hirschkop, Ken and David Shepherd, *Bakhtin and Cultural Theory* (Manchester, Manchester University Press, 1989).

Hobsbawm, Eric, 'Mass-Producing Traditions: Europe, 1870–1914' in Eric Hobsbawm & Terence Ranger (eds), *The Invention of Tradition* (Cambridge, Cambridge University Press, 1983), pp. 263–307.

Holt, Richard, *Sport and Society in Modern France* (London, Macmillan, 1981).

Hopquin, Benoît, 'Le sport français s'interroge sur son attitude sous Vichy', *Le Monde*, 11 December 1998, p. 25.

—— 'Le rugby à XIII, victime de la vindicte du régime', *Le Monde*, 11 December 1998, p. 25.

Horrocks, Roger, 'Male sport', in the same author's *Male Myths and Icons* (London, Macmillan, 1995), pp. 147–69.

Hubscher, Ronald *et al.*, *L'Histoire en mouvements: Le sport dans la société française (XIXe–XXe siècle)* (Paris, Armand Colin, 1992).

Huizinga, Johan, *Homo Ludens* (London, Routledge & Kegan Paul, 1949).

Inglis, Fred, *The Name of the Game: Sport and Society* (London, Heinemann, 1977).

—— *Popular Culture and Political Power* (London, Harvester Wheatsheaf, 1988).

Itié, F. P. (ed.), *Les Yeux du Stade: Colombes, temple du Sport* (Paris, Editions de l'Albaron, 1993).

Jarvie, Grant, 'Sport, nationalism and cultural identity' in Lincoln Allison (ed.), *The Changing Politics of Sport* (Manchester, Manchester University Press, 1993), pp. 58–83.

—— and Joseph Maguire, *Sport and Leisure in Social Thought* (London, Routledge, 1994).

—— and Irene Reid, 'Sport in South Africa' in James Riordan and Arnd Krüger, *The International Politics of Sport in the Twentieth Century* (London, E. and F. N. Spon, 1999), pp. 234–45.

Jefferson, Ann, 'Bodymatters: self and other in Bakhtin, Sartre and Barthes' in Hirschkop, Ken and David Shepherd, *Bakhtin and Cultural Theory* (Manchester, Manchester University Press, 1989), pp. 152–77.

Kedward, H. R. and Roger Austin, *Vichy France and the Resistance: Culture and Ideology* (London, Croom Helm, 1985).

Kidd, William and Siân Reynolds (eds), *Contemporary French Cultural Studies* (London, Arnold, 2000).

Krüger, Arnd, 'The homosexual and homoerotic in sport' in James Riordan and Arnd Krüger, *The International Politics of Sport in the Twentieth Century* (London, E. and F. N. Spon, 1999), pp. 191–216

Laborderie, Renaud de, *Le Rugby dans le sang* (Paris, Calmann-Lévy, 1968).

Lacouture, Jean, *Le Rugby, c'est un monde* (Paris, Seuil, 1979).

—— *Voyous et gentlemen: Une histoire du rugby* (Paris, Gallimard, 1993).

Laget, Françoise, Lionel, and Serge, *Rugby en toutes lettres* (Biarritz, Atlantica, 1999).

Bibliography

Lagorce, Guy, *Le Train du soir* (Paris, Grasset, 1983).

Lagrée, M., 'Sport et sociabilité catholique en France au début du XXe siècle' in Pierre Arnaud and Jean Camy (eds), *La Naissance du mouvement sportif associatif en France: sociabilités et formes de pratiques sportives* (Lyons, P.U. de Lyon, 1986), pp. 327–37.

Lalanne, Denis, *Le Grand Combat du quinze de France* (Paris, La Table Ronde, 1959).

—— *Les Conquérants du XV de France* (Paris, La Table Ronde, 1970).

—— and Jean Chouquet, *Allez la Rafale!* (Paris, Antenne 2 and Editions Mengès, 1977).

Lanfranchi, Pierre, 'Mekloufi, un footballeur français dans la guerre d'Algérie', *Actes de la Recherche en Sciences Sociales*, no.103, June 1994, p. 70.

Lavigne, S.-R., *L'Auvergnat marque un essai* (Paris, Editions Guy Authier, 1978).

Le Bras, Hervé, *Les Trois France* (Paris, Éditions Odile Jacob, 1986 and 1995).

—— and Emmanuel Todd, *L'Invention de la France: atlas anthropologique et politique* (Paris, Livre de Poche, 1981).

Le Galès, Patrick, 'The regions' in Malcolm Cook and Grace Davie (eds), *Modern France: Society in Transition* (London, Routledge, 1998), pp. 91–112.

Le Roy Ladurie, Emmanuel, *Montaillou, village occitan de 1294 à 1324* (Paris, Gallimard, 1975); *Montaillou: Cathars and Catholics in a French Village, 1294–1324* (trans. Barbara Bray; London, Scolar Press, 1978).

Londres, Albert, *Tour de France, tour de souffrance* (Paris, Le Serpent à Plumes, 1996).

Mackaman, Douglas Peter, *Leisure Settings: Bourgeois Culture, Medicine, and the Spa in Modern France* (Chicago, University of Chicago Press, 1998).

MacKay, Hugh (ed.), *Consumption and Everyday Life* (London, Sage and Open University, 1997).

Mac Orlan, Pierre, *La Clique du Café Brebis* (Paris, Renaissance du Livre, 1918; Paris, NRF/Gallimard, 1951 and 1991)

McRae, Donald, *Winter Colours: Changing Seasons in World Rugby* (Edinburgh, Mainstream, 1998).

Maguire, Joseph, 'Globalisation, sport and national identities: "The Empire strikes back"?', *Loisir et société*, vol. 16, no. 2, 1993, pp. 293–322.

—— and Jason Tuck, 'Global sports and patriot games: rugby union and national identity in a United Sporting Kingdom since 1945', Mike Cronin and David Mayall (eds), *Sporting Nationalisms: Identity, Ethnicity, Immigration and Assimilation* (London, Frank Cass, 1998), pp. 103–26.

Maigne, Jacques and Marie-Ange Rodeaud, 'Lapasset veut en finir avec l'amateurisme marron', *Libération*, 19 September 1994, p. 29.

Mauroy, Pierre, *Léo Lagrange* (Paris, Denoël, 1997).

Mérillon, Jean, *Le Challenge Yves du Manoir* (Paris, Chiron, 1990).

Montels, Louis, *Graulhet: 80 ans de rugby* (Graulhet, Sporting Club Graulhétois, 1988).

Montherlant, Henry de, *Les Bestiaires* (Paris, Gallimard, 1954).

Moorhouse, Geoffrey, *At The George and Other Essays on Rugby League* (London, Hodder & Stoughton, 1989).

Bibliography

Nauright, John and Timothy J. L. Chandler (eds), *Making Men: Rugby and Masculine Identity* (London, Frank Cass, 1996).

Nicaud, Jean, *Cent ans de rugby régional* (Bourg-en-Bresse, Les Editions de la Taillanderie, 1992).

Nier, Olivier, 'Professionnalisation du rugby et stratégies de clubs de l'élite européenne' (unpublished doctoral thesis), Université Claude Bernard – Lyon 1, Lyons, 1998.

Nye, Robert, *Crime, Madness, and Politics in Modern France: The Medical Concept of National Decline* (Princeton, NJ, Princeton University Press, 1984).

—— *Masculinity and Male Codes of Honour in Modern France* (Oxford, Oxford University Press, 1993).

O'Donnell, Hugh and Neil Blain, 'Performing the Carmagnole: negotiating French national identity during France 98', *Journal of European Area Studies*, vol. 7, no. 2, November 1999, pp. 211–25.

Ory, Pascal, *L'Aventure culturelle française* (Paris, Flammarion, 1989).

—— 'Naissance des loisirs' in Yves Lequin, *Histoire des Français: XIXe–XXe siècles: III. Les Citoyens et la démocratie* (Paris, A. Colin, 1984), pp. 264–72.

Pascot, Jep, *Six maillots de rugby* (Paris, Aux Horizons de France, 1944).

Pastre, Georges, *Histoire générale du rugby* (5 volumes), (Toulouse, Midi-Olympique, 1968–1971).

—— *Rugby, capitale Béziers* (Paris, Solar, 1972).

—— *Les Ovaliques* (Paris, Editions Dehedin, 1990).

Paxton, Robert O., *Vichy France: Old Guard and New Order, 1940–1944* (New York, Alfred A. Knopf and London, Barrie & Jenkins, 1972).

Pech, Rémy and Jack Thomas, 'La Naissance du rugby populaire à Toulouse (1893–1914)' in Pierre Arnaud and Jean Camy (eds), *La Naissance du mouvement sportif associatif en France: sociabilités et formes de pratiques sportives* (Lyons, P.U. de Lyon, 1986), pp. 97–126.

—— 'Pratiques sportives et antagonismes sociaux: Le rugby à Carmaux, 1920–1933' in Société Française de Sociologie du Sport, *Sport et changement social* (Talence, Maison des Sciences de l'Homme d'Aquitaine, 1987), pp. 217–27.

Pociello, Christian, *Le Rugby ou la guerre des styles* (Paris, A. M. Métailié, 1983).

Potter, Alex and Georges Duthen, *The Rise of French Rugby* (London, Bailey & Swinfen, 1961).

Prouteau, G., *L'Equipe de France (anthologie)* (Paris, Plon, 1972).

Rearick, Charles, *Pleasures of the Belle Epoque* (London and New Haven, CT, Yale University Press, 1985).

Renoir, Edmond, 'Un match de foot-ball', 1892, reproduced in E. Baschet (ed.), *L'Illustration, Histoire d'un siècle, 1843–1944: VII. Années 1892–1898* (Paris, Le Livre de Paris, 1988), pp. 36–7.

Rey, Jean-Paul, *Tarbes, le rugby en rouge et blanc* (Paris, Solar, 1973).

—— *Qu'ont-ils fait de notre rugby?* (Paris, Solar, 1997).

Riordan, James and Arnd Krüger, *The International Politics of Sport in the Twentieth Century* (London, E. & F. N. Spon, 1999).

Rioux, Jean-Pierre (ed.), *La Vie culturelle sous Vichy* (Paris, Editions Complexe, 1990).

Rosjean, D., *L'Ovalie: Histoire et légende du rugby* (promotional video for Autoroutes du Sud de la France, 1997).

Ross, Kristin, *Fast Cars, Clean Bodies: Decolonization and the Reordering of French Culture* (Cambridge, MA and London, MIT Press, 1995).

Rousso, Henry, *Le Syndrome de Vichy de 1944 à nos jours* (2nd edn, Paris, Seuil, 1990).

Rylance, Mike, *The Forbidden Game: The Untold Story of French Rugby League* (Brighouse, League Publications, 1999).

Sagan, Françoise, 'Cette enfance naturelle et drôle' in Roger Couderc and Pierre Albaladejo, *Le Livre d'or du rugby 1981* (Paris, Solar, 1981), pp. 3–4.

Sansot, Pierre, *La France sensible* (Paris, Editions du Champ Vallon, 1985 and Paris, Editions Payot and Rivages, 1995).

—— *Les Formes sensibles de la vie sociale* (Paris, PUF, 1986).

—— 'Le rugby et les nouvelles pratiques sportives' in Collective, *L'Univers du rugby: Actes du Colloque de Larrazet* (Montauban, Edicopie, 1988), pp. 63–74.

—— *Le Rugby est une fête: Au monde de l'ovale* (Paris, Plon, 1990).

Saouter, Anne, *"Etre rugby": Jeux du masculin et du féminin* (Paris, Editions de la Maison des Sciences de l'Homme, 2000).

Shennan, Andrew, *Rethinking France: Plans for Renewal, 1940–1946* (Oxford, Clarendon, 1989).

Sheringham, Michael, 'Attending to the everyday: Blanchot, Lefebvre, Certeau, Perec', *French Studies*, vol. LIV, no. 2, April 2000, pp. 187–99.

Smith, Sean, *The Union Game: A Rugby History* (London, BBC, 1999).

Société Française de Sociologie du Sport, *Sport et changement social* (Talence, Maison des Sciences de l'Homme d'Aquitaine, 1987).

Souchon, Paul, *Les Chants du stade* (Paris, Editions Tallandier and Commissariat Général à l'Education Générale et aux Sports, 1943).

'Sport For All' Clearing House (CDDS/Council of Europe), 'France', in *Sports Structures in Europe: Situation in the Countries of the Committee for the Development of Sport of the Council of Europe*, 1993, F.2, pp. 1–4.

Stallybrass, Peter and Allon White, *The Politics and Poetics of Transgression* (London, Methuen, 1986).

Stierlé, Christian, *Lire le rugby: Bibliographie thématique – Répertoire d'ouvrages publiés en France des origines à 1994* (Editions MIRE and Académie Provençale de Recherches et de Créativité Littéraire, 1995).

Terret, Thierry, 'Learning to be a man: French rugby and masculinity' in Timothy J. L. Chandler and John Nauright (eds), *Making the Rugby World: Race, Gender, Commerce* (London, Frank Cass, 1999), pp. 63–87.

Tillinac, Denis, *Rugby blues* (Paris, La Table Ronde, 1993).

Todd, Emmanuel, *The Making of Modern France: Ideology, Politics and Culture* (trans. Anthony and Betty Forster; Oxford, Blackwell, 1991).

Trempé, Rolande, *Les Mineurs de Carmaux* (Paris, Éditions Ouvrières, 1971).

Van Esbeck, Edmund, *The Story of Irish Rugby* (London, Stanley Paul, 1986).

Vigarello, Georges, 'Le Tour de France' in Pierre Nora (ed.), *Les Lieux de mémoire: III. Les France: traditions* (Paris, Gallimard, 1992), pp. 884–925.

Voivenel, Paul, *L'Ame de la France* (Toulouse, Editions de l'Héraklès, 1941).

—— *Mon beau rugby: L'Esprit du Sport* (Toulouse, Editions de l'Héraklès, 1942; Toulouse, Editions Midi Olympique, 1962).

Weber, Eugen, 'Gymnastics and sports in *fin-de-siècle* France: opium of the classes?', *The American Historical Review*, 76/1, February 1971, pp. 70–98.

—— *Peasants into Frenchmen: The Modernization of Rural France, 1870–1914* (London, Chatto & Windus, 1977).

—— 'Pierre de Coubertin and the introduction of organized sport', in idem, *My France: Politics, Culture, Myth* (Cambridge, MA and London, Belknap/Harvard University Press, 1991), pp. 207–25.

White, P. G. and A. B. Vagi, 'Rugby in the 19th-century boarding school system: a feminist psychoanalytic perspective' in M. Messner and D. Sabo (eds), *Sport, Men and the Gender Order: Critical Feminist Perspectives* (Champaign, IL, Human Kinetics, 1990).

Williams, Gareth, 'From William Webb Ellis to World Cup – the social history of rugby union', in the same author's *1905 and All That: Essays on Rugby Football, Sport and Welsh Society* (Llandysul, Gomer Press, 1991).

Winter, Jay M., *Sites of Memory, Sites of Mourning: The Great War in European Cultural History* (Cambridge, Cambridge University Press, 1995).

Zeldin, Theodore, *France, 1848–1945: II. Intellect, Taste and Anxiety* (Oxford, Clarendon Press, 1977).

Appendix 1

Location of Leading French Rugby Clubs, 2000–2001

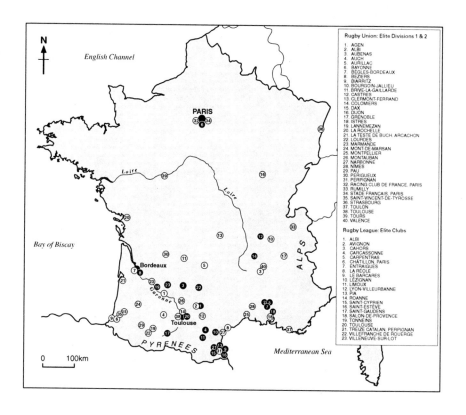

Appendix 2

French Club Championship Winners, 1892–2000

1892	Racing Club de France
1893	Stade Français
1894	Stade Français
1895	Stade Français
1896	Olympique
1897	Stade Français
1898	Stade Français
1899	Stade Bordelais
1900	Racing Club de France
1901	Stade Français
1902	Racing Club de France
1903	Stade Français
1904	Stade Bordelais
1905	Stade Bordelais
1906	Stade Bordelais
1907	Stade Bordelais
1908	Stade Français
1909	Stade Bordelais
1910	FC Lyon
1911	Stade Bordelais
1912	Stade Toulousain
1913	Aviron Bayonnais
1914	AS Perpignan

1915–1919: Championship suspended

1920	Stadoceste Tarbais
1921	US Perpignan
1922	Stade Toulousain

1923   Stade Toulousain
1924   Stade Toulousain
1925   US Perpignan
1926   Stade Toulousain
1927   Stade Toulousain
1928   Section Paloise
1929   US Quillan
1930   SU Agen
1931   RC Toulon
1932   Lyon OU
1933   Lyon OU
1934   Aviron Bayonnais
1935   Biarritz Olympique
1936   RC Narbonne
1937   CS Vienne
1938   USA Perpignan
1939   Biarritz Olympique

1940–1942: Championship suspended

1943   Aviron Bayonnais
1944   USA Perpignan
1945   SU Agen
1946   Section Paloise
1947   Stade Toulousain
1948   FC Lourdes
1949   Castres Olympique
1950   Castres Olympique
1951   US Carmaux
1952   FC Lourdes
1953   FC Lourdes
1954   FC Grenoble
1955   USA Perpignan
1956   FC Lourdes
1957   FC Lourdes
1958   FC Lourdes
1959   Racing Club de France
1960   FC Lourdes
1961   AS Béziers
1962   SU Agen
1963   Stade Montois

1964   Section Paloise
1965   SU Agen
1966   SU Agen
1967   US Montauban
1968   FC Lourdes
1969   CA Bègles-Bordeaux
1970   La Voulte Sportive
1971   AS Béziers
1972   AS Béziers
1973   Stadoceste Tarbais
1974   AS Béziers
1975   AS Béziers
1976   SU Agen
1977   AS Béziers
1978   AS Béziers
1979   FC Narbonne
1980   AS Béziers
1981   AS Béziers
1982   SU Agen
1983   AS Béziers
1984   AS Béziers
1985   Stade Toulousain
1986   Stade Toulousain
1987   RC Toulon
1988   SU Agen
1989   Stade Toulousain
1990   Racing Club de France
1991   CA Bègles-Bordeaux
1992   RC Toulon
1993   Castres Olympique
1994   Stade Toulousain
1995   Stade Toulousain
1996   Stade Toulousain
1997   Stade Toulousain
1998   Stade Français
1999   Stade Toulousain
2000   Stade Français

Appendix 3

French Achievements in International Competitions

Five Nations Championship

1954 Joint Winner (with England and Wales)
1955 Joint Winner (with Wales)
1959 Outright Winner
1960 Joint Winner (with England)
1961 Outright Winner
1962 Outright Winner
1967 Outright Winner
1968 Outright Winner and 1st Grand Slam
1970 Joint Winner (with Wales)
1973 Joint Winner (five-way tie)
1977 Outright Winner and 2nd Grand Slam
1981 Outright Winner and 3rd Grand Slam
1983 Joint Winner (with Ireland)
1986 Joint Winner (with Scotland)
1987 Outright Winner and 4th Grand Slam
1988 Joint Winner (with Wales)
1989 Outright Winner
1993 Outright Winner
1997 Outright Winner and 5th Grand Slam
1998 Outright Winner

World Cup Results

1987 Runners-Up (to New Zealand)
1991 Quarter-Finalists (knocked out by England, losing finalists to Australia)
1994 Semi-Finalists (knocked out by South Africa, the eventual winners)
1999 Runners-Up (to Australia)

European Club Championship

1996 Winners: Stade Toulousain
1997 Winners: CA Brive
1998 Runners-Up (to Bath): CA Brive
1999 Runners-Up (to Ulster): US Colomiers

Index

Index

see also gender
World Cup
  rugby league
    1954, 117
  rugby union
    1987, 159, 179, 183

    1991, 172–3, 176, 179, 196
    1995, 166–7, 180–1
    1999, 3–4, 20
  see also football

Ybarnégaray, Jean, 106